Upgrading to MS-DOS® 6

BRIAN UNDERDAHL

Upgrading to MS-DOS 6

Library of Congress Catalog No.: 93-83028

ISBN: 1-56529-211-1

96 95 94 93 4 3 2 1

Interpretation of the printing code: the rightmost double-digit number is the year of the book's printing; the rightmost single-digit number, the number of the book's printing. For example, a printing code of 93-1 shows that the first printing of the book occurred in 1993.

Screens in this book were created using Collage Plus from Inner Media, Inc., Hollis, NH.

Upgrading to MS-DOS 6 is based on MS-DOS Version 6.0.

Publisher: Lloyd J. Short

Associate Publisher: Rick Ranucci

Operations Manager: Sheila Cunningham

Plan Manager: Thomas H. Bennett

Book Designer: Scott Cook

Graphic Image Specialists: Jerry Ellis, Dennis Sheehan, Susan VandeWalle

Figure Specialist: Wilfred Thebodeau

Production Analyst: Mary Beth Wakefield

Production Team: Claudia Bell, Julie Brown, Jodie Cantwell, Laurie Casey, Brook Farling, Heather Kaufman, Bob LaRoche, Jay Lesandrini, Caroline Roop, Susan Shepard, Greg Simsic, Tina Trettin

DEDICATION

I never imagined I would become an author. It took a very special person named Darlene to help me find that dream. When you find someone like that, there's no limit to what your dreams may hold or what your future may be.

CREDITS

Title Manager
Walter R. Bruce, III

Product Director
Timothy S. Stanley

Senior Acquisitions Editor
Chris Katsaropoulos

Production Editor
Fran Blauw

Editor
Joy M. Preacher

Technical Editor
Jerry Ellis

Formatter
Jill Stanley

Editorial Assistant
Elizabeth D. Brown

Composed in *Cheltenham* and *MCPdigital* by Que Corporation.

ABOUT THE AUTHOR

Brian Underdahl is an author and independent consultant based in Reno, Nevada. He is the author of Que's best-selling *Upgrading to MS-DOS 5*; *Using Quattro Pro for Windows*; *Que's Guide to XTree*; *1-2-3 for DOS Release 3.1+ Quick Reference*, and *Easy Paradox for Windows*. He was also a contributing author to Que's *Using Symphony*, Special Edition; *1-2-3 Beyond the Basics*; *1-2-3 for DOS Release 3.1+ Quick Start*; *1-2-3 Power Macros*; *Using 1-2-3 Release 3.1*; *Using 1-2-3 for DOS Release 3.1+*, Special Edition; *Using 1-2-3 for Windows*; and *Using 1-2-3 Release 2.4*, Special Edition. He has also served as technical editor for Que on *Using 1-2-3 Release 2.3*; *Batch File and Macros Quick Reference*; and *Computerizing Your Small Business*.

ACKNOWLEDGMENTS

Upgrading to MS-DOS 6, like every Que book I've had the pleasure of participating in, is the result of the hard work and dedication of many individuals. I'd like to thank them for helping me so much:

Tim Stanley, product development specialist, for his many hours helping me make this book the best it could be.

Chris Katsaropoulos, senior acquisitions editor, for making it possible to fit *Upgrading to MS-DOS 6* into my schedule.

Stacey Beheler, acquisitions coordinator, for keeping the office running in spite of overwhelming demands on her time.

Fran Blauw, production editor, for making sure *Upgrading to MS-DOS 6* is a book you can actually read. Good editors are the backbone of a project like this one.

Jerry Ellis, technical editor, for making certain that everything you read in this book is true—not an easy task with new, changing software.

Lloyd Short, publisher, and **Rick Ranucci**, associate publisher, for giving me a home at Que.

Patty Brooks, for coordinating beta acquisitions with Microsoft, so we could have *Upgrading to MS-DOS 6* ready when you need it.

Microsoft, for allowing us the opportunity to examine DOS 6 early enough to complete this book on time.

Trademarks

CONTENTS AT A GLANCE

TABLE OF CONTENTS

Introduction

MS-DOS Version 6 (referred to in this book as *DOS 6*) is the latest in a series of advancements in operating systems for the IBM-PC and compatible computer systems. DOS 6 remains fully compatible with earlier versions of MS-DOS and PC DOS, but includes many new and advanced features. Many of these new features take advantage of the increasing power and sophistication of today's more powerful PCs, while other new features apply to all PCs—new or old.

Upgrading to MS-DOS 6 introduces the new features and enhancements to DOS 6. This book provides an overview of DOS 6, while concentrating on those areas that have changed from earlier DOS versions. Instead of in-depth coverage of all aspects of DOS, *Upgrading to MS-DOS 6* focuses on the new features of DOS 6. This book shows you how to take maximum advantage of the opportunities available to you when you upgrade your operating system.

You'll find tips and techniques in this book to help you get a fast start with DOS 6, and you'll learn concepts such as the following:

- Using the enhancements available in DOS 6 on your system
- Taking advantage of the newest memory-management techniques and gaining the most space possible for your programs
- Gaining more space on your hard disk without the expense of purchasing new hardware
- Increasing the performance of your PC with DOS 6
- Protecting your programs and data

- Using the new connectivity features included in DOS 6
- Understanding the differences between commands new to MS-DOS 6 and commands in earlier versions

In short, you'll find what you need to know about DOS 6 in *Upgrading to MS-DOS 6*, without wasting a lot of your time. This book is intended to help you get a running start with DOS 6.

Who Should Read This Book?

Upgrading to MS-DOS 6 shows you what you need to know to upgrade to DOS 6. It shows you how to make the most of the time and money you spend upgrading to DOS 6. If you're interested in using DOS 6 immediately without wasting too much time, this book is for you.

Millions of people use PCs, and each PC user has a different reason for upgrading to DOS 6. Some users are interested in making their PCs easier to use, others want to make their current system last a little longer, some need to connect their systems to other PCs, and others want to learn about all the new features. Whatever your reason for being interested in DOS 6, *Upgrading to MS-DOS 6* is for you.

Whether you've upgraded your PC's operating system in the past (perhaps to DOS 5), or you're using the same software that originally came on your PC, you'll find that this book provides the information you need to get started. You'll learn how to upgrade your system easily, how to use the new features, and what you may need to do before you upgrade to DOS 6.

Although *Upgrading to MS-DOS 6* is not intended as a complete reference to DOS 6, it does provide all the information needed by most PC users who want to upgrade their operating systems, or who want to help other users upgrade their systems. You won't find a lot of boring technical details, but you will find the information you need.

If you're a Microsoft Windows user, you'll find that DOS 6 offers special features that help you use Windows. *Upgrading to MS-DOS 6* includes coverage of the new Windows utility programs included in DOS 6.

What Is Covered in This Book?

Upgrading to MS-DOS 6 is designed to answer questions you may have as you install, configure, and use DOS 6. The information you'll find in this book includes the following topics.

Enhancements to DOS 6

DOS 6 includes many enhancements, such as new commands, additional options for existing commands, easy-to-use memory configuration options, built-in disk compression, and the capability to easily connect two or more PCs in order to share files and printers. This book shows you what those enhancements are and gives you examples so that you can see how to apply those enhancements to your advantage.

This book also examines new features of DOS 6 that, in many cases, eliminate the need for expensive and complicated programs many PC users have needed in the past to perform functions. The new DBLSPACE command, for example, effectively increases the size of your hard disk—often doubling the space available—without requiring you to purchase a utility program such as Stacker or SuperStor. The new antivirus and backup programs make it easier to protect your data.

If your PC is connected to a network, or if you have two PCs (perhaps a laptop PC and a desktop system) you'll be interested in the new capabilities of DOS 6 that enable you to connect PCs. *Upgrading to MS-DOS 6* examines these features and shows you how to take advantage of them—whether or not you have a network.

Tips on System Optimization

DOS 6 offers many opportunities for customization and optimization that were not available or were very difficult to implement in previous versions of DOS. You can gain more memory for your programs by placing DOS, device drivers, and some programs into high memory (if it is available on your system), for example. DOS 6 includes a new program, MEMMAKER, designed to help you gain this additional memory automatically.

In many cases, you simply can sit back and allow MEMMAKER to optimize your system's configuration. In other cases, you may want to take more control of your system's configuration options. Regardless of the method you choose, *Upgrading to MS-DOS 6* includes the information you'll need to proceed.

Computer Systems That Can Run DOS 6

If you have been using a previous version of MS-DOS or PC DOS, you should be able to upgrade to DOS 6 without any difficulty. DOS 6 is an upward-compatible enhancement of earlier versions of DOS, and should be able to run any programs that ran under an earlier version of DOS.

If you have been using Microsoft Windows, you can continue to use your current version of Windows and all of your Windows programs after you upgrade to DOS 6. In fact, you will find that DOS 6 is designed to enhance Windows—especially Windows 3.1.

If you have been using OS/2, you can upgrade to DOS 6, too. OS/2 and DOS 6, however, are very different types of operating systems. Any OS/2 application programs you use will not run on DOS 6, but any DOS programs you have been running on OS/2 will run under DOS 6.

Upgrading to DOS 6 requires a minimum level of hardware and software on your system. You must have DOS or OS/2 installed, for example. You cannot install DOS 6 on computers that are not IBM compatible, such as a Macintosh. Upgrading to DOS 6 requires at least the following hardware:

- 440K of memory.
- 4.2M of free disk space (if you want to install all the options and you are upgrading to a hard disk system).

If you do not have enough hard disk space for a complete installation, you can skip the optional programs and install DOS 6 with about 2M of space, if necessary. You then can use DBLSPACE to increase your available disk space and install the optional programs later.

- Three high-density floppy disks, if you're upgrading by installing DOS 6 on a floppy disk system. If necessary, you can order low-density DOS 6 installation disks.
- One blank floppy disk (or possibly two 360K floppy disks) for hard disk system installation. You use this disk during the installation process, to uninstall DOS 6 if necessary, or to recover from installation problems.

Although it is not required, you should consider backing up your hard disk before installing DOS 6. Installation problems are rare, but a current set of backup disks can save you from losing your important files in the unlikely event that something does go wrong. After you install DOS 6, you will find that making backups using the new Backup for DOS and Backup for Windows programs is easier than ever before. Even so, backing up your important files *before* installing DOS 6 is a wise move.

What Does This Book Contain?

Now that you have an idea of what's included in *Upgrading to MS-DOS 6*, it's time for a closer look at the new DOS 6 features covered in each chapter:

Chapter 1, "Introducing DOS 6," provides a short introduction to the enhancements included in DOS 6. The new features are summarized, and the command changes relative to earlier DOS versions are shown in two tables.

Chapter 2, "Upgrading to DOS 6," takes you through the steps of installing DOS 6 on your system and shows you how to deal with problems that may arise while you're installing DOS 6.

Chapter 3, "Customizing Memory Usage with DOS 6," covers the different types of memory DOS 6 can use and shows you how to take maximum advantage of these types. You learn how to optimize your system's memory usage and how to fine-tune the configuration.

Chapter 4, "Optimizing Your Hard Disk with DOS 6," introduces disk compression, disk caching, and disk optimization. These features help you get more out of your PC's hardware without requiring you to spend any extra money.

Chapter 5, "Backing Up Your Data," describes DOS 6's new Backup for DOS and Backup for Windows programs. These programs help you protect your work from disk failures and human errors.

Chapter 6, "Using Virus Protection," explains computer viruses and shows you how to protect your system using the antivirus programs new to DOS 6.

Chapter 7, "Recovering Deleted Files," shows you how to recover files that were deleted accidentally. You also learn how to use DOS 6's enhanced methods for recovering lost files and directories.

Chapter 8, "Connecting PCs with Interlnk," covers a totally new area of DOS. With DOS 6, you can share files and printers, without connecting to a network.

Chapter 9, "Controlling Configurations," shows you how to set up your system with different configuration options and how to create program selection menus.

Chapter 10, "Using DOS 6 on Your Laptop PC," covers the features of DOS 6 that are of special interest to owners of laptop PCs.

Appendix A, "Connecting PCs with Workgroup Connection," shows you how to use the separately sold Microsoft Workgroup Connection to share files and printers, and to send and receive electronic mail over a network.

How Can You Learn More About DOS 6?

This book provides an overview of the features new to DOS 6. It does not attempt to cover all areas of DOS. After you upgrade to DOS 6, you may be interested in some other fine Que books on DOS, including the following:

- *MS-DOS 6 Quick Reference*
- *Easy DOS 6*
- *MS-DOS 6 QuickStart*

What Conventions Are Used in This Book?

Certain conventions are followed in this book to help you more easily understand the discussions, use of commands, and syntax.

Special Typefaces and Representations

In most cases, the keys on your keyboard are represented as they appear on your keyboard. Arrow symbols, such as ↑ and their corresponding terms, such as *up arrow*, are used to represent the arrow keys.

Ctrl+Z indicates that you press the Ctrl key (which may appear as Control on your keyboard) and hold it down while you also press the Z key.

Words or phrases that are defined for the first time appear in *italic* characters. Words or phrases you type appear in **boldface** characters.

Uppercase characters are used to distinguish file names and DOS commands. Although uppercase characters are shown in the examples, DOS does not distinguish between uppercase and lowercase characters; you can use either case.

All screen displays and on-screen messages appear in the following special typeface:

```
This is a screen message
```

Command Syntax

The notation for issuing commands and running programs appears, in fullest form, in lines such as the following:

d:path\DEFRAG *drive /switches*

In any syntax line, not all elements of the syntax can be represented in a literal manner. For example, *d:* represents the drive where the DEFRAG command is on your system, *path*\ represents the path to your subdirectory where DEFRAG is located, *drive* represents the drive you want to defragment, and */switches* indicates the various switches you may use with the DEFRAG command. To execute the command DEFRAG.EXE, for example, you must type the word **DEFRAG**. To use the DEFRAG command with the /F (full) switch and process the files on drive C, you can type the following:

DEFRAG C: /F

Any literal text you type in a syntax line is shown in uppercase characters. Any text you can replace with other text (variable text) is shown in lowercase characters. Note the following syntax line, for example:

DEFRAG *d:*

This line indicates that you type the **DEFRAG** command followed by a drive letter. You substitute the letter of the drive you want defragmented for *d:*.

Mandatory versus Optional Parts of a Command

Not all parts of a syntax line are essential when typing a command. Any portion of a syntax line shown in regular type is mandatory; you must always issue this part of the command. In the preceding example, to issue the DEFRAG command, you must type the word **DEFRAG**.

Many commands have optional portions. These are shown in a syntax line in *italic characters*. You supply these items only when needed. In the previous example, you substitute a drive letter for *d:* to specify the drive letter on the command line instead of selecting the drive letter after the DEFRAG command starts execution.

In most cases, if you do not type an optional item, DOS uses a default value or setting for the item. In a few cases, DOS displays the proper syntax or an option menu instead of using a default value.

1

CHAPTER

Introducing DOS 6

This chapter looks at the enhancements included in DOS 6 and explains how these enhancements can benefit you and improve the operation of your PC. Later chapters cover each enhancement in greater detail and show you how to use each of them. You can use this chapter as your quick guide to learning the basics of what's new in DOS 6, and then read the later chapters when you're ready to install and use DOS 6.

As you read Chapter 1, keep in mind that DOS 6 runs on many different types of PCs, and all of the new features may not currently apply to your system. When a feature does require more than a basic PC, however, the text will indicate the type of hardware that is required.

Although a few advanced features of DOS 6 benefit only owners of the newer, more powerful PCs, most of the enhancements are available to all PC users. The following sections of this chapter describe DOS 6's enhancements, which include

- Advanced memory management, including automatic upper memory optimization
- New disk-management features, including disk compression, caching, and optimization

- Data protection, including virus protection, easier backups, and improved file-recovery capabilities
- Built-in connectivity features for networked and non-networked PCs
- Support for multiple system configurations, including options enabling users to choose from menus
- Many new or enhanced commands

Memory Management

The memory-management enhancements included in DOS 6 are intended primarily to benefit users with PCs based on 80386, 80486, and higher processors. DOS 6 provides easier memory management and more flexibility for owners of these types of systems.

If your PC has an 80286 processor and your current operating system is a version of DOS earlier than DOS 5, you will find some advanced memory management features in DOS 6 that may offer benefits to your system, too. The benefits of DOS 6's advanced memory-management features are aimed primarily at the newer PC systems, however.

Easier Memory Management

DOS 5 provided an important breakthrough in DOS memory management. For the first time, DOS 5 enabled the PC user to use more than the 640K of conventional memory available to programs in earlier versions of DOS. Unfortunately, making use of the high memory area (HMA) and upper memory blocks (UMBs) was almost a black art. Not only was the terminology confusing, but you almost had to be a computer scientist to make the best use of the DOS 5 memory-management options. If you made a mistake, you could end up with less memory available, or even be unable to start up your computer.

DOS 6 includes a new program, MemMaker, intended to make memory-management hassles a thing of the past. After you execute the MemMaker program, it examines your system's configuration, considers many possible options, and tries the most promising ones. When the program finishes its task, it makes the necessary changes in CONFIG.SYS and AUTOEXEC.BAT. Although the term *upper memory block* may sound like something that makes you forget the names of people who live in tall buildings, MemMaker can use UMBs to quickly give your programs more memory space.

The MemMaker program runs on PCs with an 80386, 80486, or higher processor, and 1M or more of random-access memory (RAM). This category includes most of the PCs sold in the past few years.

More Options in Memory Usage

Even though the DOS 6 MemMaker program can do an excellent job of supplying more memory for your programs (up to 104K more than is available with DOS 5), some PC users still may want to try adding their own fine-tuning to their system configurations in an attempt to squeeze out those last few bytes of memory. DOS 6 provides several tools to make this possible.

DOS 6 enables you to specify exactly which memory block is used for each device driver or memory-resident program. Because upper memory often is fragmented into a number of blocks, this enables you to move and juggle your configuration settings until every possible byte of *conventional* memory (memory below 640K used to run programs) is freed. To make this task a little easier, the DOS 6 MEM command has been enhanced to provide more useful information.

Chapter 3 covers DOS 6's memory-management options in detail. Whether you're a novice PC user or an expert with a pocket protector, DOS 6 makes it easier than ever to manage your PC's available memory.

Disk Management

The term *DOS* is an acronym for *disk operating system*. It's no wonder, then, that the latest version of DOS has advanced disk-management capabilities built into the program. The newest features of DOS 6's disk management are similar to separate utility programs, such as Stacker, SuperPCK, and Speed Disk in The Norton Utilities.

Added Disk Space with DoubleSpace

DoubleSpace is a disk compression program similar to Stacker and SuperStor that greatly increases the apparent space available on your disks. DoubleSpace makes more space available by compressing files as they're stored on your disks, and then uncompressing those files as they're loaded into memory.

When you use a disk-compression program, the same size disk can store much more information. Because different types of files compress by varying percentages, it's difficult to say how much extra space DoubleSpace provides. On the average, however, it's probably safe to guess that with DoubleSpace, your files will use about one-half as much disk space. A 65M hard disk, for example, probably will be able to hold about 130M of files by using DoubleSpace.

Although other disk-compression software existed before DoubleSpace, the earlier programs were much more difficult to use because they weren't as closely integrated with DOS as is DoubleSpace.

You may be familiar with file-compression programs, such as PKZIP, that compress files and store them in archives. These types of programs require you to manually specify files to compress and uncompress—unlike DoubleSpace, which works automatically with every program on your PC.

Increased Performance with Smartdrv

Accessing information from your hard disk is hundreds of times slower than accessing the same information already in memory. Floppy disks are even slower than hard disks. One of the best ways to make your system perform at a faster rate is to somehow reduce the number of times your system has to read information from the disk drives.

Disk caching, storing information read from a disk in a special location in memory, is one of the techniques DOS 6 uses to increase your PC's level of performance. Although versions of Smartdrv, the disk-caching program, are provided with earlier versions of DOS and Windows, the DOS 6 Smartdrv program is the best yet. It not only offers higher speed than earlier versions of the same program, but it also was designed to work with both DoubleSpace and Windows.

If you have an earlier version of Smartdrv installed on your system, be sure to upgrade to the DOS 6 Smartdrv program when you install DOS 6. Earlier versions of Smartdrv are not designed to work with disk-caching programs like DoubleSpace, and may cause damage to your files if you use DoubleSpace.

Optimized Disks with Defrag

When you first add files to a new disk, each file is stored in one contiguous area. As you use your system, you probably delete old files and add new ones. When DOS allocates space for files, it does so on a space-available basis; this system often causes larger files to be stored in several small pieces in various locations on your disk. Files stored in several pieces are said to be *fragmented*, and take longer to access than files stored in one piece. In addition, fragmented files that have been accidentally deleted are much harder to recover.

You may not notice the effects of file fragmentation for quite some time after you first start using a PC, but eventually you may find that your files take longer to save and to load. DOS 6 includes a program, Defrag, that *defragments* the files on your disk. This process often is called *optimizing* a disk, because it results in faster disk operation.

Chapter 4 covers the disk-management features new to DOS 6 and shows you how to effectively apply them to your system. You can gain from DOS 6's new disk-management capabilities regardless of the type of PC you use.

Data Protection

For most PC users, the data generated and stored on their systems has a value far beyond the cost of the hardware. The protection of that data is very important, but often is treated as a minor issue. DOS 6 adds new features to make protecting your data much easier.

Data protection falls into three general areas: backing up your files, preventing their destruction by computer viruses, and recovering files that were accidentally erased. The following sections examine the DOS 6 enhancements in each of these areas.

Easier Backups

Most PC users know they should back up their files, but very few people are ever as conscientious about backups as they should be. Backing up files can take quite a bit of time, it's a lot of work, and you need a large number of floppy disks.

Earlier versions of DOS include a program called Backup to make backup copies of the files on your hard disk. These early versions offer an advantage compared to simply copying those same files to floppy disks: files don't have to fit on a single floppy disk. If you want to back up 20M of hard disk files, for example, you simply make sure that you have enough floppy disks to hold all that data. Of course, you also must change floppy disks quite a few times, label those disks, and spend quite a bit of time making your backups.

DOS 6 still backs up your hard disk files to floppy disks, but this version makes the whole process much easier and more reliable with two new backup programs. *MS Backup for DOS* backs up your files from the DOS command line, and *MS Backup for Windows* backs up your files using all the features of the graphical Windows interface. Actually, the two programs are really just two versions of the same program, and include the same operating features.

The new MS Backup for DOS and MS Backup for Windows programs have several new features that make backing up your files much easier, and therefore more likely that you actually will perform the backups. These features fall into several areas:

- Selecting files for backups is easier because you can quickly select the directories and files you want to back up. You can select complete disks, individual directories, or even individual files within directories simply by tagging the entire disk, selected directories, or selected files. This approach is much more flexible than selecting files by using wild cards.
- Fewer floppy disks are required because the backup programs offer optional file compression during backups. Depending on the types of files you are backing up, you may find that you need only half as many floppy disks.
- If your floppy disk drives send a signal to your PC after you change a disk (most high-density drives do), the MS Backup programs sense when you change a floppy disk. This saves you time because you don't have to change disks and then press Enter. Instead, the backup process continues as soon as you insert the new floppy disk.
- A new option enables you to make *differential* backups. A differential backup includes all files changed since the last *full* backup. In the past, you had a choice between a full backup (all selected files) and an *incremental* backup (all files changed since the last full or incremental backup). Differential backups give you a useful third option, especially if you often update the same files.
- Backup sets and backup catalogs provide new methods of managing your backups. A named backup set, for example, enables you to quickly back up the same group of files without having to respecify each of those files. Backup *catalogs* are databases of

information about the files that have been backed up. Catalogs enable you to select specific files or versions of the same file for restoration.

- Finally, MS Backup ensures that your data is backed up properly, and that even if floppy disk errors occur, you probably will be able to restore your files. Error-correction codes can be stored with your backed-up files to ensure the safe recovery of the data.

Chapter 5, "Backing Up Your Data," covers DOS 6's backup programs and their options in detail.

Virus Protection

Computer viruses are big news. These programs, designed to cause loss or corruption of data, can enter your system from many sources—including infected floppy disks, programs you download from on-line services, or even from your company's local area network (LAN). Regardless of the source, having a computer virus invade your PC is no fun.

Protecting your computer from viruses involves many steps; some steps are very easy, while others require extra effort. Knowing whether your system is infected, however, often requires special antivirus programs—especially if you want to detect and remove viruses before they have the opportunity to do any damage.

DOS 6 includes two programs: *MS Anti-Virus for DOS* and *MS Anti-Virus for Windows*. These programs can detect and, in most cases remove, more than 1,000 known computer viruses. These programs protect you from the most common viruses, and can be updated as new viruses are released. In addition, DOS 6 includes another program, *VSafe*, which constantly monitors your system for the types of activities that make viruses so dangerous. MS Anti-Virus protects you from known viruses and VSafe protects you from new, unknown viruses.

Chapter 6, "Using Virus Protection," explains the details of DOS 6's antivirus programs and shows you how to protect your data from viruses.

Lost File Recovery

The third part of DOS 6's data-protection trio is an enhanced ability to recover files that were accidentally deleted. Deleted files are not erased from a disk, but simply are *marked* as erased. DOS 5 included a new command, UNDELETE, that enabled you to recover many deleted files. DOS 6 goes a few steps further, and makes it much more likely that you can recover accidentally deleted files. In addition, DOS 6 now can recover directories that have been accidentally deleted.

Undelete for DOS and *Undelete for Windows* have a new option, called *Delete Sentry*, that guarantees the recovery of deleted files—regardless of how many new files you have saved to the disk. Delete Sentry saves deleted files in a special hidden directory, making it possible to recover those files completely intact. If you don't feel that you need such complete protection, Undelete for DOS and Undelete for Windows still can recover most deleted files quickly and easily.

Chapter 7, "Recovering Deleted Files," shows you how to recover accidentally deleted files.

Networking

Connecting two or more PCs is fast becoming very important to many PC users. Whether you want to share files and printers on a network, quickly move files between your desktop and laptop PCs, or simply use electronic mail, connectivity is a vital issue. DOS 6 is the first version of DOS designed to make connecting PC systems an easy and integral part of the operating environment.

Easy Connections to Networks

An optional feature of DOS 6, the *Workgroup Connection*, enables you to use the features of a network without all the complications often involved in networked computing. If you have a network adapter card installed in your PC and you install the Workgroup Connection, you can share files and printers with others on the network while still using your standard DOS and Windows programs. You also can send electronic mail to and receive electronic mail from other users on your network.

The Workgroup Connection makes it very easy to connect to a network. It recognizes most common network adapter cards, connects to many different types of networks, and enables you to connect or disconnect from the network without leaving your application programs.

Network Advantages Without a Network

Even if you don't have your PC connected to a network, you may want to share files or printers between two PCs. If you have a laptop PC that you take on business trips and a desktop PC in your office or home, for example, you probably want to share files. You also may have a report that you generated on your laptop, but that you want to print on your desktop's laser printer.

DOS 6 hasn't ignored the needs of PC users who want to perform these types of file- and printer-sharing tasks, but don't want to install a network. The Interlnk program enables two PCs to share disk drives and printers, and requires only a cable between serial or parallel ports. Interlnk isn't a full-blown network program, but it suits the needs of a great many PC users.

Chapter 8, "Connecting PCs with Interlnk," shows you all the exciting new connectivity options available in DOS 6, whether you're networked or simply want to connect two PCs.

Multiple Configurations

Managing different system configurations has, in the past, been a difficult but often necessary evil. One application program may have required your PC to use certain options that were incompatible with those required by another program. A spreadsheet program may have required that your system's memory be configured as extended memory, while a game program may have required that memory be configured as expanded memory. A network adapter may have required you to load a device driver into memory, but this may have left too little memory for a computer aided design (CAD) program.

To make matters worse, you may have found that certain system configuration options were completely incompatible. If you loaded your network adapter card driver and a special driver for your scanner, your system may have locked up when you tried to boot. You then had to find and use your emergency boot floppy in order to restart your system. DOS 6 has much better options.

New Booting Options

When you *boot* (start up) your PC, DOS looks for two special configuration files in the root directory of the boot disk. These files, CONFIG.SYS and AUTOEXEC.BAT, control which device drivers are loaded, determine whether any memory-resident programs are loaded, and specify several other important system settings. Unfortunately, it's fairly easy to make changes in CONFIG.SYS or AUTOEXEC.BAT that can prevent you from starting DOS.

In DOS 6, however, you can instruct your system to bypass specific commands in CONFIG.SYS, or to completely ignore all of the commands in CONFIG.SYS or AUTOEXEC.BAT. If you have created a set of system configuration commands that don't enable you to boot your PC, these options enable you to start your system without executing the configuration commands that are causing the problems.

Even if you never make any changes to CONFIG.SYS or AUTOEXEC.BAT, many application programs have installation programs that do make these types of changes. With DOS 6, you can start your system even if an installation program makes inappropriate changes to CONFIG.SYS or AUTOEXEC.BAT.

Menus in CONFIG.SYS and AUTOEXEC.BAT

Before DOS 6, each command in CONFIG.SYS and AUTOEXEC.BAT was executed every time you booted your system. If you needed to load a different set of device drivers, to load different memory-resident programs, or to create a different set of environment variables, you had to have several different sets of CONFIG.SYS and AUTOEXEC.BAT files. You may have used a number of floppy disks to boot your system with different configurations, or you may have copied those special CONFIG.SYS and AUTOEXEC.BAT files to your hard disk's root directory whenever you needed to use a special configuration.

With DOS 6, however, these cumbersome methods of changing your system configuration to meet special program requirements are a thing of the past. DOS 6 enables you to create configuration option menus in CONFIG.SYS and AUTOEXEC.BAT. You can specify a standard configuration that is selected automatically after a specified period of time, and you can add color to the menus. If your network adapter card and your scanner card cannot coexist, you can specify which device driver you want to load. If your spreadsheet program requires a different type of memory than your favorite game, you can select that option as well.

Chapter 9, "Controlling Configurations," shows you how to create menus that enable you to select different configuration options. The chapter also tells you what to do if certain options prove incompatible with your system.

Command Differences in DOS 6

DOS 6 has quite a few new command options. DOS 6 contains several new commands and new options for existing commands. DOS 6 also has replaced some commands, and does not include other commands. Tables 1.1, 1.2, and 1.3 summarize the command differences in DOS 6. Later chapters of *Upgrading to MS-DOS 6* cover each of these command differences in more complete detail.

Table 1.1 Commands New to DOS 6

Command	Description
CHOICE	Waits for the user to select a choice in a batch file. Use CHOICE to create menus in AUTOEXEC.BAT.
DBLSPACE	Compresses files to create more effective space on your disks.
DEFRAG	Reorganizes files on a disk to unfragment the files and optimize disk performance.
DELTREE	Deletes a directory and any files or subdirectories it contains. You no longer have to delete the files in a directory before deleting the directory.
DOSHELP	Provides on-line information about DOS commands. For more detailed information, use the HELP command.
EXPAND	Decompresses the compressed DOS 6 files from the installation disks. These files are not usable until you decompress them.
INCLUDE	Includes the contents of a *configuration block*—a block of commands contained in CONFIG.SYS. You use the INCLUDE command to define multiple configurations within a single CONFIG.SYS file.
INTERLNK	Connects two PCs using their serial or parallel ports, enabling you to share files and printers. You must install the INTERLNK.EXE device driver in CONFIG.SYS before you can use this command. You use the INTERLNK command on the computer on which you will be entering commands.

continues

Table 1.1 Continued

Command	Description
INTERSVR	Starts the Interlnk server, which provides serial or parallel file-transfer capability through redirected drives, and printing through redirected printer ports. You use the INTERSVR command on the computer on which you will not be entering commands.
MAIL	Starts Microsoft Mail, an electronic mail program. MAIL is installed only if you are connected to a network and install the Workgroup Connection.
MEMMAKER	Optimizes your system's memory by moving device drivers and memory-resident programs to upper memory. To use MemMaker, your computer must have an 80386, 80486, or Pentium microprocessor and extended memory.
MENUCOLOR	Sets the text and background colors for a startup menu you create in CONFIG.SYS. The startup menu is a list of choices that appears when you start your computer and makes it possible to start your computer with a variety of configurations.
MENUDEFAULT	Specifies the default menu item on a startup menu you create in CONFIG.SYS, and sets an optional time-out value.
MENUITEM	Defines an item on a startup menu you create in CONFIG.SYS. You can have up to nine menu items per menu.
MICRO	Starts a memory-resident program that notifies you when new mail messages arrive. You must install the Workgroup Connection and set up Microsoft Mail on your computer before you can use Micro.
MOVE	Moves files and renames directories and files. You can move individual files, move groups of files, or rename an entire directory.
MSAV	Scans your files searching for computer viruses. Optionally removes any viruses it discovers.
MSBACKUP	Runs the MS Backup for DOS program. MSBACKUP is the enhanced DOS 6 replacement for the BACKUP command.
MSCDEX	A device driver that you can load from AUTOEXEC.BAT to access your CD-ROM drive.

Command	Description
MSD	Obtains detailed technical information about your computer's installed hardware and software. Diagnoses system problems and helps you optimize your PC's configuration.
NUMLOCK	Specifies whether the NUM LOCK setting of the numeric keypad is initially set to ON or OFF. Can be used only within a menu block in the CONFIG.SYS file.
POWER	Reduces power consumption on a laptop PC when applications and devices are idle. POWER is most useful on PCs that conform to the Advanced Power Management (APM) specification.
SIZER	A program that only MemMaker uses to determine the size of TSRs and device drivers.
SUBMENU	Defines an item in a startup menu you create in CONFIG.SYS that, when selected, displays another set of choices. Use the SUBMENU command to create nested menu options.
VSAFE	Loads a memory-resident program that continuously monitors your computer for viruses. Displays a warning if it finds a virus.

Table 1.2 Command Options New to DOS 6

Command	Option	Description
COMMAND	/K	Runs a specified program or batch file and then displays the command prompt.
DEVICEHIGH	/L:*x*	Specifies the number of the UMB region in which to load a device driver. By default, DOS loads drivers into the largest free UMB, but you can use the /L switch to load a device driver into a specific region of memory or to specify which region(s) the driver can use.
DEVICEHIGH	/S	Shrinks the UMB to its minimum size while the driver is loading. Using /S makes the most efficient use of memory. You can use the /S switch only with the /L switch, and

continues

Table 1.2 Continued

Command	Option	Description
		/S affects only UMBs for which a minimum size was specified.
DIR	/C	Displays the compression ratio of compressed files stored on Dblspace volumes. DOS 6 ignores the /C switch if it is used with the /W or /B switch.
FDISK	/STATUS	Displays the partition information for your PC's hard disk(s).
LOADHIGH	/L:*x*	Specifies the number of the upper memory block region into which to load a memory-resident program. By default, DOS loads programs into the largest UMB, but you can use the /L switch to load a program into a specific region of memory or to specify which region(s) the program can use.
LOADHIGH	/S	Shrinks the UMB to its minimum size while the memory-resident program is loading. Using /S makes the most efficient use of memory. You can use the /S switch only with the /L switch, and /S affects only UMBs for which a minimum size was specified.
MEM	/F /FREE	Lists the free areas of conventional and upper memory, showing the segment address and size of each free area of conventional memory, and the largest free UMB in each region of upper memory.
MEM	/M program /MODULE program	Shows how a program is currently using memory. You must specify the program name after the /M switch. MEM /M lists the areas of memory the program has allocated, and shows the address and size of each area.
MEM	/P	Pauses the display of the MEM command after each screen of output.

Command	Option	Description
SWITCHES	/F	Skips the two-second pause before CONFIG.SYS commands execute after the `Starting MS-DOS ...` message appears during startup.
SWITCHES	/N	Prevents you from using the F5 or F8 key to bypass startup commands.
SWITCHES	/W	Specifies that the WINA20.386 file has been moved to a directory other than the root directory. You need this switch only if you are using Windows 3.0 in enhanced mode, and you have moved the WINA20.386 file.
UNDELETE	/DS	Recovers only those files listed in the SENTRY directory.
UNDELETE	/LOAD	Loads the Undelete terminate-and-stay-resident (TSR) program into memory. UNDELETE /LOAD replaces the DOS 5 MIRROR command.
UNDELETE	/PURGE	Deletes the contents of the \SENTRY directory on the specified drive or the current drive. The \SENTRY directory is a special hidden directory that stores files you have deleted.
UNDELETE	/STATUS	Displays the type of delete protection in effect for each drive.
UNDELETE	/Tdrive-#	Loads the TSR portion of the UNDELETE program that records information used to recover deleted files, using the delete-tracking method. The drive parameter is required. The optional # parameter specifies the maximum number of entries in the deletion-tracking file (PCTRACKR.DEL).
UNDELETE	/U	Unloads the TSR portion of the Undelete program from memory, disabling the capability to restore deleted files.

Table 1.3 Commands Deleted from DOS 6

Command	Replacement
BACKUP	MSBACKUP
MIRROR	UNDELETE /LOAD
RECOVER	none

Chapter Summary

DOS 6 has many important enhancements. This chapter provided a quick overview of the new features in DOS 6. The remaining chapters show you how to take advantage of these new features on your PC.

2

CHAPTER

Upgrading to DOS 6

This chapter shows you how to upgrade to DOS 6. The chapter starts by explaining how to determine whether your system meets the necessary hardware and software requirements before you begin installing DOS 6. Next, you learn how to add the DOS 6 files to your system quickly and automatically, and you learn what options are available if the Express Setup option is not correct for your PC. Although you shouldn't have any problems installing DOS 6, the next section tells you how to handle any problems that may arise. You also see how to uninstall DOS 6 if necessary. Finally, you learn how to delete your old version of DOS and free the disk space it occupied.

Before Upgrading to DOS 6

You install DOS 6 using the SETUP program—an easy and straightforward process. During the installation procedure, SETUP examines your system to learn what hardware and software is installed. In most cases, you don't have to worry about the details, because the default settings are correct.

You may, however, want to start out by making some system checks to help you determine whether your PC is ready to upgrade to DOS 6. These simple checks provide information you can use to decide whether you need to make some changes before you begin installing DOS 6.

If you normally load certain types of programs automatically whenever you start your PC, you may need to temporarily disable the command lines in CONFIG.SYS or AUTOEXEC.BAT that load those programs.

The following sections show you the steps you should take before you install DOS 6.

Checking Your Current DOS Version

You can use the DOS 6 upgrade package to install DOS 6 only on a PC that currently is running MS-DOS, PC DOS, or OS/2. You can determine whether your PC is using a version of MS-DOS or PC DOS by typing the **VER** command at the command prompt.

DOS responds with a message similar to the following:

```
MS-DOS Version 5.00
```

Your system may show a different version number, or it may include your PC manufacturer's name, but as long as you see some variation of this message you should be able to upgrade to DOS 6. If the message does include the PC manufacturer's name, you may want to contact the manufacturer to see if it is offering a special version of DOS 6 that contains features specific to your brand of PC. Some manufacturers, for example, include special utility programs that offer increased functionality—such as the capability to control screen displays or keyboard click sounds—on their systems.

Determining Disk Space and Memory Needs

To install DOS 6, you must have at least 440K of RAM and 4M of space available on your hard disk.

To install DOS 6 on floppy disks instead of a hard disk, you must have 440K of RAM, a high-density (1.2M or 1.44M) drive A, and three high-density floppy disks.

You can use the CHKDSK program in your current version of DOS to determine whether you have enough memory (RAM) and hard disk space to install DOS 6. To get this information, type the following command at the DOS prompt:

CHKDSK C:

The CHKDSK command responds by displaying several pieces of information about your system's hard disk and memory. You may see information similar to that shown in figure 2.1, for example.

```
Volume Fixed C      created 04-28-1992 11:15a
Volume Serial Number is 1963-712A

1037795328 bytes total disk space
  52822016 bytes in 5 hidden files
   3162112 bytes in 193 directories
 287195136 bytes in 5750 user files
 694566912 bytes available on disk

     16384 bytes in each allocation unit
     63342 total allocation units on disk
     42393 available allocation units on disk

    655360 total bytes memory
    577824 bytes free
```

Fig. 2.1
CHKDSK shows your disk space and memory usage.

The two important lines in figure 2.1 are those that show the number of bytes available on your disk and the number of bytes free (which also may appear as largest executable program size). You must have at least 4,200,000 bytes available on your disk and 450,560 bytes free before you can install DOS 6.

Freeing Disk Space

If the CHKDSK command shows less than 4,200,000 bytes available on the hard disk, copy some of your files to floppy disks, and then delete the files from the hard disk before installing DOS 6. You will be able to recover some of the disk space used to install DOS 6 after you successfully complete the installation, but make sure that you have at least 4,200,000 bytes available on your hard disk before you begin.

Freeing Memory

If the CHKDSK command shows less than 450,560 bytes of available RAM, look at the line just above the one that indicates the number of bytes that are free. This line shows how much total conventional memory is installed in your system. In most cases, this line should say `655360 total bytes memory` (640K), but it must say at least `524288 total bytes memory`, which is equal to 512K.

If your PC has less than 512K total bytes of memory, you must install additional RAM before you can upgrade to DOS 6. See your dealer or manufacturer for information about adding memory to your system.

If your PC has at least 512K total bytes of memory but has less than 450,560 bytes available, you probably are loading device drivers or memory-resident programs when you start your system. You will need to disable the lines in CONFIG.SYS or AUTOEXEC.BAT that load these device drivers or memory-resident programs before you can install the upgrade to DOS 6.

The next section provides more information on temporarily preventing device drivers and memory-resident programs from loading. For now, however, you must decide which device drivers and memory-resident programs to disable in order to free enough memory to install DOS 6. Don't disable any device drivers necessary to access your hard disk, such as CONFIG.SYS commands that load Disk Manager. You can, however, disable lines that load such items as a mouse driver, a disk cache, fax-board drivers, and CD-ROM drivers. None of these items is needed during the DOS 6 installation.

Temporarily Disabling Problem Programs

The DOS 6 SETUP program is incompatible with most disk-caching, delete-protection, and antivirus programs. If you load any of these programs in CONFIG.SYS or AUTOEXEC.BAT, you must temporarily disable the commands that load the programs before you install DOS 6. If necessary, you can reactivate these commands after you successfully complete the installation.

You don't need to disable the Smartdrv disk-caching program before installing DOS 6.

To temporarily disable a command in CONFIG.SYS or AUTOEXEC.BAT, type **REM** and a space at the beginning of the line you want to disable. To disable the following line in CONFIG.SYS:

```
DEVICE=C:\DOS\BAD.SYS
```

change the line to:

```
REM DEVICE=C:\DOS\BAD.SYS
```

You can use any text editor, such as EDIT in DOS 5 or EDLIN in any DOS version, to make this change. When you are satisfied that you have made the correct modifications, save the file and restart your system (changes you make in CONFIG.SYS or AUTOEXEC.BAT take effect only when you restart or *reboot* your system).

Upgrading the Easy Way

When you are sure that you have enough memory and disk space available to install DOS 6 properly, you can proceed with the upgrade. The DOS 6 Setup program makes this process easy.

Important Backup Information

Before you begin the installation process, you may want to back up your files. You are not likely to encounter problems that would cause a loss of data, but if you have files that you cannot afford to lose or work that you don't want to repeat if a problem does occur, this would be a good time to finally make a backup. Your backup doesn't need to include your program files. You always can reinstall your programs using the original program disks, but your backup should include any data files that you don't want to lose.

Using Express Setup

For most upgraders, the easiest method of upgrading to DOS 6 is to use the Express Setup option. When you use this option, the Setup program first examines your system to determine the type of hardware you have on your PC. Next, the program locates your current DOS version's files and determines whether you have Windows installed. After these tests have been completed, the Setup program installs DOS 6.

Unless you must install DOS 6 on floppy disks, or you have tried to install DOS 6 on your hard disk and were unsuccessful, you should use the Express Setup option to install DOS 6. To use this option, follow these steps:

1. If you are running any programs or are using Windows, exit completely from the program or from Windows. You cannot run Setup successfully from the Windows MS-DOS prompt.
2. Make certain that you have enough available memory and disk space (see "Determining Disk Space and Memory Needs," earlier in this chapter).
3. Label a blank floppy disk *Uninstall*. This disk must be compatible with drive A. If this disk is a 360K disk, you will need two disks, which you should label *Uninstall 1* and *Uninstall 2*.
4. Insert the disk labeled *Disk 1/Setup* into drive A and close the drive door. If your DOS 6 upgrade disks are incompatible with drive A, insert the *Disk 1/Setup* disk into drive B.
5. Type the command **A:** and press Enter. (If *Disk 1/Setup* is in drive B, type the command **B:** and press Enter instead.)
6. Type the command **SETUP** and press Enter.

The Setup program now examines your system. Follow the instructions on your screen. As the installation continues, you are instructed to insert your Uninstall disk into drive A. You must use drive A for the Uninstall disk, because this disk is used to restart your system if any problems occur.

You are instructed to change disks several times during the DOS 6 setup. Watch the screen prompts carefully and make sure that you are inserting the proper disk. Using the correct disk is especially important when you are prompted to insert the Uninstall disk, because the Setup program writes copies of some of your existing DOS files to this disk. If you are uncertain, always double-check to make sure that the disk you are inserting is the one requested by the screen prompt.

The files on the DOS 6 upgrade disks are compressed and cannot be used until they are expanded. The Setup program expands the files as it copies them to your hard disk. If you must install any files manually, use the EXPAND command rather than the COPY command. For further information on the EXPAND command, type **EXPAND /?** at the command prompt and press Enter.

Using Setup Options

Although the Express Setup option correctly and successfully installs DOS 6 on most systems, the Setup program has several options that may help in unusual situations. This section covers the options that are available with the Setup program.

Using the /B Switch

If you attempt to run the Setup program and cannot easily read the screen, you can use the command SETUP /B to display the setup screens in monochrome instead of color. This option probably is most useful on laptop PCs.

Using the /E Switch

If you chose not to install the optional programs when you installed DOS 6, you can use the command SETUP /E to install these programs later. You also use this command to install the Windows versions of the optional programs if you installed Windows after you upgraded to DOS 6.

The three optional programs, MS Anti-Virus, MS Backup, and MS Undelete, can be installed for use from the DOS command prompt, from Windows, or from both. If you have limited disk space, you may want to install only the DOS versions of each program. If you use Windows, however, you probably will find the Windows versions easier to use.

Using the /F Switch

In some cases, you may find it necessary to install DOS 6 on floppy disks rather than on your hard disk. If your PC doesn't have a hard disk, this is your only option. You also must install DOS 6 on floppy disks if your existing DOS version doesn't support hard disk partitions larger than 32M and you want to repartition your hard disk to take advantage of larger partitions.

To install DOS 6 on floppy disks, use the command SETUP /F. You will need three high-density disks, which you should label as *Startup /Support*, *Help/BASIC/Edit/Utility*, and *Supplemental*.

If you install DOS 6 on floppy disks, you will not be able to install MS Anti-Virus, MS Backup, and MS Undelete on the floppy disks.

If you are installing DOS 6 on floppy disks because you intend to repartition your hard disk, make sure that you back up the files on your hard disk before you make any changes to the existing disk partitions. All files contained in disk partitions that are removed or resized will be lost.

Using the /G Switch

When you upgrade to DOS 6, Setup creates an Uninstall disk and updates your network drivers, if they are out of date. You can bypass this process, however, by using the /G switch when running Setup. Generally speaking, you should not use this switch. The purpose of the Uninstall disk is to enable you to return to your previous operating system if, for some reason, DOS 6 does not operate on your computer.

Using the /I Switch

If you experience problems with the Setup program due to an unusual hardware setup, you may need to use the command SETUP /I to turn off the Setup program's automatic hardware detection. If you do need to use this command switch, you must specify the types of hardware installed on your system.

Using the /M Switch

If you cannot free enough space on your startup disk (usually drive C) for a complete DOS 6 installation, you can use the command SETUP /M to perform a minimal setup. The minimal setup adds just enough of the DOS 6 files to enable you to boot your system using DOS 6 (COMMAND.COM, IO.SYS, and MSDOS.SYS).

After you perform a minimal setup, you can boot from DOS 6 and manually install the balance of the DOS 6 files—perhaps to another disk with more available space—by using SETUP with the /Q switch. (See the next section, "Using the /Q Switch.")

If possible, you should avoid using the SETUP /M command. Not only is using SETUP /M more time-consuming (because you must manually expand the DOS 6 files), but using this command will prevent you from using the commands (such as FORMAT) from your previous DOS version. Instead, free additional space on your startup disk by copying files to floppy disks and then deleting those files from your hard disk. If you cannot copy and delete files, use the DBLSPACE command described in Chapter 4, "Optimizing Your Hard Disk with DOS 6," to free additional disk space; then set up DOS 6 normally.

Using the /Q Switch

When you use SETUP with the /Q switch, you can instruct SETUP to install the DOS utilities to any drive attached to your computer that has enough space available. Generally, you use the /Q switch after you have used the /M switch to install a minimal DOS setup.

Suppose that your computer contains two hard disks: drive C and drive D. Drive C is the hard disk from which you normally boot the computer. Because drive C is nearly full, you used SETUP /M to install the DOS boot files to drive C. After the DOS 6 files have been transferred to drive C, issue the command SETUP /Q and press Enter. As SETUP runs, you can specify where the DOS utilities should be installed. You can specify a directory on drive D to install the DOS files to—for example, D:/DOS. SETUP creates the directory you specified on drive D and copies the utilities to that directory.

Using the /U Switch

The final Setup program option, SETUP /U, enables you to install DOS 6 even if Setup detects disk partitions—such as Novell, UNIX, or XENIX partitions—that may be incompatible with DOS 6. Use caution with this option, because it destroys any existing files in the incompatible partitions. Be sure that you back up any important data first.

Handling Upgrade Problems

Although you probably will not have problems installing DOS 6, a hardware failure, a damaged disk, or a power failure may prevent you from completing the upgrade. If you experience a problem during setup, remove the DOS 6 upgrade disks and insert the Uninstall disk into drive A. Restart your PC and follow the instructions on-screen for reverting to your old version of DOS.

If an event such as a power failure prevents you from successfully completing the DOS 6 setup, you can just start again after you revert to your old DOS version. If a hardware failure prevents you from completing the DOS 6 setup, make any necessary repairs before attempting to restart the Setup program. If you think that you have a damaged DOS 6 Setup disk, contact your vendor for a replacement.

The DOS 6 Setup program cannot install DOS 6 on your system if you have the DOS files for your old version of DOS in the root directory of your startup disk. Before you can upgrade to DOS 6, you must create a directory for these files and move them from the root directory. If you have the DOS files for your old version of DOS in the root directory of your startup disk, follow these steps to move them to a new directory:

1. Make the startup disk (the disk you use to start DOS) the current disk. In most cases this is drive C, so you should type **C:** and press Enter.
2. Make certain that the root directory is the current directory by typing **CD ** and pressing Enter.
3. Create a new directory for the DOS files by typing **MD DOS** and pressing Enter.
4. Copy the files to the new directory by typing **COPY *.* DOS** and pressing Enter.
5. Insert a new, blank floppy disk into drive A, and enter the following command to create a system disk:

   FORMAT A: /S

6. Next, copy AUTOEXEC.BAT and CONFIG.SYS to the floppy disk by typing the following commands:

   COPY AUTOEXEC.BAT A:

   COPY CONFIG.SYS A:

7. Press Ctrl+Alt+Del to restart your system.
8. Make drive C the current drive by typing **C:** and pressing Enter.
9. Delete all files from the root directory of C by typing **DEL *.*** and pressing Enter. When the prompt informs you that all files will be deleted, press Y to delete the files.
10. Copy the three files back from the floppy disk by entering the following commands:

    COPY A:AUTOEXEC.BAT

    COPY A:COMMAND.COM

    COPY A:CONFIG.SYS

11. Remove the floppy disk from drive A and insert the DOS 6 Upgrade disk labeled *Disk 1/Setup*. You now are ready to try the Setup program again.

If you are unable to solve your problems with the DOS 6 installation and require additional support, Microsoft provides technical support for DOS 6 free for the first 90 days after you purchase DOS 6. Support is available from 6:00 a.m. to 6:00 p.m. Pacific time, Monday through Friday, by calling (206) 646-5104. When you call this number, make sure that you have the serial number that is printed on the inside back cover of the DOS 6 User's Guide. Also, be prepared to tell the support person the exact wording of any error messages that were displayed, the type of PC hardware you are using, and the steps you have taken to try to solve the problem.

If you are deaf or hard of hearing, you can contact Microsoft Product Support Services via a TDD/TT line by calling (206) 635-4948 during the same time period listed in this section for voice calls.

Uninstalling DOS 6

DOS 6 offers many advantages, but you can uninstall DOS 6 easily, if necessary, by inserting the Uninstall disk into drive A and restarting your system. Follow the screen instructions to revert to your old version of DOS.

You will not be able to use the Uninstall disk to return to your old version of DOS, however, if you repartitioned your hard drive to use a larger partition size, if you reformatted your hard drive, or if you removed the old DOS version from your hard drive.

If you are considering returning to an earlier version of DOS because a program displays the message `Incorrect DOS version`, consider using the SETVER command instead. The SETVER command enables most older programs to run under DOS 6. Don't, however, use the SETVER command to run old versions of disk utility programs that don't recognize the larger partition sizes available in DOS 6. Contact the manufacturer for a DOS 6 compatible upgrade to the utility program.

Deleting Your Old DOS Version

After you successfully upgrade to DOS 6 and verify that it is fully compatible with your system, you can delete your old version of DOS. The Setup program creates a new directory for your old version DOS files. These files are used with the Uninstall disk if you must revert to your old DOS version. Once you no longer need these files, you can remove them from your hard disk to free up the space they occupy.

To remove the old DOS version files from your hard disk, type the command **DELOLDOS** and press Enter. Press Y to confirm that you want to remove the old DOS files.

Chapter Summary

This chapter gave you a brief look at the first steps you need to take to upgrade to DOS 6. Installing DOS 6 on your system is only the first step, however. In the following chapters, you learn how to gain even more benefits from the new and enhanced features of DOS 6. You learn how to optimize your system's memory usage, how to improve disk operations, and even how to connect your PC to other PCs.

3

CHAPTER

Customizing Memory Usage with DOS 6

In this chapter, you learn about the different types of memory supported by DOS 6, as well as the new MEMMAKER program designed to optimize your system's memory usage. In addition, you learn how to use the new features of DOS 6 to add your own memory optimization touches manually.

Before You Begin

Changing your PC's memory usage can provide many benefits, but you may accidentally make changes that could prevent your system from functioning properly. Before experimenting, consider the following important points:

- Always make certain that your hardware supports a feature before trying to include that feature in your system configuration. If your system has an 8088 processor, for example, it will not be able to use features that require an 80386 or 80486.

- If you make a change that causes your system to "lock up" instead of properly starting DOS 6, press the F8 key after your system displays the message `Starting MS-DOS` as it boots. Pressing F8 enables you to specify whether each CONFIG.SYS command line should be executed, and whether the commands in AUTOEXEC.BAT should be executed. If you want to bypass CONFIG.SYS and AUTOEXEC.BAT, press F5 after your system displays the message `Starting MS-DOS` as it boots.
- When you turn on or reboot your PC, it immediately searches the root directory for two files: CONFIG.SYS and AUTOEXEC.BAT. These files are optional, but they serve the important purpose of enabling you to customize your system's operation. CONFIG.SYS normally contains commands and directives that cannot be typed at the DOS command line or that should be used only once per session. AUTOEXEC.BAT is a batch file, and therefore contains commands that you can type at the DOS command line.
- COMMAND.COM is a special DOS program that processes your commands, and is referred to as the *command processor*. Because COMMAND.COM processes your commands, it must be loaded whenever you boot your PC, or you see the message

  ```
  Bad or missing command interpreter
  ```

  and your system halts.

Understanding DOS 6 Memory Terms

You can use many different terms to describe the types of memory available in PCs. All PCs have conventional memory; extended and expanded memory, the high memory area, and upper memory blocks are available on more advanced types of PCs. DOS 6 uses all types of memory as long as you have the correct system hardware and software configuration.

The following sections describe the types of memory important to DOS 6 users. The terms in these sections can be confusing because they often are quite similar. Table 3.1 summarizes the types of memory used by DOS 6.

Table 3.1 Descriptions of Memory Terms

Memory	Description
Conventional	The first 640K of memory addresses on a PC. Available on all PC processors.
Expanded	Paged memory used to provide extra memory for data. Also called LIM or EMS memory. Can be installed using an expanded memory board on 8086, 8088, and 80286 PCs. Can be emulated on 80386 and 80486 PCs.
Extended	Memory addressed in a linear fashion above the 1M memory address. Available only on 80286, 80386, and 80486 PCs.
HMA	High Memory Area. The first 64K block of extended memory managed under XMS. The place where the DOS kernel is loaded when the DOS=HIGH directive is used. Available only on 80286, 80386, and 80486 PCs.
XMS	Extended Memory Specification. A memory management specification for extended memory. HIMEM.SYS is the DOS 6 XMS memory manager. Available only on 80286, 80386, and 80486 PCs.
UMB	Upper Memory Blocks. Unused blocks of memory in the area above the 640K conventional memory and below the 1M address. Used to load device drivers and TSR programs. EMM386.EXE is the UMB provider supplied with DOS 6. Available only on 80386 and 80486 PCs unless you obtain another UMB provider.

Conventional Memory

Personal computer capabilities have increased greatly in a relatively short time. Today's PCs, with 32-bit processors and megabytes of memory, have power that only the mainframe computers of the 1980s could provide. Even with all this power, one limitation of the first design of the IBM-PC still exists: a 640K limit on conventional memory. DOS 6 has a number of ways to stretch this limit.

Early versions of DOS could address only 1M of memory because the Intel 8086 and 8088—the leading microprocessors when the IBM-PC was developed—had only 20 address lines. Because memory addressing is binary (consisting of 2 states), 20 address lines can access

1,048,576 bytes, or 1M (2 to the 20th power bytes). The later 80286, 80386, 80486, and Pentium processors have more address lines and can address far more memory.

Early versions of DOS allocated 640K of the 1M of memory addresses for applications programs, which seemed quite adequate at the time. The remaining 384K was reserved for various device drivers, ROM (read-only memory), graphics adapters, and other functions.

By the time the more advanced 80286 and 80386 microprocessors began to appear in PCs, DOS already had a huge installed user base. To accommodate the larger memory capacity of the newer CPUs, DOS would have had to abandon the installed base of users with 8086- and 8088-based PCs. DOS designers chose not to change the basic arrangement of DOS and to keep DOS uniform with the installed base.

Two basic methods were developed to give programs access to more memory. The first method, *expanded memory*, accesses memory through a device driver. The second method uses *extended memory* addressing. DOS 6 supports the EMS (Expanded Memory Specification) standard for expanded memory and the XMS (eXtended Memory Specification) standard for extended memory. Expanded and extended memory are explained in the following two sections.

Expanded Memory

Expanded memory enables even the 8086 to take advantage of more RAM. Some DOS programs (such as 1-2-3 release 2.4) access the contents of expanded or EMS memory as addresses within the first 1M of memory. Using expanded memory, any CPU in the 8086 family can break the 1M memory barrier.

Expanded memory is accessed through a device driver as though the memory were a device. The device driver *pages* (temporarily assigns) expanded memory into memory addresses below 1M. The portion of expanded memory is called a *page* and the temporarily assigned address is called a *page frame*. More than one memory page is associated with a page frame.

When your computer addresses the page frame, it actually accesses the values in a page of expanded memory. To access all the pages of expanded memory, the driver must swap 16K pages of memory in and out of the available page frames. When a program needs to access a page of expanded memory that is not in the page frame, the device driver must swap the new page into the page frame (and the old one back to expanded memory if any changes were made).

This swapping of page frames is a processing overhead that extended-mode addressing does not have. Most programs and device drivers that can use both expanded and extended memory perform better using extended memory.

Expanded-memory operation enables specially designed programs to permit even the older Intel 8086 and 8088 processors to have access to more than 1M of memory through page frames.

Two versions of EMS exist: LIM 3.2 and LIM 4.0 both use the paged switching of expanded memory. LIM 4.0, which is supported by DOS 6, provides for more flexible page-frame location and greater expanded-memory access. You still can use an LIM 3.2 expanded memory board and driver with DOS 6, but because of the advantages of LIM 4.0, you should try to get the most recent version of the LIM software from the manufacturer of your expanded memory board.

The advanced memory-management features of the 80386, 80486, or Pentium processors can emulate an expanded-memory adapter board. DOS 6 provides expanded memory support for these processors through EMM386.EXE—an LIM 4.0 device driver. DOS 6 does not provide LIM 4.0 drivers for the expanded memory boards often installed in older PCs with 8086, 8088, or 80286 processors, because these drivers are specific to the particular expanded memory board.

Extended Memory

As a result of having 20 address lines, the Intel 8088 and 8086 processors, for which DOS was designed, can address 1M of memory. The Intel 80286 processor has 24 address lines and can address 16M of memory. The newer Intel processors have 32 address lines and can address 4G (gigabytes) of memory. Regardless of the processor, however, the first 1M of this range addresses the system's conventional memory. Addresses above 1M are called *extended-memory* addresses. Any memory at these extended addresses is called extended memory and is unavailable on systems with 8086 and 8088 processors.

The 80286, 80386, and 80486 address conventional memory as the earlier 8086 does by using an internal operating mode called *real mode*. In real mode, the microprocessors are restricted to the same 1M address range as the 8086. The newer microprocessors can enter another mode (called *protected mode*) to address the extended-memory locations.

Because DOS became a standard before the advent of protected mode, it cannot effectively take advantage of protected mode's extensive address range. Some DOS programs and device drivers, such as 1-2-3 release 3.4, Windows 3.1, and SMARTDRV, can use extended memory, however. The programs switch the CPU from real mode to protected mode. These DOS programs and device drivers cooperate in extended memory use, but many older programs that use extended memory may not.

The DOS 6 HIMEM.SYS device driver manages extended memory according to a set of rules called the *extended memory specification* or XMS. XMS includes the reserved memory between 640K and 1M, the HMA (the first 64K of extended memory), and the balance of extended memory. XMS enables DOS programs to use extended memory in a consistent manner and provides a standard method of storing data in extended memory.

High Memory Area

The first 64K of extended memory space is called the *high memory area* or HMA. If your PC has extended memory and you include the HIMEM.SYS device driver in your CONFIG.SYS file, the HMA becomes available. The HMA is unique because programs can be executed in it while in real mode (unlike the rest of extended memory, which requires protected mode).

Only a few programs besides DOS 6 can use the HMA. Later in this chapter, you learn how to place most of the DOS kernel into the HMA, freeing up considerable conventional memory.

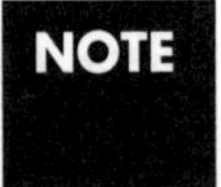

The HMA is actually 16 bytes less than 64K bytes. It starts at FFFF:10h and ends at FFFF:FFFFh, making the HMA 64K – 16 bytes.

Upper Memory Blocks

DOS addresses the first 640K of memory as conventional memory and the remaining 384K of the 1M conventional memory as *reserved memory*. This range of memory addresses contains system ROM (read-only memory), graphics adapters, and often a number of other adapters such as network or scanner adapter cards addressed at specific memory locations. Usually, however, one or more blocks of unused memory addresses exist within reserved memory. These blocks of unused memory are called *upper memory blocks* or *UMBs*.

DOS 6 can use UMBs for device drivers and TSRs (terminate-and-stay-resident programs) if you have the proper *UMB provider* (a memory manager that provides upper memory blocks). EMM386.EXE, one of the programs supplied with DOS 6, is a UMB provider for PCs with 80386 or higher processors. In order to use UMBs with EMM386.EXE, you must have an 80386 or 80486 PC, memory between the 640K and 1M addresses, and include the HIMEM.SYS and EMM386.EXE device drivers in your CONFIG.SYS file.

By placing device drivers and TSRs in UMBs, you free the conventional memory that device drivers and TSRs normally would use. This action provides more conventional memory for your applications programs and enables you to do much more with your PC. Later in this chapter, you learn how to use the MemMaker program to optimize memory usage by using UMBs.

Many 80286-based PCs and some 8086- and 8088-based PCs have memory in the space between 640K and 1M. DOS 6, however, does not provide the means to convert this memory into UMBs. Products such as QEXT.SYS, from Quarterdeck Office Systems, provide the HMA (if you have more than 1M of RAM), UMBs, and XMS extended memory on these types of systems.

Hands-Off Memory Management with MemMaker

Memory management can be very difficult even for the most expert PC user. Just the thought of trying to understand all the different memory terms, calculating the optimal position for each device driver, and trying several hundred combinations of options makes most PC users feel that memory management is a subject best left to the experts.

The MemMaker program requires an 80386 or higher processor and extended memory.

For most PC users, memory management first became an issue with the introduction of DOS 5. That version of DOS provided the first built-in capability to access additional memory in the form of the HMA and UMBs. Unfortunately, to use that additional memory, you had to make manual changes to CONFIG.SYS and sometimes AUTOEXEC.BAT, and those changes weren't always successful. In fact, if you tried some combinations, you probably found yourself with a locked-up computer system that couldn't be started without an emergency boot disk.

If you were brave enough to try optimizing memory in DOS 5, and lucky enough to not lock up your system, you probably gained quite a bit of extra conventional memory. In fact, many users gained 100K or more of conventional memory compared to earlier DOS versions. As impressive as that may be, DOS 6's MemMaker program often can do much better, and MemMaker can do it automatically.

Using MemMaker Syntax

The MemMaker command uses the following syntax:

> **MEMMAKER** */b /batch /batch2 /session /swap:drive /t /undo /w:size1,size2*

Table 3.2 summarizes the MemMaker command options.

Table 3.2 MemMaker Command Options

Option	Description
/b	Displays MemMaker in black and white instead of color.
/batch	Runs MemMaker in batch (unattended) mode.
/batch2	Runs MemMaker in batch (unattended) mode and exits when finished.
/session	Used by MemMaker during memory optimization only; do not include on the command line.
/swap:drive	Specifies the drive that was originally your start-up drive, if drive swapping is in effect.
/t	Disables detection of IBM token-ring networks.
/undo	Undoes MemMaker's most recent changes to CONFIG.SYS and AUTOEXEC.BAT, returning your system to its previous configuration.
/w:size1,size2	Specifies how much upper memory to reserve for the translation buffers used by Windows when running MS-DOS-based applications.

Using MemMaker Express Memory Optimization

Once you have installed DOS 6, you're ready to take advantage of its new features. In most cases, running the MemMaker program—if you have an 80386 or higher processor and extended memory—should be the next step. To run the MemMaker program, type the command **MEMMAKER** and press Enter. MemMaker displays the opening screen shown in figure 3.1. Press Enter again to continue to the screen shown in figure 3.2. Press Enter one more time to instruct MemMaker to begin Express Optimization.

```
Microsoft MemMaker

Welcome to MemMaker.

MemMaker optimizes your system's memory by moving memory-resident
programs and device drivers into the upper memory area. This
frees conventional memory for use by applications.

After you run MemMaker, your computer's memory will remain
optimized until you add or remove memory-resident programs or
device drivers. For an optimum memory configuration, run MemMaker
again after making any such changes.

MemMaker displays options as highlighted text. (For example, you
can change the "Continue" option below.) To cycle through the
available options, press SPACEBAR. When MemMaker displays the
option you want, press ENTER.

For help while you are running MemMaker, press F1.

          Continue or Exit? Continue

ENTER=Accept Selection  SPACEBAR=Change Selection  F1=Help  F3=Exit
```

Fig. 3.1
The MemMaker opening screen.

MemMaker first examines your hardware to determine whether your system can physically support the HMA and UMBs using the DOS 6 memory managers HIMEM.SYS and EMM386.EXE. If you have an 80386, 80486, or Pentium processor, and extended memory, your system passes the first test and MemMaker continues.

The reserved memory between 640K and 1M may contain several small or large blocks of unused address space. 80386 and higher processors have the capability to map physical memory—actual memory chips installed in your system—into different address spaces. When MemMaker examines the reserved memory, it tries to detect any unused blocks of address space. Although large portions of the reserved memory are used for ROM addresses and various adapter cards, MemMaker usually finds one or more areas it can use for UMBs.

```
Microsoft MemMaker

There are two ways to run MemMaker:

Express Setup optimizes your computer's memory automatically.

Custom Setup gives you more control over the changes that
MemMaker makes to your system files. Choose Custom Setup
if you are an experienced user.

      Use Express or Custom Setup? Express Setup


ENTER=Accept Selection  SPACEBAR=Change Selection  F1=Help  F3=Exit
```

Fig. 3.2
Selecting Express Optimization.

MemMaker next examines the device drivers and TSR programs you load in CONFIG.SYS and AUTOEXEC.BAT. After determining how much memory each device driver and TSR requires, MemMaker considers many combinations—perhaps thousands of combinations—as it calculates the best way to use the available UMBs.

After MemMaker finds the best combination, it makes temporary changes to CONFIG.SYS and AUTOEXEC.BAT. These changes adjust the memory addresses used for loading your device drivers and TSR programs, and add some special drivers to test the settings. MemMaker then reboots your system for its first test of the new settings.

If all goes well, your PC will restart and run correctly using MemMaker's optimized configuration. In some cases, however, your system may lock up or run erratically. If so, simply reboot by pressing Ctrl+Alt+Del or by turning the system power switch off and back on. MemMaker senses that a problem occurred and offers to try again. Follow the suggestions displayed on-screen.

If MemMaker is unable to properly optimize your memory configuration, press the space bar until the Undo Changes option appears. Press Enter to instruct MemMaker to undo any changes and return your system's CONFIG.SYS and AUTOEXEC.BAT to their original settings.

Using MemMaker Custom Memory Optimization

Although MemMaker tries many different combinations of memory-optimization settings, your system may include device drivers or TSR programs that cannot be loaded into UMBs; or your computer may have adapter cards located in memory address space that MemMaker does not detect. In such cases, you need to give MemMaker a little help.

MemMaker's Custom Optimization option enables you to help the program bypass problems it cannot recognize on its own. If MemMaker is unable to properly optimize your memory configuration using Express Optimization, try the Custom Optimization option.

Before you try the MemMaker Custom Optimization option, note where the problem seems to be. If your system starts to boot but then locks up when a certain device driver is loaded, for example, MemMaker probably was trying to load the device driver into a UMB, and that particular driver may not be compatible with UMBs. If your system locks up before any device drivers are loaded, MemMaker may be trying to include memory addresses already in use by adapter cards.

After you've tried unsuccessfully to use MemMaker's Express Optimization option and noted the point at which problems seemed to occur, you're ready to try the MemMaker Custom Optimization option. Type **MEMMAKER** and press Enter to begin the program. Press Enter again to move to the second screen. To select Custom Optimization, press the space bar and then press Enter. You see the following message:

```
Do you use any programs that need expanded memory (EMS)? No
```

If you do not use expanded memory, press Enter to accept the default No response. If any of your programs use EMS, press the space bar to toggle the response to Yes and press Enter. The screen shown in figure 3.3 appears.

Use the up- and down-arrow keys to select options, and press the space bar to change a selected option. After you make your selections, press Enter to start MemMaker using your selected options. The following list describes the options that appear on-screen and in figure 3.3:

- *Specify which drivers and TSRs to include during optimization:* Specifies whether specific device drivers and TSR programs should be loaded into UMBs during MemMaker's optimization attempts. If you change this option to Yes, when MemMaker begins its optimization, it asks you whether to include device drivers and TSRs. By default, MemMaker attempts to place most device drivers and TSR programs into UMBs (MemMaker uses a file named MEMMAKER.INF to identify device drivers and TSR programs it should not load into UMBs). Set this option to Yes if your system locked up when it tried to load a device driver or TSR into a UMB.

```
    Microsoft(R) MemMaker
    ____________________________________________________________________

                            Advanced Options
    ____________________________________________________________________

    Specify which drivers and TSRs to include in optimization?        No
    Scan the upper memory area aggressively?                          Yes
    Optimize upper memory for use with Windows?                       No
    Use monochrome region (B000-B7FF) for running programs?           No
    Keep current EMM386 memory exclusions and inclusions?             Yes
    Move Extended BIOS Data Area from conventional to upper memory?   Yes
    ____________________________________________________________________

    To select a different option, press the UP ARROW or DOWN ARROW key.
    To accept all the settings and continue, press ENTER.


ENTER=Accept All   SPACEBAR=Change Selection   F1=Help   F3=Exit
```

Fig. 3.3

MemMaker's Custom Optimization options.

- *Set aside upper memory for EMS page frame:* Specifies whether EMS (expanded) memory should be provided. If none of your programs require EMS memory, you can set this option to No. EMS memory support uses 64K of UMB space.
- *Scan the upper memory area aggressively:* Specifies whether MemMaker should search the largest possible address range in the reserved memory while trying to find free memory space. If possible, leave this option set to Yes so that MemMaker has the best chance at finding all available memory spaces. If your system locks up when this option is set to Yes, change it to No to instruct MemMaker to search a smaller and safer range of addresses.
- *Optimize upper memory for use with Windows:* Enables you to specify whether MemMaker optimizes upper memory for use with nonWindows programs running under Windows. If you don't use Windows, or if you only run Windows programs under Windows, you can change this option to No.
- *Use monochrome region (B000-B7FF) for running programs:* Specifies whether MemMaker uses the address range normally assigned to monochrome display adapters. If you have an EGA or VGA adapter, it's usually safe to use the monochrome region for additional UMBs by changing this option to Yes. SuperVGA adapters sometimes use this address range, and may require you to select No.

- *Keep current EMM386 memory exclusions and inclusions:* Specifies whether MemMaker uses any current I= and X= settings on the CONFIG.SYS line that loads EMM386.EXE. By changing this option to No, you allow MemMaker to attempt to create more UMB space by allowing the program to determine which areas are available. Set this option to Yes if your system locks up when you try setting this option to No.
- *Move Extended BIOS Data Area from conventional to upper memory:* Specifies whether MemMaker moves the Extended BIOS Data Area (EBDA) from the end of conventional memory to upper memory. You seldom should have a reason to change this option to No, although it may be necessary if your system locks up when you set this option to Yes.

You may have to experiment with these MemMaker options in order to find the best combination of settings for your system. If your PC locks up when MemMaker tries to optimize your system's memory, change one option at a time until you find the best combination.

Hands-On Memory Management for Optimization

Although the MemMaker program makes memory optimization much easier and automatic, DOS 6 also enables you to dig in and practice hands-on memory management. In fact, DOS 6 provides more memory-optimization options and more powerful tools for hands-on memory management than were available in any earlier DOS version.

TIP

Why You May Want To Make Hands-On Adjustments

If your system's configuration is too complex for the MemMaker program, your only options are to make some hands-on adjustments to CONFIG.SYS and AUTOEXEC.BAT, or to accept a less than optimal setup. If every MemMaker optimization attempt locks up your system, for example, you must use the hands-on approach if you need to create more conventional memory.

You also may appreciate the challenge of trying to squeeze out a little more memory than MemMaker can provide. Although MemMaker usually does a creditable job of optimizing memory, the program tries to create a safe and stable configuration rather than one that finds every last byte of memory.

Using MEM

MEM is a program introduced in DOS 4; it was enhanced in DOS 5 to show more information about how device drivers and TSR programs use memory, but its reports were meant more for engineers than for the typical PC user. In DOS 6, MEM again has been improved, and now provides information anyone can use when trying to optimize the use of memory. Table 3.3 shows the options for DOS 6's MEM command. In the next section, "Specifying Where Programs Load," you learn how to use MEM as you customize your system's configuration.

Table 3.3 MEM Options in DOS 6

Option	Description
/CLASSIFY or /C	Classifies device drivers and TSR programs by memory usage. Lists their size, summarizes memory use, and lists largest available memory block.
/DEBUG or /D	Displays status of all device drivers, TSR programs, and internal drivers in memory.
/FREE or /F	Displays information about the amount of free memory.
/MODULE or /M	Displays a detailed listing of a device driver's or TSR program's memory use. You must include the name of the device driver or TSR.
/PAGE or /P	Pauses after each full screen of information.

Figure 3.4 shows a report produced by the MEM /C command.

This report shows a large amount of information about the system's memory. The first report section shows every device driver and TSR program, along with their conventional and UMB memory use. The next section summarizes all installed memory. The final section shows that EMS (expanded) memory is available, lists the amount of conventional memory available for programs, reports the largest free UMB, and tells you that DOS is loaded into the HMA.

The MEM /D command produces a different report, as shown in figure 3.5.

```
Modules using memory below 1 MB:

  Name           Total       =   Conventional    +   Upper Memory
  ----         ---------         ---------           ---------
  MSDOS        16781   (16K)     16781   (16K)           0   (0K)
  ASPI4DOS      6672    (7K)      6672    (7K)           0   (0K)
  HIMEM         1104    (1K)      1104    (1K)           0   (0K)
  EMM386        3072    (3K)      3072    (3K)           0   (0K)
  PROTMAN        128    (0K)       128    (0K)           0   (0K)
  EXP16         8944    (9K)      8944    (9K)           0   (0K)
  SATISFAX      3968    (4K)      3968    (4K)           0   (0K)
  SMARTDRV     30832   (30K)      2480    (2K)       28352  (28K)
  COMMAND       3232    (3K)      3232    (3K)           0   (0K)
  win386       29808   (29K)     20240   (20K)        9568   (9K)
  CASMGR        5520    (5K)      5520    (5K)           0   (0K)
  WIN           1696    (2K)      1696    (2K)           0   (0K)
  COMMAND       3472    (3K)      3472    (3K)           0   (0K)
  SETVER         656    (1K)         0    (0K)         656   (1K)
  ASWCDTSH     14640   (14K)         0    (0K)       14640  (14K)
  MVSOUND       9184    (9K)         0    (0K)        9184   (9K)
  MOUSE        17120   (17K)         0    (0K)       17120  (17K)
  WORKGRP       4400    (4K)         0    (0K)        4400   (4K)
  MSCDEX       15856   (15K)         0    (0K)       15856  (15K)
  SHARE         5248    (5K)         0    (0K)        5248   (5K)
  DOSKEY        4656    (5K)         0    (0K)        4656   (5K)
  Free        578144  (565K)    578144  (565K)           0   (0K)

Memory Summary:

  Type of Memory        Size       =      Used       +      Free
  --------        ---------         ---------         ---------
  Conventional      655360   (640K)     77216    (75K)    578144  (565K)
  Upper             109680   (107K)    109680   (107K)         0    (0K)
  Adapter RAM/ROM   283536   (277K)    283536   (277K)         0    (0K)
  Extended (XMS)  15728640 (15360K)  14680064 (14336K)   1048576 (1024K)
  --------        ---------         ---------         --------

  Total memory    16777216 (16384K)  15150496 (14795K)   1626720 (1589K)

  Total under 1 MB  765040   (747K)    186896   (183K)    578144   (565K)

  EMS is active.

  Largest executable program size         578128    (565K)
  Largest free upper memory block              0      (0K)
  MS-DOS is resident in the high memory area.
```

Fig. 3.4

Using MEM /C to see how programs use memory.

```
Conventional Memory Detail:

  Segment          Total            Name           Type
  ---            --------         ------         ----
  00000          1039   (1K)                      Interrupt Vector
  00040           271   (0K)                      ROM Communication Area
  00050           527   (1K)                      DOS Communication Area
  00070          2656   (3K)       IO             System Data
                                     CON          System Device Driver
                                     AUX          System Device Driver
                                     PRN          System Device Driver
                                     CLOCK$       System Device Driver
                                     A: - C:      System Device Driver
                                     COM1         System Device Driver
                                     LPT1         System Device Driver
                                     LPT2         System Device Driver
                                     LPT3         System Device Driver
                                     COM2         System Device Driver
                                     COM3         System Device Driver
                                     COM4         System Device Driver
  00116          5072   (5K)       MSDOS          System Data
  00253         33488  (33K)       IO             System Data
                 6656   (7K)         SCSIMGR$     Installed Device=ASPI4DOS
                 2464   (2K)         _doubleB     Installed Device=SMARTDRV
                 1088   (1K)         XMSXXXX0     Installed Device=HIMEM
                 3104   (3K)         $MMXXXX0     Installed Device=EMM386
                  112   (0K)         PROTMAN$     Installed Device=PROTMAN
                 8928   (9K)         EXP16$       Installed Device=EXP16
                 3952   (4K)         $INTELFX     Installed Device=SATISFAX
                 2672   (3K)                      FILES=50
                   80   (0K)                      FCBS=1
                  512   (1K)                      BUFFERS=24
                  704   (1K)                      LASTDRIVE=H
                 3008   (3K)                      STACKS=9,256
  00A80            80   (0K)       MSDOS          System Program
  00A85            64   (0K)       COMMAND        Data
  00A89          2640   (3K)       COMMAND        Program
  00B2E            80   (0K)       win386         Data
  00B33           528   (1K)       COMMAND        Environment
  00B54           272   (0K)       win386         Data
  00B65          5520   (5K)       CASMGR         Program
  00CBE           288   (0K)       WIN            Environment
  00CD0          1408   (1K)       WIN            Program
  00D28           320   (0K)       win386         Environment
  00D3C         19520  (19K)       win386         Program
```

Fig. 3.5

Using MEM /D to see more detailed memory information.

```
  01200          304    (0K)      COMMAND         Data
  01213         2640    (3K)      COMMAND         Program
  012B8          528    (1K)      COMMAND         Environment
  012D9          304    (0K)      MEM             Environment
  012EC        87664   (86K)      MEM             Program
  02853       490176  (479K)      MSDOS           — Free —

Upper Memory Detail:

  Segment  Region     Total        Name         Type
  ———      ————     ———————      —————       ————
   0B13A      1      14624   (14K)  IO           System Data
                     14592   (14K)    CDROM1     Installed Device=ASWCDTSH
   0B4CC      1       9168    (9K)  IO           System Data
                      9136    (9K)    MVPROAS    Installed Device=MVSOUND
   0B709      1       3920    (4K)  win386       Data
   0C801      2      17104   (17K)  IO           System Data
                     17072   (17K)    MS$MOUSE   Installed Device=MOUSE
   0CC2E      2       4384    (4K)  IO           System Data
                      4352    (4K)    NET$HLP$   Installed Device=WORKGRP
   0CD40      2      28768   (28K)  SMARTDRV     Program
   0D446      2      16192   (16K)  MSCDEX       Program
   0D83A      2        240    (0K)  win386       Data
   0D849      2       5248    (5K)  SHARE        Program
   0D991      2       4656    (5K)  DOSKEY       Program
   0DAB4      2       5312    (5K)  win386       Data

Memory Summary:

  Type of Memory       Total         =       Used         +       Free
—————————  —————————   ——————————   ———————
  Conventional        655360   (640K)      77216      (75K)   578144   (565K)
  Upper               109680   (107K)     109680     (107K)        0     (0K)
  Adapter RAM/ROM     283536   (277K)     283536     (277K)        0     (0K)
  Extended (XMS)    16777216 (16384K)   15728640  (15360K)  1048576  (1024K)
  ———————  ——————————   ————————   —————
  Total memory      17825792 (17408K)   16199072  (15819K)  1626720  (1589K)

  Total under 1 MB    765040   (747K)     186896     (183K)   578144   (565K)

  EMS is active.
  Memory accessible using Int 15h              0      (0K)
  Largest executable program size         578128    (565K)
  Largest free upper memory block              0      (0K)
  MS-DOS is resident in the high memory area.

  XMS version  3.00; driver version  3.09
  EMS version  4.00
```

Fig. 3.5
Continued

In the report shown in figure 3.5, you can see more details about the actual position in memory where device drivers, TSR programs, and internal drivers are loaded. In the Upper Memory Detail section, you also can see that upper memory is divided into two separate blocks. This information is especially valuable for those who use a hands-on approach to memory management. The following section, "Specifying Where Programs Load," provides further information on the usefulness of this report.

The MEM /F command shows the size of each free conventional and upper memory area, as shown in figure 3.6.

```
Free Conventional Memory:

  Segment          Size
  ---          -------
   012D9          304   (0K)
   012EC        87376  (85K)
   02841       490464 (479K)

  Total Free: 578144  (565K)

Free Upper Memory:

  Region   Largest Free     Total Free      Total Size
  ---     --------        --------        --------
     1         0    (0K)        0    (0K)     27744  (27K)
     2         0    (0K)        0    (0K)     81936  (80K)
```

Fig. 3.6

Using MEM /F to see available memory areas.

Finally, the MEM /M command shows information about specific device drivers and TSR programs (in this case, a mouse driver), as shown in figure 3.7.

```
MOUSE is using the following memory:

  Segment  Region        Size          Type
  ---      ---      ---------     ----
   0C801      2       17072    (17K)  Installed Device=MOUSE
                     --------
  Total Size:         17072    (17K)
```

Fig. 3.7

Using MEM /M to see where a program is loaded.

If you're viewing MEM reports on-screen, add the /P switch to pause the display after each full screen. Often, a better option, especially with the /C or /D switches, is to redirect the report to your printer. To make a printed copy of the MEM /D report, for example, enter the following command:

```
MEM /D >PRN
```

Specifying Where Programs Load

Two new commands were introduced in DOS 5 that enable you to specify that device drivers and TSR programs load into UMBs on 80386 or higher CPUs with extended memory: DEVICEHIGH and LOADHIGH. DEVICEHIGH is used in CONFIG.SYS in place of the standard DEVICE directive, and LOADHIGH is used in AUTOEXEC.BAT as an addition at the beginning of a command line. Before you can use DEVICEHIGH or LOADHIGH, you must make UMBs available by including three commands in CONFIG.SYS. These three commands (assuming that your DOS files are in C:\DOS) follow:

```
DEVICE=C:\DOS\HIMEM.SYS
DEVICE=C:\DOS\EMM386.EXE
DOS=UMB
```

It is more common to use DOS=HIGH,UMB which also loads the DOS kernel into the HMA in addition to providing UMBs.

Both HIMEM.SYS and EMM386.EXE have additional options not shown in this example, but assume that their default values are acceptable for now. To see the complete range of options available, enter the commands **HELP HIMEM.SYS** and **HELP EMM386.EXE** at the command prompt.

When you use DEVICEHIGH or LOADHIGH to load device drivers and TSR programs into UMBs, the largest available UMB is used first. This may not result in the most efficient use of memory, however, because each device driver or TSR must be able to fit completely into a single memory block. Some device drivers and TSRs may use memory in a second block for data storage, but unless there is a large enough UMB available, the device driver or TSR will load into conventional memory. This can be a problem.

In the MEM /F example shown in figure 3.6, two UMBs of 27,744 bytes and 81,936 bytes were available originally. If you want to load a device driver that uses 21,504 bytes of memory and a TSR program that requires 65,536 bytes of memory, you may think that you will have no problem placing both of them into the available UMBs. Unfortunately, in DOS 5, you probably would not be able to load both the device driver and the TSR into UMBs. Device drivers are loaded using a DEVICE or DEVICEHIGH command in CONFIG.SYS; TSRs usually are loaded by commands in AUTOEXEC.BAT. When you boot your system, the commands in CONFIG.SYS are read and executed before any of the commands in AUTOEXEC.BAT. Because the largest available UMB is used first, the 21,504-byte device driver loads into the 81,936-byte UMB, leaving 60,432 bytes available in the largest UMB—far too small to load the 65,536-byte TSR.

Although this example includes only a single device driver and a single TSR, the situation is usually much more complex. Often device drivers or TSR programs must be loaded in a particular order. The device driver for a SCSI adapter, for example, must be loaded before device drivers for CD-ROM drives, which are controlled by the adapter. When each device driver or TSR you load into a UMB uses the largest available UMB, it can be very difficult to make optimal use of UMBs.

DOS 6 has new options for the DEVICEHIGH and LOADHIGH commands that address this difficulty. Each of these commands now has an optional /L:*x* parameter that you can use to specify which of the UMBs to use. By specifying which UMB to use, you can avoid the problem caused by using the largest UMB first. In the case of the 21,504-byte device driver and the 65,536-byte TSR, for example, you can specify that the device driver load into the 27,744-byte UMB, and that the TSR load into the 81,936-byte UMB. To accomplish this, you load the device driver by using a command similar to the following:

DEVICEHIGH=/L:1 *device_driver*

Because the remaining UMB is large enough for the TSR, you do not need to specify which UMB to use for loading the TSR. Including the parameter does no harm, though, so you might use the following command to load the TSR:

LOADHIGH /L:2 *tsr_program*

In this example, you used the MEM /F report to see the size of the available memory blocks. The other MEM reports also help you determine how your system's memory is being used and how you can make adjustments. The MEM /C report gives you a summary showing each of the device driver and TSRs and details the types of memory they are using. The MEM /D report shows you exactly where each device driver and TSR is loaded. Using this report, you can determine which UMB a device driver or TSR is using. Armed with this information, you can make further adjustments in both CONFIG.SYS and AUTOEXEC.BAT, and make even better use of your system's resources.

Chapter Summary

Memory management is a difficult and complex subject. As you add more components that require their own device drivers, memory—resident programs, and more advanced and sophisticated software to your PC, making room in memory for everything becomes a major undertaking. Fortunately, DOS 6 has more capabilities than any earlier version of DOS, and can optimize your system's configuration for you. In this chapter, you learned how to use MemMaker for hands-off memory management, and how to apply some hands-on memory management if necessary.

In the next chapter, you see how DOS 6 can greatly improve the performance of one of the slowest parts of your system—your disk drives. You see how to double your disk space, how to use disk caching, and how to optimize file storage using the powerful tools in DOS 6.

Chapter Summary

CHAPTER 4

Optimizing Your Hard Disk with DOS 6

Your hard disk is one of the most expensive and important components in your PC. It stores all your programs and data. If you've used your system for any length of time, you've probably thought that it would be nice to have a larger and faster hard disk. Unfortunately, larger and faster hard disks can be very expensive, and once you've purchased a hard disk, it has to be installed, partitioned, and formatted. There must be a better way!

DOS 6 includes several tools that cannot only create more effective space on your hard disk, but also can make your hard disk perform at a higher rate. In this chapter, you see how to use DoubleSpace, Smartdrv, and Defrag to double or even triple your hard disk's effective space and take much less time to load or save your files.

Creating Space with DoubleSpace

As programs become more sophisticated and easy to use, they also tend to grow larger. A simple text processor with few capabilities, for example, can fit easily on a single floppy disk. A modern Windows word processor, with extensive formatting capabilities, a context-sensitive on-line help system, built-in foreign file format conversion, what-you-see-is-what-you-get display, a spell checker and thesaurus, and several dozens of other features, may take 20M of disk space. The simple text editor may work just fine for editing batch files, but few PC users would want to use it for creating a complex business document.

As the disk space demands of new programs grow, the available space on your disk shrinks. The DoubleSpace utility in DOS 6 can help you cope with this problem by creating more space on your hard disk. In fact, if you're running short of disk space, you probably will find that DoubleSpace alone is worth the entire cost of the DOS 6 upgrade. This chapter explains how DoubleSpace works.

Understanding Disk Compression

Files are stored on your hard disk as binary data. Each piece of information takes some space on the disk. Very little information is unique—most files have considerable amounts of repeated data. A document file, for example, has many words that are repeated. If you could identify those repeated words, you could develop a shorthand method of storing them. If you replaced every instance of the word *file* with the characters *2f*, for example, you would save one half of the space necessary to store each instance of *file*.

Imagine how much space you could save if you could replace larger groups of characters with two characters. Suppose that you were able to identify patterns of 10 or 20 characters? Of course, you probably wouldn't want to make all those replacements manually, but why not teach your computer how to do the job automatically?

Essentially, that is how disk compression programs work. As files are compressed, the compression program stores repeated data in less space. Files with a large percentage of repeated data tend to compress more than files with a low percentage of repeated data.

There are two primary types of compression methods. Utility programs such as PKZIP compress files when you enter a command at the command prompt. These compressed files are stored in a format that must be uncompressed before you can use the file. DoubleSpace, the DOS 6 compression program, works in a different way. Instead of waiting for you to issue a command to compress or uncompress files, DoubleSpace works automatically and transparently to compress and uncompress files. Once you install DoubleSpace, you don't have to use any special commands to compress and uncompress files—you just use your computer as you normally would.

DoubleSpace does not make any physical changes to your hard disk, but because it stores files in less space, the disk appears to have two or three times as much space. A 65M hard disk appears to have 130M or more after you install DoubleSpace.

Even though DoubleSpace has to compress or uncompress every file you store or load from the disk, you probably will find that files take less time to store or load. The reason for this is simple—your disk drives are much slower than the rest of your computer. The time required for DoubleSpace to compress or uncompress files is very short, and less data has to be read from or written to slow mechanical disk drives.

When you install DoubleSpace, it becomes a part of DOS 6 on your computer. DoubleSpace is loaded with the DOS kernel, and is completely invisible to your programs. As far as your word processor, database manager, or favorite game is concerned, your system is unchanged except for a larger, slightly faster disk drive.

Although you can use DoubleSpace to compress both hard disks and floppy disks, avoid compressing floppy disks that you may share with other PC users. Unless the other PC users also have DoubleSpace loaded, they will be unable to read the data on your compressed floppy disks. Figure 4.1 shows what appears on-screen when a user with a PC that does not have DoubleSpace loaded requests a directory listing on a compressed floppy disk.

```
C:\>DIR A:

 Volume in drive A has no label
 Directory of A:\

DBLSPACE 000    1447035 11-21-92   2:11p
        1 file(s)    1447035 bytes
                       10240 bytes free

C:\>
```

Fig. 4.1

A screen informing users that data on compressed disks is unreadable unless DoubleSpace is loaded.

Once you compress your disks with DoubleSpace, you must always load DoubleSpace. You cannot remove DoubleSpace once it is installed on your hard disk. DoubleSpace uses approximately 50K of memory, but it can be loaded in upper memory.

Understanding DoubleSpace's Components

DoubleSpace consists of two components—DBLSPACE.BIN and DBLSPACE.SYS. DBLSPACE.BIN is the part of DOS that provides access to compressed drives, and is loaded along with the DOS kernel. Because DBLSPACE.BIN is loaded along with the DOS kernel, it provides immediate access to your compressed drives. DBLSPACE.BIN is loaded into memory before any of the device drivers (such as HIMEM.SYS and EMM386.EXE, which provide access to upper memory), so it initially is loaded into conventional memory. You can use the DBLSPACE.SYS device driver to move DBLSPACE.BIN after upper memory is made available.

The DBLSPACE.SYS device driver does not actually provide access to your compressed drives; it simply specifies where DBLSPACE.BIN is loaded into memory. DBLSPACE.BIN initially loads into the top of conventional memory; DBLSPACE.SYS enables you to move DBLSPACE.BIN to the bottom of conventional memory or to upper memory.

To move DBLSPACE.BIN to the bottom of conventional memory, add the following command line to CONFIG.SYS (substitute the correct directory and drive letter if your DOS files are not in C:\DOS):

```
DEVICE=C:\DOS\DBLSPACE.SYS /MOVE
```

To move DBLSPACE.BIN into upper memory (if it is available on your system), add the following command line to CONFIG.SYS:

```
DEVICEHIGH=C:\DOS\DBLSPACE.SYS /MOVE
```

See Chapter 3, "Customizing Memory Usage with DOS 6," for more information on making upper memory available with DOS 6.

Compressing Files in Place

It is easy to add DoubleSpace to your system. You don't have to do any special preparation, because DoubleSpace automatically adds the necessary device driver, compresses your files in place, creates a new drive for your start-up files that cannot be compressed, and then restarts your system.

To add DoubleSpace to your system and compress the files on drive C, follow these steps:

1. Exit from all programs and from Windows. DoubleSpace must restart your system, and cannot be run from the Windows MS-DOS prompt or from the DOS shell.
2. Type the command **DBLSPACE** and press Enter. The DoubleSpace welcome screen appears.
3. Press Enter to display the Express/Custom screen.
4. Press Enter to select Express Setup. The first time you use DoubleSpace, you should use Express Setup to compress drive C.
5. Press C to continue and compress drive C. Compressing a drive for the first time takes a considerable length of time—typically about 1 minute per 1M of files on the disk. If you have 30M of files on drive C, this step requires about 30 minutes.
6. When DoubleSpace finishes compressing your files, press Enter. Your system restarts with the DoubleSpace device driver loaded in CONFIG.SYS.

DoubleSpace creates a new drive letter for files that cannot be compressed, such as IO.SYS and any Windows permanent swap file. The compressed drive is called drive C. The small uncompressed drive is given a drive letter that follows the letters assigned to any existing drives, such as I.

Understanding DoubleSpace Options

In addition to compressing your drive C, DoubleSpace offers a number of options you can use to compress additional drives, control the size of compressed drives, and so on. Table 4.1 summarizes these options.

Table 4.1 DoubleSpace Options

Option	Description
/CHKDSK	Checks the internal file structure of a compressed drive.
/COMPRESS	Compresses a hard disk drive or floppy disk.
/CREATE	Creates a new compressed drive.
/DEFRAGMENT	Defragments a compressed drive.
/DELETE	Deletes a compressed drive. You cannot delete compressed drive C.
/FORMAT	Formats a compressed drive. You cannot format compressed drive C.
/INFO	Displays information about a compressed drive.
/LIST	Displays a list of all the local (non-network) drives on your computer, including compressed and uncompressed disk drives.
/MOUNT	Mounts (makes available) a compressed disk.
/RATIO	Changes the estimated compression ratio of a compressed drive.
/SIZE	Changes the size of a compressed drive.
/UNMOUNT	Unmounts a compressed drive.

You can start DoubleSpace by including the optional parameters on the command line following the DBLSPACE command, or you can select these options from the DoubleSpace menu that appears if you enter the DBLSPACE command without additional parameters (see fig 4.2).

If you prefer to use the DoubleSpace menu, you can select commands by pressing the Alt key plus the correct letter to active the menu you want to use. Or, you simply can point to the correct menu title and click the left mouse button. After you select the correct menu, use the arrow keys to highlight your choice and press Enter, or point to the command and click the left mouse button. To select the Chkdsk command, for example, activate the **T**ools menu by pressing Alt+T, move the highlight to Chkdsk, and press Enter.

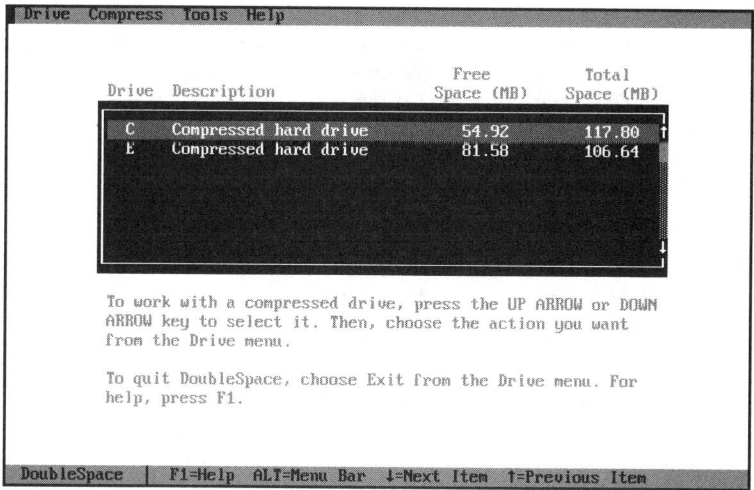
Drive Compress Tools Help
Drive Description
Free Space (MB)
Total Space (MB)
C Compressed hard drive 54.92 117.80
E Compressed hard drive 81.58 106.64
To work with a compressed drive, press the UP ARROW or DOWN ARROW key to select it. Then, choose the action you want from the Drive menu.
To quit DoubleSpace, choose Exit from the Drive menu. For help, press F1.
DoubleSpace | F1=Help ALT=Menu Bar ↓=Next Item ↑=Previous Item

Fig. 4.2
The DoubleSpace menu.

The following sections show you how to use the DoubleSpace options. As each option is discussed, both its command-line options and its DoubleSpace menu location is shown, so that you can use the method you prefer—command line or menu selection.

Verifying Compressed Files

Because the files on a compressed drive are stored in a special format, you must use the DoubleSpace Chkdsk command to find and correct errors such as lost clusters or cross-linked files on compressed drives. The DOS CHKDSK command finds and corrects similar errors on noncompressed drives. Use the following syntax to issue the DoubleSpace Chkdsk command (or select the command from the DoubleSpace **T**ools menu):

DBLSPACE /CHKDSK */F drive:*

Drive: specifies the letter of the drive you want DoubleSpace to check. If you do not specify a drive, DoubleSpace checks the current drive.

The */F* option instructs the DoubleSpace Chkdsk command to correct any errors it finds, such as lost clusters or cross-linked files.

Compressing Files on an Existing Disk

DoubleSpace automatically compresses drive C the first time you run the program, but you must manually instruct the program when you want to compress the files on other disk drives. You use the DoubleSpace Compress command to compress the files on an existing disk drive. Use the following syntax to issue the DoubleSpace Compress command (or select the command from the DoubleSpace Compress menu):

DBLSPACE /COMPRESS d1: */NEWDRIVE=d2: /RESERVE=size*

D1: is the drive containing the files you want to compress.

/NEWDRIVE=d2: is an optional argument that specifies the drive letter for the uncompressed (host) drive. If you do not specify a drive letter, DoubleSpace assigns the next available drive letter to the uncompressed drive.

/RESERVE=size specifies how many megabytes of space to leave uncompressed—the space that remains available on the uncompressed drive. A few files, such as the Windows swap file, do not work properly when stored on a compressed drive, so you must leave enough space on the uncompressed drive for these files.

You cannot compress a disk that is completely full. You must have at least 1M of free space on a hard disk or 200K of free space on a floppy disk before you can compress the files on the disk.

If you use DoubleSpace to increase the storage capacity of floppy disks, the files on the compressed floppy disk can be read only on PCs that have DoubleSpace loaded. In addition, although DoubleSpace automatically *mounts* (makes the compressed disk's files available) a floppy disk when you create the compressed disk, you must remount compressed floppy disks that have been removed from the drive. You also must remount if the system has been restarted (see the DoubleSpace /MOUNT command later in this chapter in "Mounting a Compressed Drive").

Creating a New Compressed Disk

The DoubleSpace Compress command compresses files already on a disk and assigns the existing drive letter to the compressed disk. The DoubleSpace Create command creates a new compressed drive without compressing existing files, and assigns a new drive letter to the new compressed drive. The existing uncompressed drive retains its existing drive letter. Use the following syntax to issue the DoubleSpace Create command (or select the command from the DoubleSpace **C**ompress menu):

DBLSPACE /CREATE d1: */NEWDRIVE=d2: /SIZE=size*

or

DBLSPACE /CREATE d1: */NEWDRIVE=d2: /RESERVE=size*

D1: specifies the uncompressed drive (the host drive) whose space you want to use to create the new drive.

/NEWDRIVE=d2: is an optional parameter that specifies the drive letter for the new compressed drive. If you do not specify a drive letter, DoubleSpace assigns the next available drive letter to the new compressed drive.

/SIZE=size specifies the amount of space, in megabytes, on the uncompressed drive that you want to allocate to the compressed drive. Because the files you later store on the compressed drive will be compressed, the capacity of the compressed drive will be much larger than the size you specify.

/RESERVE=size specifies the amount of space, in megabytes, that DoubleSpace should leave on the uncompressed drive. To make the compressed drive as large as possible, specify a reserve size of 0.

You can include either */SIZE=size* or */RESERVE=size*, but not both. If you omit both arguments, DoubleSpace reserves 1M of free space on the uncompressed drive.

Defragmenting a Compressed Drive

As you use a compressed drive, the file space it contains becomes fragmented. Defragmenting a compressed drive consolidates its free space, and should be done if you plan to change the compressed drive's size. Defragmenting a badly fragmented compressed drive also may improve the drive's performance and make it easier to recover accidentally deleted files. Use the following syntax to issue the DoubleSpace Defragment command (or select the command from the DoubleSpace **T**ools menu):

DBLSPACE /DEFRAGMENT *drive:*

Drive: is an optional argument that specifies the drive you want to defragment. If you do not specify a drive, DoubleSpace defragments the current drive (if it is a compressed drive).

Deleting a Compressed Drive

Deleting a compressed drive erases the entire drive and all of its files. You may need to delete a compressed drive if you created the compressed drive on a removable disk (such as a floppy disk or a cartridge drive), and you want to share files with another system that is not using DoubleSpace. Use the following syntax to issue the DoubleSpace Delete command (or select the command from the DoubleSpace **D**rive menu):

```
DBLSPACE /DELETE drive:
```

Drive: specifies the compressed drive you want to delete (you cannot delete drive C).

WARNING: Use caution when deleting compressed drives, because this also deletes all files on the compressed drive.

NOTE

In some cases, you may be able to recover an accidentally deleted compressed drive by using the Undelete command. Compressed drives are actually files (called *Compressed Volume Files* or *CVF*) on your uncompressed drive. The CVF has a file name in the form DBLSPACE.*xxx* (for example, DBLSPACE.000).

To recover an accidentally deleted compressed drive, first use the Undelete command to restore the deleted CVF. After you restore the file, remount it by using the DBLSPACE /MOUNT command (see "Remounting a Compressed Drive," later in this chapter, and Chapter 7, "Recovering Deleted Files").

Formatting a Compressed Drive

Formatting a compressed drive deletes all of its files, and is the quickest method of permanently removing all files and any directory structure on a compressed drive. You cannot unformat or recover files on a compressed drive that has been formatted. Use the following syntax to issue the DoubleSpace Format command (or select the command from the DoubleSpace **D**rive menu):

```
DBLSPACE /FORMAT drive:
```

Drive: specifies the drive you want to format. You cannot format drive C.

WARNING: If you use the DOS FORMAT command to format an uncompressed (host) drive that contains a compressed drive, the entire contents of both the uncompressed (host) drive and the compressed drive are lost.

Displaying Information About a Compressed Drive

The DoubleSpace Info command displays information about a compressed drive's free and used space, the name of its compressed volume file, and its actual and estimated compression ratios (see fig. 4.3). Use the following syntax to issue the DoubleSpace Info command (or select the command from the DoubleSpace **D**rive menu):

DBLSPACE */INFO drive:*

Drive: specifies the drive letter of the compressed drive. You must specify either the /INFO argument or the drive letter.

```
DoubleSpace is examining drive C.

Compressed drive C is stored on uncompressed drive D in the file
D:\DBLSPACE.000.

        Space used:                 192.43 MB
        Compression ratio:           1.7 to 1

        Space free:                 166.33 MB
        Est. compression ratio:      2.0 to 1

        Total space:                358.76 MB
```

Fig. 4.3

Using DBLSPACE /INFO to display information about a compressed drive.

Displaying Information on All Drives

In addition to displaying detailed information about a single compressed drive, DoubleSpace can display the current status of all local (non-network) drives on your system (see fig 4.4). Use the following syntax to issue the DoubleSpace List command (the List command does not have an equivalent on the DoubleSpace Drive menu):

DBLSPACE /LIST

Drive: specifies the drive letter of the compressed drive. You must specify either the /INFO argument or the drive letter.

Fig. 4.4

Using DBLSPACE /LIST to display information about all local drives.

```
Drive  Type                         Total Free  Total Size  CVF Filename
--     ---------------------       ----------  ----------  ------------
  A    Removable-media drive        No disk in drive
  B    Removable-media drive        No disk in drive
  C    Compressed hard drive          166.33 MB   358.77 MB  D:\DBLSPACE.000
  D    Local hard drive                 4.14 MB   202.38 MB
```

Mounting a Compressed Drive

Compressed drives must be *mounted* (made available for use) before you can access the files on the compressed drive. DoubleSpace usually mounts compressed drives automatically, but if you unmount a compressed drive or if the compressed drive is a floppy disk, you must remount it before you can access its files. Use the following syntax to issue the DoubleSpace Mount command (or select the command from the DoubleSpace **D**rive menu):

DBLSPACE /MOUNT=*nnn* d1: */NEWDRIVE=d2:*

/MOUNT=*nnn* directs DoubleSpace to mount the compressed volume file (CVF) using the optional file name extension *nnn* parameter. If you omit the *nnn* parameter, DoubleSpace attempts to mount the compressed volume file named DBLSPACE.000.

D1: specifies the uncompressed drive that contains the compressed drive you want to mount. You must specify the drive letter of the uncompressed drive.

/NEWDRIVE=d2: is an optional argument that specifies the drive letter to assign to the newly mounted compressed drive. If you don't specify a drive letter, DoubleSpace assigns the next available drive letter.

If you create compressed drives on floppy disks, you must use the DoubleSpace Mount command to make the files on those drives accessible whenever you change floppy disks.

Changing the Estimated Compression Ratio

DoubleSpace estimates the compression ratio of a compressed drive to determine how much free space the drive contains. Each time you start your system, DoubleSpace adjusts the estimated compression ratio to match the average compression ratio of the files currently stored on the drive. Because different types of files compress by differing amounts, however, you may want to change the estimated compression ratio if you store new files with a compression ratio that differs greatly from the current ratio. Use the following syntax to issue the DoubleSpace Ratio command (or select the command from the DoubleSpace **Drive** menu):

DBLSPACE /RATIO=*r.r drive:*

or

DBLSPACE /RATIO=*r.r /ALL*

/RATIO=*r.r* changes the estimated compression ratio. Use the =*r.r* argument to change the ratio to a specific number from 1.0 to 16.0. If you don't specify a ratio, DoubleSpace sets the drive's estimated compression ratio to the average actual compression ratio for all the files currently on the drive.

Drive: is an optional argument that specifies the drive you want to change. You can include either a drive letter or */ALL*, but not both. If you do not specify the drive or */ALL*, DoubleSpace changes the estimated compression ratio for the current drive.

/ALL is an optional argument that tells DoubleSpace to change the ratio of all currently mounted compressed drives.

Changing the Size of a Compressed Drive

You can enlarge or reduce the size of a compressed drive, depending on your storage needs. If the uncompressed host drive contains plenty of unused free space, for example, you may want to enlarge the size of the compressed drive. If you need more free space on the host drive, perhaps to hold a larger Windows swap file, you may want to reduce the size of the compressed drive. Use the following syntax to issue the DoubleSpace Size command (or select the command from the DoubleSpace **Drive** menu):

DBLSPACE /SIZE=*size* drive:

or

DBLSPACE /SIZE */RESERVE=size* drive:

/SIZE=*size* changes the size of the specified drive. You can specify the new amount of space that the drive's compressed volume file uses on the uncompressed (host) drive, in megabytes, using the *size* parameter. If you include /SIZE but not the *=size* parameter, DoubleSpace makes the drive as small as possible.

/RESERVE=size specifies how many megabytes of free space you want the uncompressed (host) drive to contain after DoubleSpace resizes the drive. If you do not include the */RESERVE* switch or the /SIZE=*size* parameter, DoubleSpace makes the drive as small as possible.

You can specify the drive's new size by using either /SIZE=*size* or */RESERVE=size*, but not both.

Unmounting a Compressed Drive

Unmounting a compressed drive makes it temporarily unavailable, and prevents access to its files. DoubleSpace automatically unmounts floppy disks when you turn off your system's power, but you may want to unmount a compressed drive if you want to assign it a different drive letter (you cannot unmount drive C). Use the following syntax to issue the DoubleSpace Unmount command (or select the command from the DoubleSpace **D**rive menu):

DBLSPACE /UNMOUNT *drive:*

Drive: is an optional argument that specifies the drive you want to unmount. If you omit the drive letter, DoubleSpace unmounts the current drive (unless the current drive is C).

Viewing Compression Statistics with DIR /C

DoubleSpace compresses different types of files with varying degrees of compression. To see how well DoubleSpace was able to compress different files, you can use the DIR /C command, as shown in figure 4.5.

Figure 4.5 shows compression ratios from 1.2 to 1 up to 16.0 to 1. Below the file listings, an overall compression ratio of 2.0 to 1 is indicated.

The /C switch is ignored if the drive is not a compressed drive, or if the /B or /W switches are used.

DoubleSpace increases the available space on your disk drives by compressing files. Another program provided with DOS 6, SMARTDrive, speeds up disk operations, regardless of whether they are compressed. The next section examines SMARTDrive.

Increasing Performance with SMARTDrive

Another performance enhancement included with DOS 6, SMARTDrive, can make your PC seem much faster by adding *disk caching*. You can apply this technique to any PC, whether or not you want to use disk compression. The version of SMARTDrive included with DOS 6 is the latest version of this utility, and offers some major advances compared to earlier disk-caching programs.

Understanding Caching

SMARTDrive, a disk-caching program provided with DOS 6, helps speed up system performance by removing the bottleneck that most often slows system performance: hard disk reads and writes. When SMARTDrive reads information from disk, it holds that information in memory. If a program tries to again access the same information from your hard drive, SMARTDrive instead supplies the information from RAM—which is much faster than re-reading it from the disk.

```
 Volume in drive C is FIXED C
 Directory of C:\

AUTOEXEC BAT       499 11-21-92  12:01p  16.0 to 1.0
AUTOEXEC OLD       470 11-03-92   4:01p  16.0 to 1.0
BEFSETUP MSD     34253 11-03-92   8:57a   2.5 to 1.0
COMMAND  COM     53022 10-26-92   6:00a   1.2 to 1.0
CONFIG   OLD       677 11-03-92   3:57p   8.0 to 1.0
CONFIG   SYS       844 11-21-92  11:59a   8.0 to 1.0
CONFIG   TXT       832 11-03-92   3:34p   8.0 to 1.0
DSVXD    386      5741 10-26-92   6:00a  16.0 to 1.0
IO       SYS     39590 10-26-92   6:00a   1.4 to 1.0
MSDOS    SYS     37416 10-26-92   6:00a   1.3 to 1.0
PARADOX  NET      8076 04-13-92   8:42p  16.0 to 1.0
SD       INI      2497 02-29-92   3:12p   8.0 to 1.0
SFINSTAL DIR       430 02-07-91  12:00p  16.0 to 1.0
TREEINFO NCD       555 11-13-92   4:58p  16.0 to 1.0
WINA20   386      9349 04-09-91   5:00a   5.3 to 1.0
                   2.0 to 1.0 average compression ratio
       15 file(s)     194251 bytes
                    50495488 bytes free
```

Fig. 4.5

Using the DIR /C command to show file compression ratios on compressed drives.

The newest version of SMARTDrive, which is included with DOS 6, increases performance even more by using *write caching*—temporarily holding data in memory to be written to disk when your system isn't busy. SMARTDrive can wait up to five seconds before writing data to disk, but usually it writes the data much sooner. Although write caching doesn't really speed up disk operations, it increases overall system performance by enabling you to continue working instead of waiting until all data has been written to disk.

Using SMARTDrive's Defaults and Options

Earlier versions of SMARTDrive were installed as a device driver using a command in CONFIG.SYS. The DOS 6 version of SMARTDrive can be loaded from the command prompt or from a command line in AUTOEXEC.BAT. Usually the best method is to include a command line in AUTOEXEC.BAT.

Because SMARTDrive uses some of your system's memory to cache disk reads and writes, the size of the SMARTDrive cache depends on how much RAM is installed. Table 4.2 shows the default values for initial cache size and Windows cache size based on the amount of extended memory on your computer.

Table 4.2 Default SMARTDrive Cache Sizes

Extended Memory	DOS Cache Size	Windows Cache Size
Up to 1M	All extended memory	Zero (no caching)
Up to 2M	1M	256K
Up to 4M	1M	512K
Up to 6M	2M	1M
6M or more	2M	2M

SMARTDrive's disk caching enhances the performance of both DOS programs and Windows programs, but because few DOS programs use extended memory, more of the extended memory can be allocated safely to SMARTDrive when Windows is not running. Windows programs do use extended memory, so on systems with less than 6M of extended memory, less memory is allocated to SMARTDrive when Windows is running.

The version of SMARTDrive included with Windows 3.1 is very similar to the version included with DOS 6, but you should use the DOS 6 version of SMARTDrive—especially if you use DoubleSpace. The Windows 3.1 version of SMARTDrive was not designed to work with compressed disks.

The DOS 6 Setup copies SMARTDrive to your DOS directory and adds the SMARTDrive command line to your AUTOEXEC.BAT file during installation. It also may add a line to CONFIG.SYS to install *double buffering*. SMARTDrive's double buffering option is discussed in the following section, "Using Double Buffering."

The default settings probably will work very well, but there are several options you can use to fine-tune SMARTDrive's operations to best suit your system. The following syntax shows SMARTDrive's command-line options:

> *d:path***SMARTDRV** *drive +– size winsize /B: buffersize*
> */E: elementsize /C /R /L /Q /S /V?*

Table 4.3 summarizes the elements of this command line.

Table 4.3 SMARTDrive Command-Line Parameters

Parameter	Meaning
d:path	The drive and path where SMARTDRV.EXE is located, usually C:\DOS.
/E:elementsize	Specifies in bytes the amount of the cache that SMARTDrive moves at a time. Valid values are 1024, 2048, 4096, and 8192. The default value is 8192. The larger the value, the more conventional memory SMARTDrive uses.
/B:buffersize	The size of the read-ahead buffer that SMARTDrive uses to read and hold information in memory until a program calls for it. If a program reads 512K of information from a file, SMARTDrive then reads the amount of information specified in buffersize and saves it in memory. The default size of the read-ahead buffer is 16K, but a larger value greatly increases SMARTDrive's efficiency. Its value can be any multiple of *elementsize*. The larger the value of buffersize, the more conventional memory SMARTDrive uses.
drive	The drives you want to cache. You can specify multiple drives.

continues

Table 4.3 Continued

Parameter	Meaning
+	Enables read-caching and write-caching. Use the plus (+) sign to override the default settings. If you specify a drive letter without a plus or minus sign, read-caching is enabled and write-caching is disabled.
–	Disables read-caching and write-caching. Use the minus (–) sign to override the default settings. If you specify a drive letter without a plus or minus sign, read-caching is enabled and write-caching is disabled.
size	The cache size in kilobytes while Windows is not running.
winsize	The cache size in kilobytes while Windows is running.
/C	Writes all write-cached information to disk. Normally, SMARTDrive writes information from memory to the hard disk at times when other disk activity has slowed. You may use this option if you turn off your computer and want to ensure that all cached information has been written to the hard disk.
/R	Clears the contents of the existing cache and restarts SMARTDrive.
/L	Prevents SMARTDrive from loading into upper memory blocks (UMBs), even if UMBs are available. If you are using SMARTDrive's double-buffering feature and your system appears to be running slowly, try loading SMARTDrive with the /L switch.
/Q	Prevents SMARTDrive information from appearing on-screen when it is first loaded, usually in AUTOEXEC.BAT.
/S	Displays detailed information about the status of SMARTDrive.
/V	Displays status messages when starting SMARTDrive.
/?	Displays on-line Help for SMARTDrive options.

If you don't specify a drive letter, floppy disk drives and drives created using Interlnk are read-cached but not write-cached; hard disk drives are both read-cached and write-cached. SMARTDrive does not read- or write-cache CD-ROM drives, network drives, or Microsoft Flash memory-card drives.

SMARTDrive does not normally cache compressed drives, but it does cache the physical drive on which the compressed volume file is located. SMARTDrive is capable of caching compressed drives, but this slows down your system, because the data would have to pass through SMARTDrive's disk cache twice.

Although SMARTDrive does not normally write-cache floppy disk drives, you can direct the program to do so. SMARTDrive does not normally write-cache floppy disk drives for safety reasons—if SMARTDrive delays writing to a floppy disk, you may remove the disk before the data is completely written. You may think that your data is stored safely on the floppy disk, when in fact it is not!

You can use the /S switch to see how efficiently SMARTDrive is caching disk reads. Figure 4.6 shows a typical SMARTDrive status screen displayed after a system has been running for some time.

In this case, SMARTDrive's default settings are providing very good performance. The status screen in figure 4.6 reports that of 93,803 times various programs requested information from disk, 81,680 requests were satisfied by supplying data already in the cache—*cache hits*. The screen also reports that 12,123 requests required reading data from disk—*cache misses*. Almost nine out of ten disk reads were eliminated by using SMARTDrive!

The status screen also shows that drives A and B (floppy disk drives) have read-caching enabled but not write-caching. Drive C (a hard disk) has both read- and write-caching enabled. The final column in the status report, `buffering`, indicates that none of the drives is using double-buffering.

Because write-caching delays the writing of data for a short time, you must use a certain amount of caution to ensure that all data has been written to disk before you turn off the power to your system. SMARTDrive automatically *flushes*—writes its buffers to disk—whenever you press Ctrl+Alt+Del to reboot your system. It does not, however, have the capability to sense when the power will be turned off. You can ensure that all data is written by waiting five seconds after issuing any commands that write to disk, or by entering the command **SMARTDRV /C** before you turn off the power. After the drive light on your hard drive goes off, you safely can turn off your computer.

If you use a batch file that copies files and then reboots your system, add the SMARTDRV /C command line to the batch file to clear SMARTDrive's buffer before the command line that reboots your PC. This will make certain that the copied files are closed before the system reboots.

Using Double Buffering

Double buffering provides compatibility for hard-disk controllers that cannot work with memory provided by EMM386.EXE or Windows when running in 386 enhanced mode. Hard disk controllers that use direct memory access (DMA), sometimes cannot deal correctly with the virtual memory addressing used in *protected mode*—a type of processor mode used by EMM386.EXE or Windows when running in 386 enhanced mode. Usually this is a problem only if you are using a small computer system interface (SCSI) adapter for your hard disk or other device, but double buffering also can be necessary with an enhanced system device interface (ESDI) or microchannel architecture (MCA) device.

```
C:\>SMARTDRV /S
Microsoft SMARTDrive Disk Cache version 4.1
Copyright 1991,1992 Microsoft Corp.

Room for 256 elements of 8,192 bytes each
There have been 81,680 cache hits
    and 12,123 cache misses

Cache size: 2,097,152 bytes
Cache size while running Windows: 2,097,152 bytes

             Disk Caching Status
drive   read cache   write cache   buffering
--------------------------------------------
  A:       yes          no            no
  B:       yes          no            no
  C:       yes          yes           no

For help, type "Smartdrv /?".

C:\>
```

Fig. 4.6

Using the status screen for an update on SMARTDrive's efficiency.

If the DOS 6 Setup program detects an adapter that may require double buffering, it adds the following line to CONFIG.SYS:

DEVICE=C:\DOS\SMARTDRV.EXE /DOUBLE_BUFFER

If you add an adapter that may require double buffering after you upgrade to DOS 6, you should add the same line to CONFIG.SYS manually. SMARTDrive's double-buffering component uses only 2K of conventional memory, and can prevent data loss if your system does require double buffering for safe operation.

Most hard-disk controllers, however, do not need to use double buffering. If you are not sure whether your hard disk needs double buffering, follow these steps:

1. Add the SMARTDRV double-buffer command to your CONFIG.SYS:

   DEVICE=C:\DOS\SMARTDRV.EXE /DOUBLE_BUFFER

2. If necessary, add the command to AUTOEXEC.BAT to load SMARTDRV:

   C:\DOS\SMARTDRV

3. Use the MEM /C command to confirm that upper memory is in use.
4. Type **SMARTDRV** and press Enter.
5. Look at the column labeled `buffering`.

   If any line in this column reads `yes`, you need to keep the SMARTDrive double-buffering command in CONFIG.SYS.

   If every line says `no`, you can remove the SMARTDrive double-buffering command from CONFIG.SYS.

   If any line contains the minus sign character (–), SMARTDrive is unable to detect whether double buffering is needed, and you should continue to use double buffering.

SMARTDrive's double buffering must be loaded in conventional memory—not upper memory. Use the DEVICE= command to load double buffering, not DEVICEHIGH.

If your system seems to be running slowly when double buffering is installed, try adding the /L switch to the SMARTDrive command in AUTOEXEC.BAT. This will load SMARTDrive into conventional memory instead of upper memory.

SMARTDrive adds considerable performance to your system by using memory to speed up access to information on your disk drives. SMARTDrive is one of the most trouble-free enhancements you can use on your PC. In the next section, you learn about Defrag—another DOS 6 enhancement that improves disk drive operations.

The DOS 6 Setup program adds SmartMon, a Windows program that is a companion application to SMARTDrive, to your DOS directory. SmartMon provides a graph showing how efficiently SMARTDrive is functioning, and then enables you to alter the cache mode of each cacheable drive.

Although SmartMon is copied automatically to your DOS directory, you must use the Windows Program Manager File Run command to execute SMARTMON.EXE, or add SmartMon to a program group and then select its icon to run the program. SmartMon includes an on-line Help file to help you understand its options.

Optimizing Disks with Defrag

The third of DOS 6's disk-optimization tools deals with *file fragmentation*. The Defrag program, which is licensed from Symantec, not only improves system performance, but reduces wear on your disk drives and makes recovering accidentally deleted files more likely.

Understanding File Fragmentation

One problem with disks is that, after much use, your files can become *fragmented*. Fragmentation occurs when DOS stores part of a file in one cluster, a part in the next available cluster, and so on, when the disk does not have enough space to store the file in one contiguous area. When the files on a disk are fragmented, access to the hard disk can slow considerably because DOS must search several places to find all the parts of a file.

Because slower data access caused by fragmentation is a common problem, DOS 6 offers a solution: the DEFRAG command. The Defrag program safely reorganizes the files on your disk without erasing or losing any data. If your disk drive seems to operate more slowly than it used to, you often can regain speed by using the DEFRAG command. DEFRAG *optimizes* a disk by rearranging the disk's files so that each file is stored in contiguous clusters. DOS can save a file to or read a file from an optimized disk much faster than it can to or from a fragmented disk.

Using Defrag

Because Defrag drastically reorganizes your disk, you should take some precautions before you execute the program:

- Run Chkdsk to verify that no current problems exist on your hard disk.
- If you are using a disk-caching program other than SMARTDrive, disable the disk-caching program before running Defrag.
- If you are using FASTOPEN, always reboot immediately after running Defrag. FASTOPEN remembers where files *were*, and Defrag moves files to *new* locations on your disk.
- Get rid of unnecessary files, such as backup files, to help speed up the defragmentation process. The more free space you have on your computer from eliminating unneeded files, the faster Defrag works. The fuller your disk, the greater the likelihood of disk fragmentation.

The DEFRAG command uses the following syntax:

> *d:path*\DEFRAG *drive: /F /Sorder /U /B /S /SKIPHIGH /LCD /BW /G0 /H*

Table 4.4 summarizes the DEFRAG command parameters.

Table 4.4 DEFRAG Command-Line Parameters

Parameter	Meaning
d:path	The drive and path where DEFRAG.EXE is located, usually C:\DOS.
drive:	Drive letter of disk to be optimized.
/F	Full optimization.
/U	Unfragments files only.
/B	Reboots computer after optimization.
/S	Sorts files by one of the following: N Name, E Extension, D Date and time, S Size. Add a minus sign (–) following the sort key to reverse the sort order.
/SKIPHIGH	Skips loading data in high memory.
/LCD	Uses LCD display color set.
/BW	Uses monochrome display color set.
/G0	Disables the graphic mouse and graphic character set.
/H	Instructs Defrag to move hidden files.

NOTE You cannot use Defrag to optimize network drives or drives created with INTERLNK.

You can use Defrag in two ways. If you do not specify a drive letter, Defrag reads data from system memory and then displays a dialog box showing the drives available for optimization. By using this method, you interact with the program to make your selections. You also can specify a drive letter and any optimization options that you want Defrag to apply.

Using Defrag Interactively

After you begin Defrag without specifying a disk drive, the program displays a dialog box showing the drives available for optimization (see fig 4.7). In the drive list box, highlight the name of the disk you want to optimize and press Enter, or double-click the drive name.

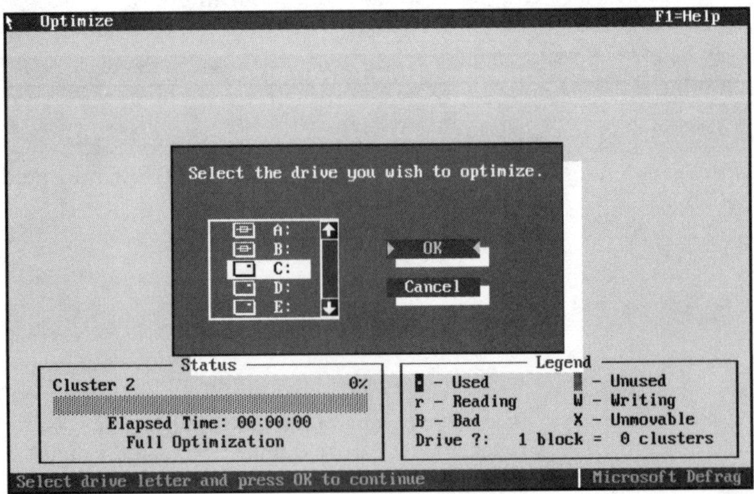

Fig. 4.7

Selecting a drive to defragment.

After you choose the drive, Defrag analyzes the data on the drive and displays a recommended course of action (see fig 4.8). For example, Defrag may recommend full optimization, that it unfragment files only, or that no optimization is necessary. To accept the recommendation, press Enter or click the Optimize option. To choose another optimization method from Defrag's menus, choose Configure (Alt+C). To end the program, press Esc three times.

If you never have optimized your disk, Defrag probably will recommend full optimization the first time you use the program. Full optimization is the most thorough method and takes the longest time. Depending on your hard disk size and the number of files your disk contains, full optimization may require considerable time to complete. After you fully optimize your disk, you may want to run Defrag weekly and accept the program's recommended approach. When used frequently, Defrag may recommend the faster Unfragment Files Only approach that takes only a few minutes.

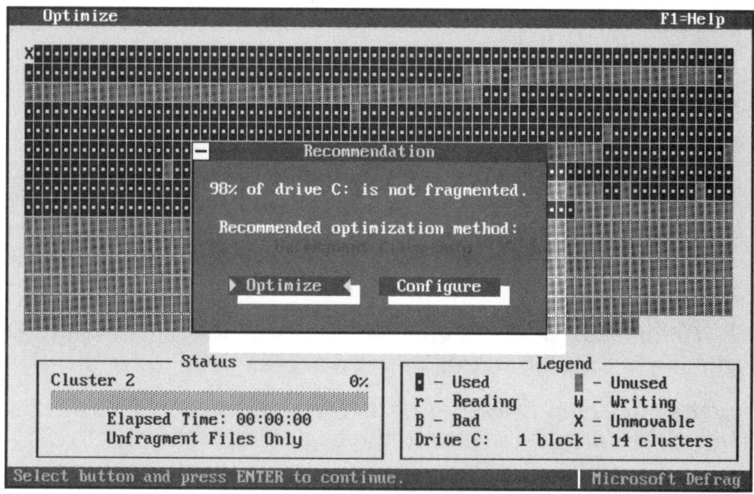

Fig. 4.8

Defrag recommending which type of optimization to use.

Although Defrag offers you several options through its pull-down menu, the easiest way to use the program is to accept Defrag's recommendation on how to optimize your disk. After you accept the recommended optimization method, Defrag immediately begins the optimization process. After optimization begins, do not turn off your computer. If you need to stop the program, press Esc, and then choose Cancel or Resume at the prompt.

During the optimization process, you see a screen that represents a map of the computer's disk space. The legend at the bottom right of the screen explains what each symbol on the map means. During the process, you can follow the movement of used clusters to the top of the map and the movement of unused clusters to the bottom. For full optimization, all unused clusters are positioned at the bottom of the map.

Using Defrag Options

If you do not want to accept the recommended optimization method, choose the Configure (Alt+C) option from the Recommendation dialog box. Choosing the Configure option puts Defrag in menu mode, which means that you can access the program's Optimize menu and choose Defrag options.

The Defrag Optimize menu contains the following options:

- ***B**egin Optimization:* Begins the optimization process. Notice that you also can press Alt+B to begin optimization, even if this menu is not pulled down.
- ***D**rive:* Enables you to choose the drive to optimize.
- ***O**ptimization Method:* Displays the Select Optimization Method dialog box. Use the up- or down-arrow key to highlight the radio button of the method you want, and then press the space bar to select the option. Then, press Enter to lock the option or Esc to cancel your selection on this menu. (Alternatively, you can click an option's radio button and then click OK.)

  Full eliminates all file fragmentation and places all files at the beginning of the disk so that you can access them faster.

  Unfragment Files Only tries to defragment as many files as possible but moves only some files to the beginning of the disk.
- ***F**ile Sort:* Enables you to specify how files are sorted within directories, based on the Sort Criterion and Sort Order options you select from the File Sort dialog box. By reorganizing your file names, you can find files quickly and easily.
- ***M**ap Legend:* Presents a dialog box that explains the symbols included on the disk map displayed during disk optimization.
- ***A**bout Defrag:* Displays a dialog box showing the Defrag copyright information.
- *e**X**it:* Exits Defrag and returns you to the DOS prompt.

Don't choose the **B**egin Optimization option until you finish choosing all your other settings.

Selecting File Sort Order

The **F**ile Sort option enables you to specify how files are sorted within directories, based on the Sort Criterion and Sort Order options you select from the File Sort dialog box. By reorganizing your file names, you can find files quickly and easily.

When you create a file, DOS locates an empty spot in the disk directory and places the file's name and information in the directory. Usually, but not always, files are listed in a directory in the order in which they were created. The **F**ile Sort option enables you to organize the files so that you can find specific files faster. You also can specify criteria to determine quickly which files are smallest or largest, which files were created last or first, and so on.

The options available in the File Sort dialog box are quite easy to use. If you choose the Name option, for example, Defrag sorts the files alphabetically by name. The Ascending option sorts the files from smallest to largest or in normal alphabetical order; the Descending option sorts from largest to smallest or in reverse alphabetical order. The Unsorted and Ascending options are selected by default. After you select the order you want, choose OK (Alt+O) to return to the menu.

During a disk optimization, certain files—called *unmovable files*—are not physically moved. When Defrag analyzes your disk, the program marks all hidden files and files related to copy-protection schemes with an X to note that they are unmovable. DOS 6 has two unmovable files: IO.SYS and MSDOS.SYS. If you use Windows in 386 enhanced mode and have configured a permanent swap file, the permanent swap file is called 386SPART.PAR and is located in the root directory of the swap drive. This file also is unmovable.

Using Defrag from the DOS Prompt

You can bypass the menu interface and use Defrag from the DOS prompt by entering the DEFRAG command followed by a drive letter and any options you want to use. Table 4.4 lists the options available with the DEFRAG command.

For example, to perform full optimization on drive C, verifying that all files were correctly written, and then rebooting the system when optimization is complete, you can use the following command:

```
DEFRAG C: /F /V /B
```

Defrag optimizes your disks so that you can more quickly access your files. Using Defrag on a regular basis can prevent file fragmentation and enhance your computer's productivity. In addition, Defrag can optimize your disks in much less time if you use the program regularly.

Chapter Summary

DOS 6 includes three powerful tools to help you optimize your hard disk. DoubleSpace increases the effective space on your hard disk by transparently compressing and uncompressing files as you work. SMARTDrive speeds disk operations by using system memory to reduce the number of times data must be read from disk. Defrag reduces file fragmentation to make all disk operations more efficient. In this chapter, you learned how to use all three of these tools to improve the performance of your PC.

In the next chapter, you are introduced to DOS 6's new Backup for DOS and Backup for Windows programs. These programs make protecting your data from loss much easier than ever before, and may even convince you to back up your files on a regular basis!

5

CHAPTER

Backing Up Your Data

Regardless of how expensive your PC system was to purchase, its cost was probably a small fraction of the value of your data. Your data files represent the total of all the time and effort spent gathering and processing information—possibly thousands of hours of work. Yet without an adequate set of backups, all of your accumulated efforts easily could be destroyed by any number of problems—including hard disk failure, accidental erasure, and viruses.

Backing up your data has always been quite a chore. The BACKUP command in previous versions of DOS was difficult to use, time-consuming, and required large numbers of floppy disks. Few PC users were willing to make backups, even though they knew how important backups were!

DOS 6 includes a powerful new tool designed to make backing up your data easier, faster, and more reliable. This chapter introduces the many new features of MS Backup and shows you ways to customize its two closely related versions—MS Backup for DOS and MS Backup for Windows—to run most efficiently for you.

MS Backup for DOS is the character-based version of MS Backup, and MS Backup for Windows is the graphical version of the same utility program. Regardless of whether you use the DOS or Windows version, the two versions offer the same options, virtually identical menus, and they both perform the same function. In fact, the two versions of the program are so similar that once you learn to use either version, you will find that you know how to use the other.

MS Backup for DOS and MS Backup for Windows are optional programs that you can choose whether to install when you upgrade to DOS 6. If you did not choose to install MS Backup for DOS or MS Backup for Windows, you can install the programs at any time by using the SETUP /E command. See Chapter 2, "Upgrading to DOS 6," for more information.

Regardless of the program version you intend to use, read through the following section to learn how to configure the program, choose the type of backup to perform, select the files you want to back up, and restore your files. A later section, "Using MS Backup for Windows," shows you the specifics of using the Windows-based version of MS Backup.

If you want to back up your files from Windows, you *must* use MS Backup for Windows. MS Backup for DOS cannot function properly in the Windows environment.

Using MS Backup for DOS

MS Backup is a modern replacement for the BACKUP command included in previous versions of DOS. The following sections show you how to configure, use, and customize MS Backup for DOS to make backing up your data much easier. Even if you prefer to use MS Backup for Windows, however, the following sections provide the basics of MS Backup that you should understand before you go on to the Windows version.

Configuring MS Backup for DOS

You must configure MS Backup before you start using it. Configuration involves telling MS Backup the type of backup device you use. Then, MS Backup can perform tests to determine how the device is used.

You can configure MS Backup the first time you use the program and when you add or change a backup drive. The first time you use MS Backup, the program automatically performs the configuration, with some input by you. You also can reconfigure when you add a new backup drive.

To begin automatic configuration with MS Backup for DOS, start the program by typing the command **MSBACKUP** and pressing Enter. An alert box prompts you to configure MS Backup for DOS (see fig. 5.1). If necessary, use the arrow keys or the mouse pointer to select Start Configuration and press Enter.

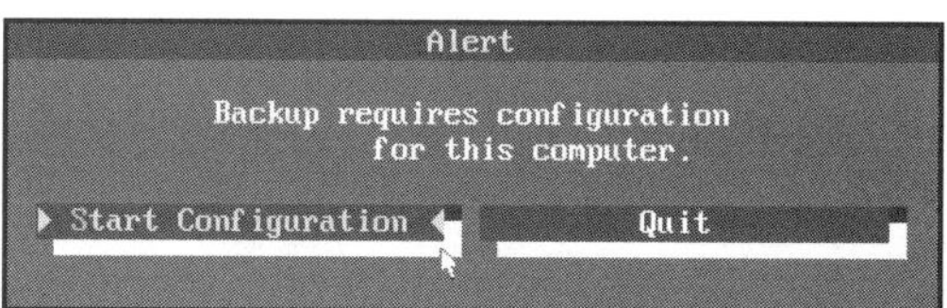

Fig. 5.1

An alert box prompting you to configure MS Backup for DOS.

The program first configures itself to your system by running tests. These tests determine the default setup and tell MS Backup how fast it can perform the exchange of information. The tests consist of the following steps:

- Selecting the program complexity level
- Configuring the screen and mouse
- Selecting backup devices
- Configuring and testing backup devices

As automatic configuration runs, you can sit back, watch the configuration, and press Enter after you are prompted to continue. Your interaction is minimal unless you decide to change some of the choices that MS Backup makes.

The first set of options enables you to configure the screen and mouse (see fig. 5.2).

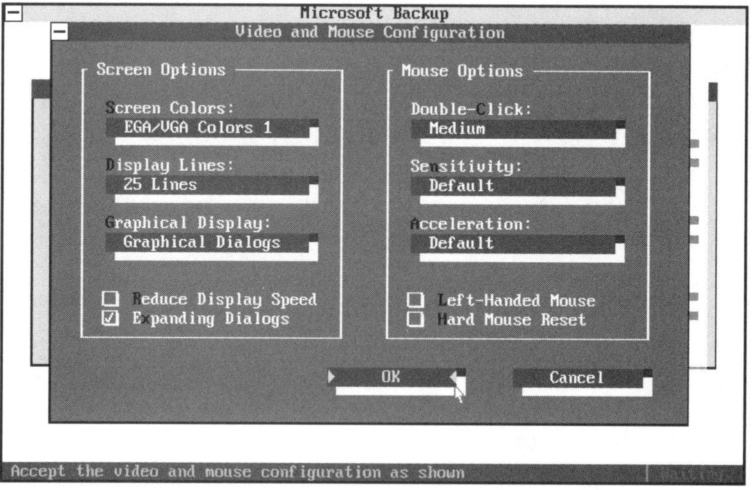

Fig. 5.2

Configuring video and mouse options.

You can change the following screen options:

- *Screen Colors (Alt+S):* If you choose this command button, you see a dialog box from which you can choose one of the alternate screen palettes.
- *Display Lines (Alt+D):* Choose this command button to change the number of lines displayed.
- *Graphical Display (Alt+G):* Choose this command button to display graphical elements that emulate Microsoft Windows or to display simple text elements.
- *Reduce Display Speed (Alt+R):* Select this check box to eliminate snow that appears on some video monitors.
- *Expanding Dialogs (Alt+X):* Use this check box to change the size of dialog boxes.

To select or deselect the check-box options, highlight the option and then press the space bar, or click the option. A check mark or X in the box indicates that the option is selected.

You can change the following mouse options:

- *Double-Click (Alt+C):* Choose this command button to change the speed at which you must click the mouse button twice in succession to choose an item.
- *Sensitivity (Alt+N):* With this command button, you can change the speed that the mouse pointer moves on-screen when you move the mouse.
- *Acceleration (Alt+A):* Use this command button to change whether the mouse pointer accelerates on-screen in relation to the speed changes of the mouse.
- *Left-Handed Mouse (Alt+L):* Select this check-box option to switch the actions of the mouse buttons.
- *Hard Mouse Reset (Alt+H):* Use this check-box option only if you are experiencing erratic problems with your mouse. Such problems may include a lack of mouse-pointer response to mouse movement, or mouse clicks with no results.

After you make all the changes you want for the screen and the mouse, choose OK.

Next, the automatic configuration searches for disk drives and determines the maximum capacity of the drive—for example, the program determines if your drive A is a 3 1/2-inch, high-density drive. The program then tests to see whether it can detect when a floppy disk has been changed. When MS Backup for DOS is ready to make this test, it displays the Floppy Drive Change Line Test dialog box shown in figure 5.3. After this test, MS Backup for DOS displays the dialog box shown in figure 5.4.

MS Backup tests to see whether it can detect when a floppy disk has been changed because if it can detect this change, you do not have to press Enter after you change disks. This feature enables MS Backup to continue backing up your files as soon as a new disk is inserted, without waiting for you to press Enter.

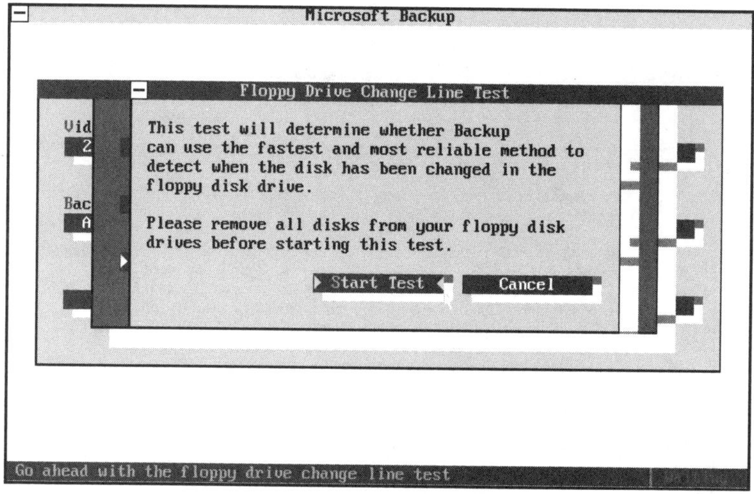

Fig. 5.3

The Floppy Drive Change Line Test dialog box.

MS Backup must know how to access your hard disk and floppy disk. The program makes this determination by a direct memory access (DMA) test. Most computers enable MS Backup to access the hard disk and the floppy disk at the same time, which greatly increases backup speed. Press Enter to start the DMA test, which takes just a moment. You see the results of the test after the test finishes.

MS Backup then runs a compatibility test to verify the configuration (see fig. 5.5). The compatibility test does an actual backup and comparison. Be prepared to insert two disks sequentially during the test. Press Enter to start the test. Watch the screen as MS Backup makes backup choices. The compatibility test pauses at the Backup To window and enables you to select a drive for the test. Insert the disks and press Enter as the program prompts you during the test.

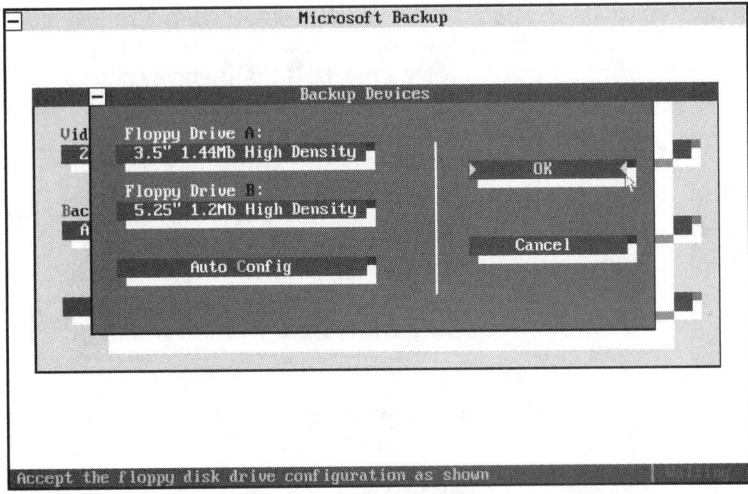

Fig. 5.4

MS Backup for DOS displaying the floppy drive configuration.

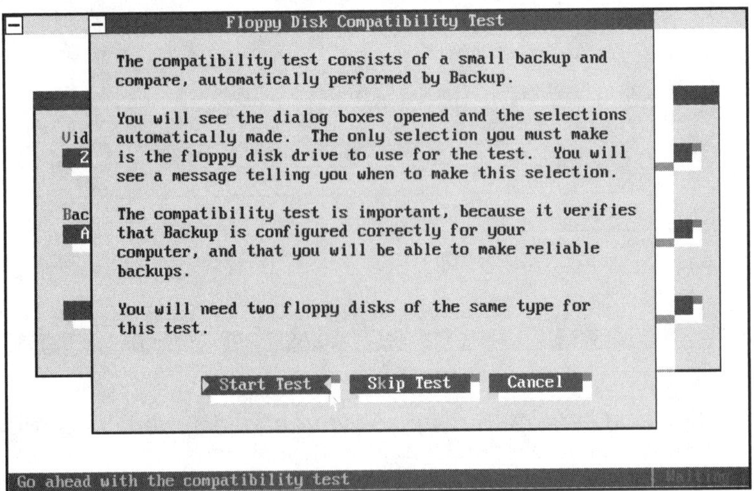

Fig. 5.5

MS Backup for DOS verifying the configuration by running a compatibility test.

During the test, MS Backup for DOS displays a screen similar to figure 5.6, which shows the success of the backup portion of the test. Press Enter to continue.

Next, the program compares the backups to the files on your hard disk and displays the results in a screen similar to figure 5.7. Press Enter to continue.

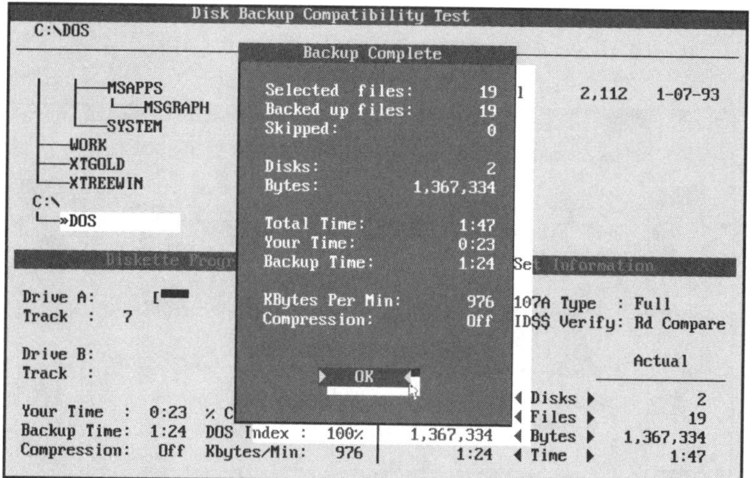

Fig. 5.6 MS Backup for DOS showing the success of the backup portion of the test.

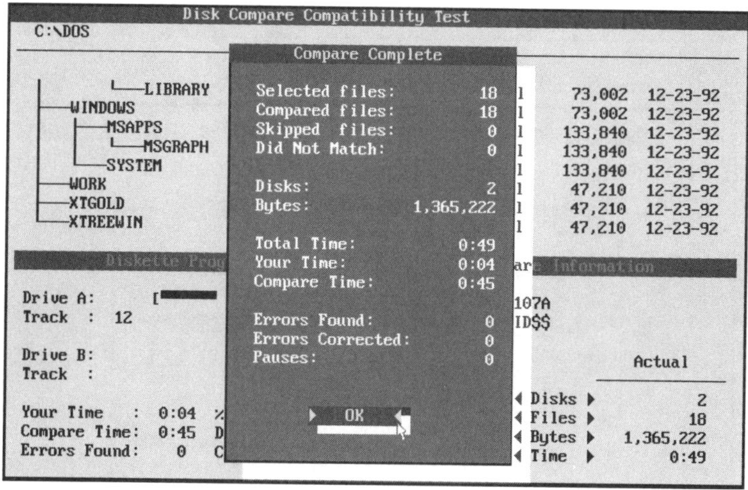

Fig. 5.7 MS Backup for DOS showing the success of the compare portion of the test.

After the compatibility test is finished, MS Backup for DOS displays the dialog box shown in figure 5.8. This dialog box tells you that the compatibility test was successful, and you can reliably make backups. Press Enter twice to continue and save the settings.

If you receive an error message box instead of the dialog box that tells you the compatibility test was successful, press F1 for more information.

You then see the MS Backup for DOS main menu screen (see fig. 5.9). MS Backup for DOS now is ready to back up your data.

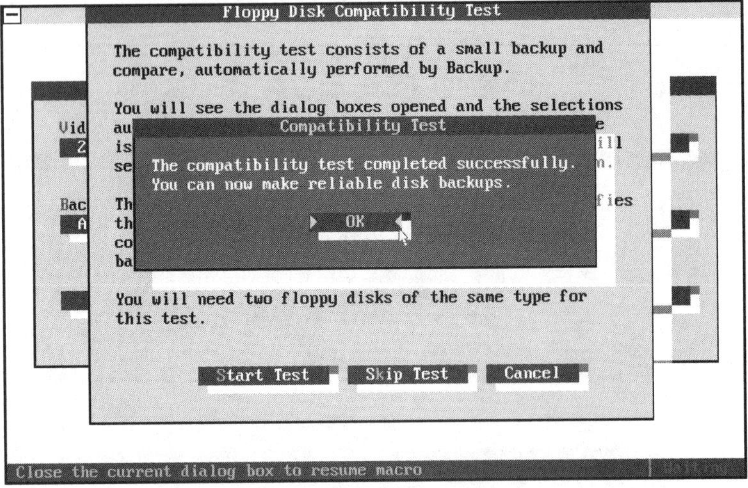

Fig. 5.8

The successful Compatibility Test dialog box.

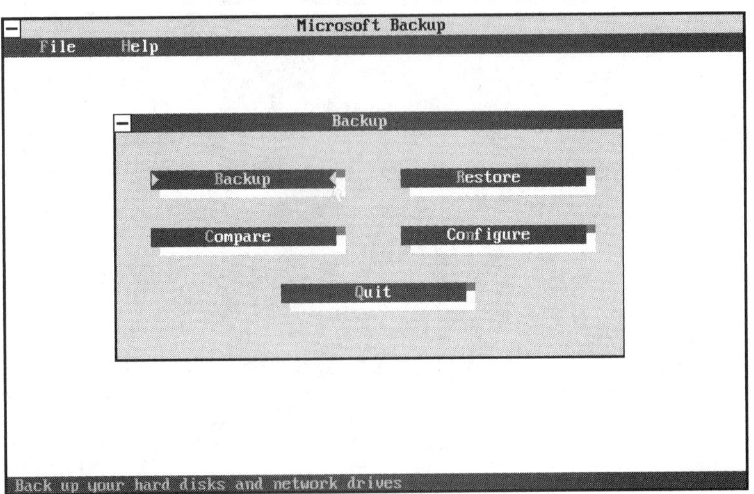

Fig. 5.9

The MS Backup for DOS main menu screen.

Making Backups with MS Backup for DOS

The **F**ile and **H**elp menus on the menu bar provide additional options to use with MS Backup. The **F**ile menu provides options that enable you to open, save, delete, and print setup files (SET) used in MS Backup. The **H**elp menu contains on-line help for working with all aspects of the MS Backup program.

The MS Backup opening menu displays the following five options:

Option	Description
Backup	Enables you to set up and run backups tailored to your individual needs. See the following section, "Backing Up Files," for more information.
Restore	Enables you to return backup files to a hard disk in cases of hard disk data loss. You also use this option to transport data from one computer to another. See "Restoring Backup Files," later in this chapter, for more information.
Compare	Compares backup files to originals to ensure data integrity. See "Using Compare," later in this chapter, for details.
Co**n**figure	Displays a dialog box containing the default setup determined by the data MS Backup used in the initial system configuration tests. You can change the default settings through this dialog box. See "Configuring MS Backup for Windows," earlier in this chapter, for more information.
Quit	Returns you to DOS.

The following sections examine the options on the MS Backup opening menu. Each section explains the use and purpose of each option in order to familiarize you with the option's operation.

Backing Up Files

If you choose the **B**ackup option on the MS Backup for DOS opening menu, you see the MS Backup for DOS dialog box (see fig. 5.10). Through this dialog box, you can choose drives and files to back up. You can back up a complete drive or just a few files.

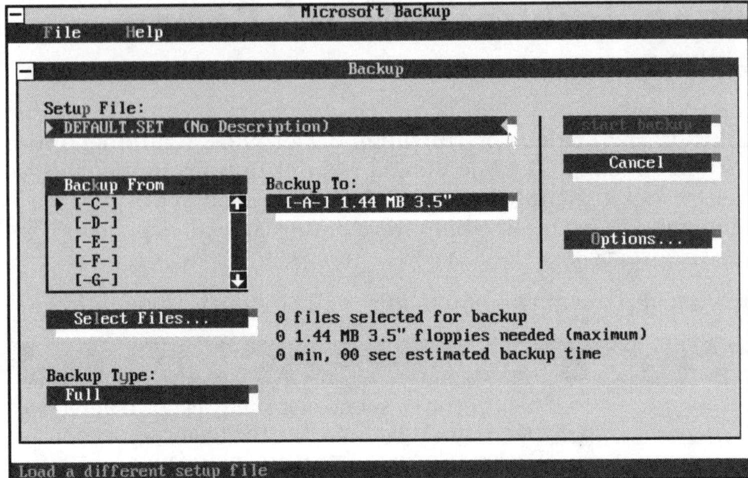

Fig. 5.10

The MS Backup for DOS dialog box.

This section takes you right into the steps for making a backup of your drive C. After you have a basic understanding of the procedure, the various steps are explained so that you will understand the different types of backups that exist. You also learn about selecting files and other options, such as data verification and compression, so that MS Backup conforms to your needs as it helps you protect your data.

Performing a Quick Backup

The following exercise creates a backup of drive C. The exercise should help familiarize you with the backup process. Follow these steps:

1. From the MS Backup opening menu, choose **B**ackup. The MS Backup for DOS dialog box appears (refer to fig. 5.10).
2. Choose the Bac**k**up From list box (Alt+K).
3. From the list of drives, use the arrow keys or the mouse to choose drive C, and press Enter.
4. Use the arrow keys or the mouse to select files or complete directories. Press the space bar or click the right mouse button to mark a directory's files for backup. In this case, select the root directory on drive C.
5. Press Tab until the OK button is highlighted and press Enter, or point to the OK button and click the left mouse button.
6. Choose the B**a**ckup To box (Alt+A).

7. Use the arrow keys to highlight the drive and disk type to use for backups ([-A-] 1.44 MB 3.5") and press the space bar. Or, point to the drive and disk type and click the left mouse button. Then press Enter.

8. Check the Backup Type box to make sure that Full backup is selected. If necessary, select Backup Type (Alt+Y) and correct the setting.

   The MS Backup for DOS dialog box also gives you information for the backup you select, including the number of files selected for backup, the number of floppy disks required, and the approximate time it will take to perform the backup.

9. Choose the **S**tart Backup command button (Alt+S) to begin.

MS Backup prompts you when to insert new disks or tapes into your drive. Be sure to number your disks or tapes so that you know the correct order. You may not want to take the time to back up your hard drive now. If you don't, choose Cancel or press Esc. If you decide to continue with the backup, make sure that you have an adequate number of disks.

Understanding Backup Types

Although you can perform a full backup of all your files, MS Backup offers other options that enable you to customize your backups to suit your needs. You can perform three types of backups, each with its own purpose. You begin by backing up your files with a full backup—a full backup is required by subsequent types of backups. You choose the Backup Type command button in the MS Backup for DOS dialog box to bring up the list of backups available (see fig. 5.11).

Descriptions of the three backup types follow:

- *Full:* A complete backup that backs up all selected files, whether or not you have changed the files since the last backup. After backup, archive flags are set to Off. A full backup doesn't require backing up the entire hard disk. You can choose a full backup of a subdirectory or a few files.

DOS uses an *archive flag* to indicate whether a file has been changed since it was last backed up. After a file is changed or created, DOS sets the archive flag to On, to signal that the file hasn't been backed up.

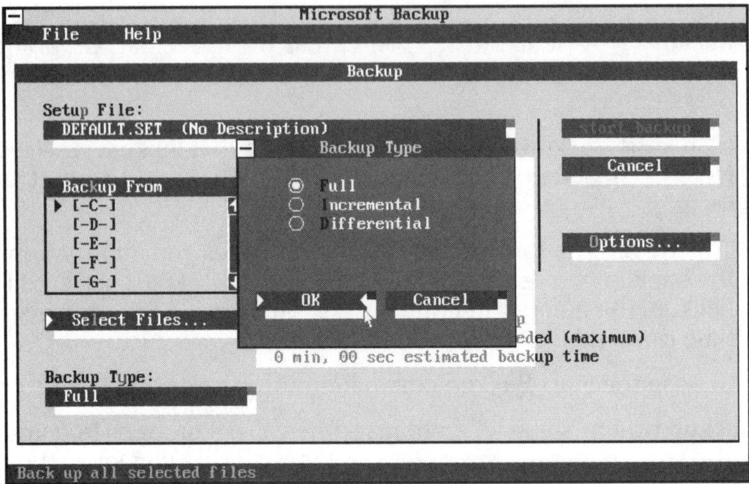

Fig. 5.11

The Backup Type dialog box.

- *Incremental:* A partial backup that backs up only those files that have been changed or created since the last full or incremental backup. An incremental backup looks only for files with the archive flag set to On. After backup, it sets the flag to Off. You must use the incremental type of backup with a full backup to maintain complete protection.

You must not use the same incremental backup disks more than once between full backups, and you must keep all sets of incremental backup disks created between full backups. If you reuse the disks before performing a full backup, you overwrite previous data with new data.

- *Differential:* Also a partial backup. A differential backup backs up files that have changed since the last full backup. Unlike the incremental backup, however, the archive flag is left On, so all files that have changed since the full backup are backed up again with each subsequent differential backup. You therefore do not need to maintain several sets of differential backups. You can reuse the same set of differential backup disks each time. You need only maintain two sets up backup disks—the full backup set and a single differential backup set.

A differential backup overwrites previous differential backups if the same disks are used. This feature isn't normally a problem because a differential backup continues to back up the same files. A problem develops, however, for people who want to maintain older file versions. If you need to keep old file versions, use the incremental backup as described earlier.

Now that you understand the three types of backups available, the following steps show how to choose the type of backup in the MS Backup for DOS dialog box. To change the type of backup, follow these steps:

1. Choose Backup Type (Alt+Y). The Backup Type dialog box appears.
2. Choose one of the types listed in the dialog box.
3. Choose OK to accept the selected backup type.

After you return to the MS Backup for DOS dialog box, the Backup Type button reflects the backup type you selected.

TIP

If you normally work with the same set of files, a differential backup probably will be your best choice. If you normally work with many different files, however, an incremental backup will better suit your needs.

Selecting Files To Back Up

You may not want to back up your entire hard drive each time you use MS Backup. Sometimes, you may want to back up only files you have been working on that day. If you are working on a special project, for example, you may want to back up only project files. MS Backup provides an easy method to select the drives, directories, subdirectories, and files you want to back up.

Choose the Select Files command button (Alt+L) from the MS Backup for DOS dialog box to begin selecting what to back up. The Select Backup Files dialog box appears (see fig. 5.12).

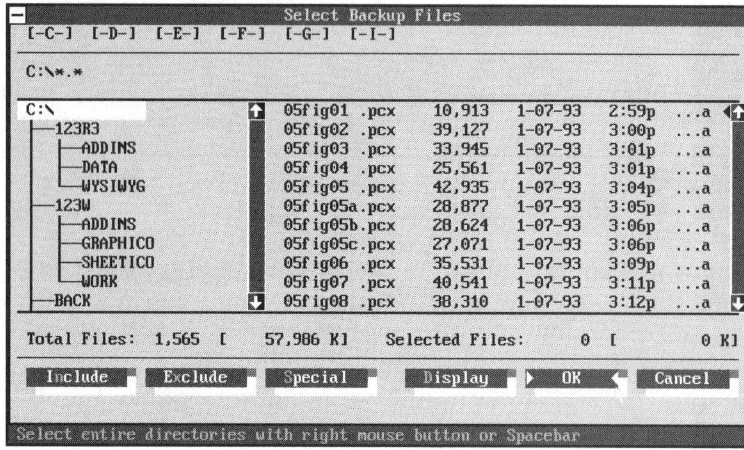

Fig. 5.12

The Select Backup Files dialog box.

The drive list at the top of the dialog box (just below the title bar) shows the drives that you can select to back up. Notice that the screen in figure 5.12 shows the available hard drives: C, D, E, F, G, and I. Press Shift+Tab, use the arrow keys to select the hard drive you want, and then press Enter. Or, simply click the drive.

On the left side of the dialog box is a directory tree, which lists all directories and subdirectories for the currently selected hard drive. To the right of the directory tree is the file list, which lists the files within a selected directory or subdirectory. You can scroll through the items in the directory tree and file list by using the arrow keys or the scroll bars.

To make a selection in one of these areas, use the mouse and click the desired area or press Tab until the highlight moves to the desired area. Next, select the drive, directory, or file you want by double-clicking it with the mouse or by highlighting the drive, directory, or file you want and then pressing the space bar.

You also can make selections by choosing the I**n**clude command button at the bottom of the Select Backup Files dialog box. Choosing this command displays a dialog box with which you can choose to include or exclude all subdirectories. The default setting is to include—that is, to back up—all subdirectories of the selected directory. An E**x**clude command button that removes a file from the backup list also is available.

In addition to choosing files by name, you also can select files by date created. The **S**pecial command button displays the Special Selections dialog box, in which you can select all files within a certain date range by filling in the From and To text boxes. The program selects all files that fall between the two dates. You can back up all files created or modified on a specified day, week, month, or year. The Special Selections dialog box also enables you to exclude files that are copy-protected, read-only, system, or hidden, from the files selected within the date range.

After you make a selection, an arrow appears to indicate the selected directory or subdirectory, and a check mark appears before selected files in the file list. As you select files for backup, a message appears in the dialog box showing the total number of files on the hard drive and the number of files selected for backup.

The **D**isplay command button is another option that can aid you in selecting files. This button calls up the Display Options dialog box, from which you can control the way that the files are displayed in the Select Backup Files dialog box.

From the Display Options dialog box, you can choose to sort the files by name (the default setting), extension, size, date, or attribute. You also can create a filter to display only certain files and to display all selected files as a group. This filter is useful when you are trying to find and back up specific file types.

Suppose that you want to back up a selected group of files according to the following conditions:

- Each file to be backed up has a WB1 file extension.
- You want to back up files regardless of their locations on your hard disk.
- You don't want to back up any files that start with the letter T.
- You want to back up only files created between April 15, 1993, and June 15, 1993.

Begin by selecting the I**n**clude button (press Alt+N or point to the I**n**clude button and click the left mouse button). Press Alt+F to select the **F**ile text box and then type ***.WB1**. If the Include All **S**ubdirectories check box is not checked, press Alt+S, or click the check box to add a check to the box. Press Enter or click OK.

Next, select the E**x**clude button (press Alt+X or point to the E**x**clude button and click the left mouse button). Press Alt+F to select the **F**ile text box and then type **T*.***. If the Exclude All **S**ubdirectories check box is checked, press Alt+S, or click the check box to remove the check in the box. Press Enter or click OK.

Finally, select the **S**pecial button (press Alt+S or point to the **S**pecial button and click the left mouse button). If the **A**pply Date Range check box is not checked, press Alt+A, or click the check box to add a check to the box. Press Alt+F to select the **F**rom text box and type **4-15-93**. Press Alt+T to select the **T**o text box and type **6-15-93**. Press Enter or click OK.

You can use these same techniques to select any group of files for backup or to change the selected group. Be sure to return the **F**ile text box in the Include dialog box to *.*, remove the entry from the **F**ile text box in the Exclude dialog box, and remove the check from the **A**pply Date Range check box in the Special dialog box. If you do not remove these selections, your backups will include only the files selected by the options you selected in this example.

Choosing Backup Options

You can choose a number of options with MS Backup. You can compress the backed-up data, password-protect the backed-up data, and add error-correction information to the backed-up data, for example.

You can set the options by choosing the **O**ptions button (or pressing Alt+O) from the MS Backup for DOS dialog box. Choosing **O**ptions displays the Disk Backup Options dialog box (see fig. 5.13).

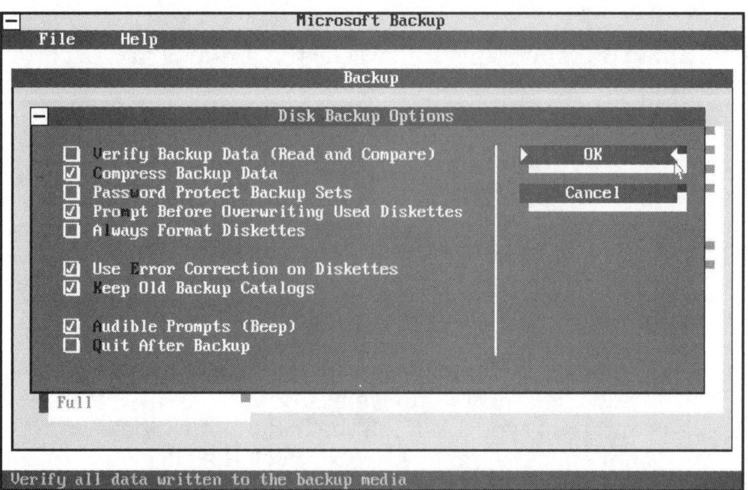

Fig. 5.13
The Disk Backup Options dialog box.

The first option on the Disk Backup Options dialog box is **V**erify Backup Data (Read and Compare) (Alt+V). This option enables you to activate or deactivate the program's data-verification feature. You choose the option to ensure the integrity of your backed-up data.

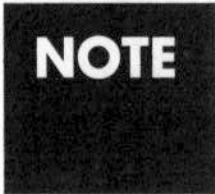

The term *data verification* describes the process of checking the backed-up data to see whether it matches the original. Any discrepancies found in the data are corrected.

Using data verification slows the backup process by approximately 50 percent. The increased integrity of your data may justify this decrease in speed, however.

The next option, **C**ompress Backup Data, enables MS Backup to compress your data onto fewer disks. Select the **C**ompress Backup Data check box (Alt+C) to compress the data you are backing up.

You don't have to do anything special to compressed backup data before restoring it. When you restore the data, the program expands the files, returning them to normal size. See "Restoring Backup Files," later in this chapter, for more information.

Select the next option, Pass**w**ord Protect Backup Sets, to include a password with the backup set. When you select this option, MS Backup prompts you to type the password twice when you perform the backup. Asterisks appear each time you type the password. After you enter the password the second time to ensure that you correctly entered it, choose OK to save the password. If you include a password with your backup, the information cannot be restored if you do not know the password. Passwords can contain up to eight characters and are case-sensitive. ***Do not forget your password***.

The next option, Pro**m**pt Before Overwriting Used Diskettes (Alt+M), specifies whether MS Backup prompts you when a floppy disk already contains data. If you are reusing floppy disks and do not want MS Backup to stop and prompt you each time it determines that a floppy disk already contains data, deselect this option.

Use A**l**ways Format Diskettes (Alt+L) if you want MS Backup to format floppy disks regardless of whether they already are formatted. Using this option will slow your backups considerably.

The Use **E**rror Correction on Diskettes (Alt+E) option adds an error-correction code to the data as it is saved. This option enables MS Backup to recover your data even if a disk error occurs, and is usually worth the small performance penalty.

The **K**eep Old Backup Catalogs (Alt+K) option is useful if you keep your old backup sets. If you keep the old backup catalogs, you can restore earlier versions of files that were backed up. By default, MS Backup creates a new master catalog (replacing any existing master catalog) when you do a full backup. Backup catalogs created by incremental or differential backups are added to this master catalog.

The **A**udible Prompts (Beep) (Alt+A) option determines whether MS Backup sounds a beep to draw your attention to the computer when it displays a prompt. If you prefer to not hear the beeps, deselect this option.

The final option, **Q**uit After Backup (Alt+Q), specifies whether to remain in MS Backup for DOS or to return to the DOS prompt when the backup is complete. You may want to select this option if you execute MS Backup for DOS from a batch file.

After you make your selections, click OK or press Enter.

Working with Setup Files

Because everyone has different backup needs, MS Backup enables you to create a customized file called a *setup file*. A setup file is used when you back up and restore files. MS Backup uses a default setup file named DEFAULT.SET if you don't specify a specific setup file.

From the MS Backup for DOS dialog box, you have many choices that enable you to customize the way you back up files. You can choose the backup type you want to perform, the drives and files you want to back up, and to which floppy disk to send the backed-up files. You probably want to make different types of backups at different times. You will not want to do a full backup every time you back up; perhaps you want to back up only the files that have changed since your last full backup.

You can create a setup file by selecting different backup options and then saving these options. You can open the setup file the next time you want to perform the same type of backup. To create a setup file, follow these steps:

1. Choose the backup options you want to include in the backup set. You can include any of the backup options such as the drive, directories, and files to back up; the type of backup; the drive to back up to; and the various data-compression and error-correction choices.

2. From the **F**ile menu at the top of the screen, choose Save Setup **A**s to display the Save Setup File dialog box.

3. Type a new file name for your selections in the File Name text box.

4. Press Alt+C to access the Des**c**ription text box, and type a description of the setup.

5. Choose the **S**ave command button to save your setup file.

If you use setup files to implement regular backup procedures, remember that new files will be included in partial backups (Incremental or Differential) only if the drive or directory containing the new files is selected in the setup file, or the new files are referenced by an Include statement in the setup file. In a directory where individual file selections are made, new files will not be included automatically.

Protecting Backup Sets

As you back up your data, MS Backup creates a *catalog*. The catalog contains information about the backup, such as the file names that you backed up and their directory structures.

You use catalog files when restoring backup files. You load the catalog file that corresponds to the backed-up data in order to restore it. You can find more information on catalog files in the next section.

If you select the **K**eep Old Backup Catalogs option, information from previous backups is maintained in the master catalog. Keeping previous catalogs enables you to restore an earlier version of a file, if necessary. You must have the backup disks that correspond to the previous catalog, however.

Restoring Backup Files

The **R**estore command on the MS Backup opening menu places your backed-up files onto your hard disk. After you choose the **R**estore command, the Restore dialog box appears (see fig. 5.14).

Catalog files are very important to the backup and restore process. The following section examines catalog files and the restore options.

Using Catalogs with Restore

After you complete a backup, MS Backup creates a *backup catalog* file for the backup. MS Backup stores these catalog files in two places: in the MS Backup directory and on the last disk of the actual backup.

Backup catalogs contain the names of all the backed-up files and the directory structure from which the files originated. Backup catalogs have the extensions FUL, INC, or DIF, which correspond to the various types of backups you can perform: Full, Incremental, or Differential (see "Understanding Backup Types," earlier in the chapter). These types of files are the ones that MS Backup looks for when you initiate the Restore command.

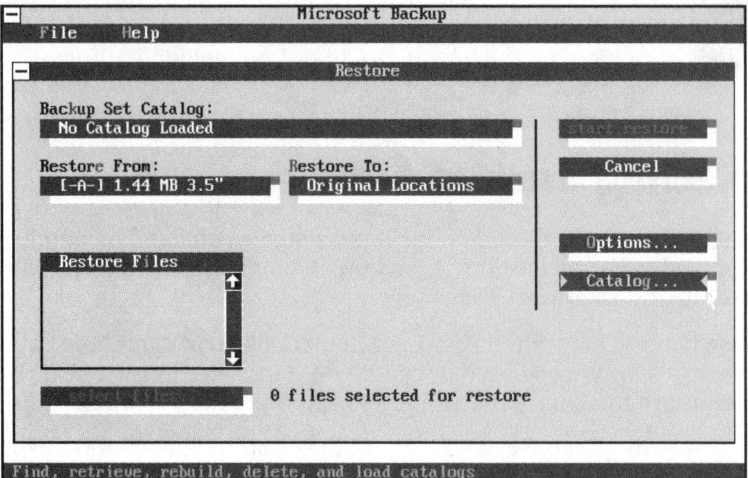

Fig. 5.14

The Restore dialog box.

Understanding how a backup catalog file is named is important so that you later can determine the file's contents. When you look at the catalog list, you see file names like CC30221A.FUL. Table 5.1 explains the meaning of the characters in the file name.

Table 5.1 Backup Catalog File Names

Character	Meaning
C	Stands for the first drive backed up in the file. In this case, the first drive backed up was drive C.
C	Indicates the last drive backed up in the file (in this case, drive C). If you back up one drive only, this letter is the same as the first letter.
3	Denotes the last digit of the year in which the backup was performed—for this file, 1993.
02	Corresponds to the month the backup was performed—for this file, February.
21	Indicates the day the backup was performed. Combining this information with the preceding year and month information tells you that the backup was performed on February 21, 1993.

Character	Meaning
A	A sequence letter that distinguishes between catalogs of the same name. Because this file is the first file created under this name, the next file has the letter B, and so on, to the letter Z.
FUL	An extension that tells you the type of backup performed

The other catalog type, the *master catalog*, coordinates the information when you restore files to the hard drive. The master catalog maintains a list of the backup catalog files. A master catalog takes the same file name as the setup file, except that a CAT extension is used (see the section "Working with Setup Files," earlier in this chapter).

Restoring Data

Now that you understand the two types of catalogs, you can get to know the MS Restore dialog box better (refer to fig. 5.14). Although this dialog box looks similar to the MS Backup for DOS dialog box, the options are different. The MS Restore dialog box provides the following options:

Option	Description
Bac**k**up Set Catalog	Displays a list of catalogs containing the files you want to restore.
Restor**e** From	Selects the drive that contains the backup disks.
Restore To	Selects the destination on the hard drive to which you want to restore. You can make the following selections: *Original Locations* to restore to the same location from which the files were backed up, *Other Drives* to restore to a different drive, or *Other Directories* to restore files to a different directory.
Restore F**i**les	Displays the name of the drive as supplied by the catalog file.
Se**l**ect Files	Chooses specific files to restore from the catalog.
Options	Selects advanced Restore options.
Catalo**g**	Loads, finds, or rebuilds a catalog.

Restoring is similar to backing up. The difference is that you are moving information from backup disks back to the hard drive. Selecting the catalog to use is much like selecting the setup file to use when backing up. Selecting files to restore is exactly the same as selecting files to back up.

After you set all your restoration parameters in the Restore dialog box, choose the **S**tart Restore command button. MS Backup restores the files to the drive and directory you selected.

Setting Restore Options

You also can customize Restore using the **O**ptions command button, which displays the Disk Restore Options dialog box. The dialog box, shown in figure 5.15, lists all the options you can change for Restore.

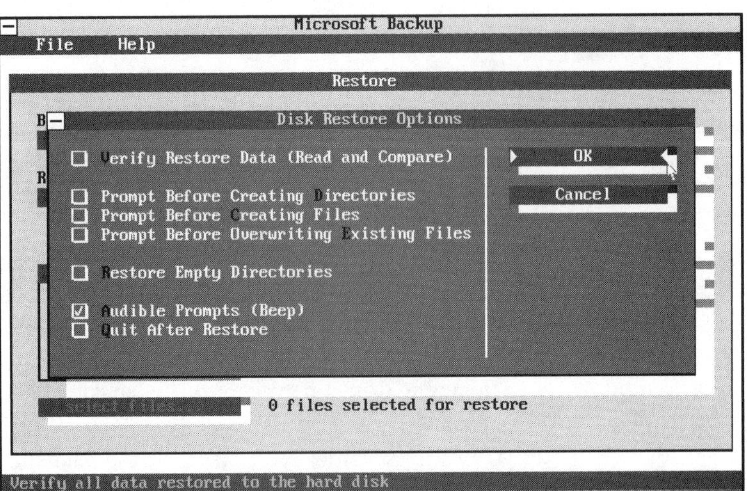

Fig. 5.15

The Disk Restore Options dialog box.

The options in the Disk Restore Options dialog box are similar to their backup counterparts (see "Choosing Backup Options," earlier in this chapter, for more details). Table 5.2 lists the options available.

Table 5.2 Restore Options

Option	Description
Verify Restore Data (Read and Compare)	Verifies data before it's restored
Prompt Before Creating Directories	Prompts user before a directory is created
Prompt Before Creating Files	Prompts user before a file is created
Prompt Before Overwriting Existing Files	Prompts user before an existing file is overwritten
Restore Empty Directories	Creates directories even though no files are stored in them
Audible Prompts (Beep)	Specifies whether to use a beep when prompting for user specifications
Quit After Restore	Immediately quits MS Backup for DOS after a Restore procedure is completed

Restoring Your Files

After you select the Restore options you want to use, you are ready to restore your backed up files. Follow these steps to restore files:

1. If necessary, select **R**estore from the MS Backup main menu.
2. If the correct backup set catalog name is not displayed, select the Bac**k**up Set Catalog button (Alt+K) and then choose the correct backup set catalog.
3. If the correct backup drive is not indicated, select the Restor**e** From button (Alt+E) and then choose the correct backup drive.
4. If the correct destination for the files is not indicated, select the **R**estore To button (Alt+R) and then choose the correct destination.
5. Choose the Se**l**ect Files button (Alt+L) to display the Select Files dialog box.
6. Choose the files to restore. You can select an entire directory by pointing to the directory and clicking the right mouse button.
7. Press Enter or click OK after you select files to restore.
8. Choose the **S**tart Restore button (Alt+S).

9. Press Enter or click Continue to begin restoring your files. Watch for MS Backup to prompt you to insert the backup disks and change disks as required.
10. Press Enter or click OK to return to the MS Backup main menu when the restore operation is complete.

Using Compare

The **C**ompare command on the MS Backup for DOS opening menu matches backed-up files to the originals to ensure that the backup is an exact duplicate. After you choose the **C**ompare command, you see the Compare dialog box (see fig. 5.16).

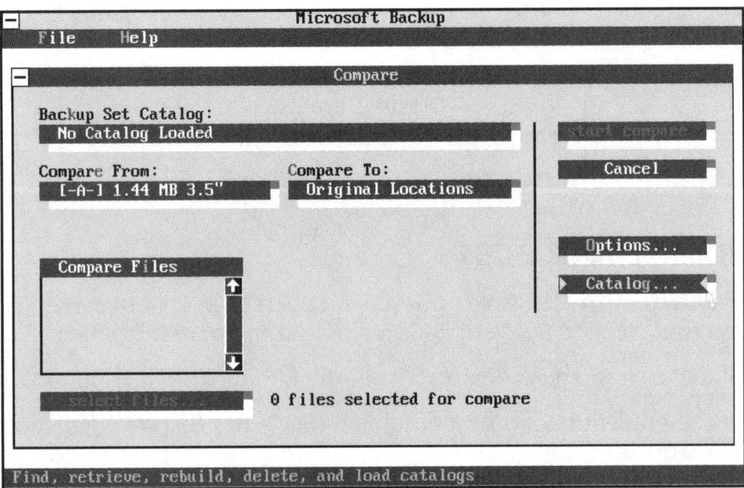

Fig. 5.16

The Compare dialog box.

The Compare dialog box is nearly identical to the Restore dialog box discussed in the preceding section, and the process of using the **C**ompare command is the same as using the **R**estore command.

First, choose the catalog that corresponds to the files you want to compare by using the Bac**k**up Set Catalog option. After you select the catalog containing the files you want to compare, double-check the Compar**e** From and **C**ompare To options to make sure that the source and destination of the files are correct. Then, select the **S**tart Compare option to activate your selections and begin comparing your backed-up files to the hard drive.

MS Backup has many enhancements and is much easier to use than the BACKUP command provided in earlier versions of DOS. In the next sections you learn about MS Backup for Windows. The Windows version of MS Backup is very similar to the DOS version, but is even easier to use.

Using MS Backup for Windows

MS Backup for Windows works identically to MS Backup for DOS. However, it has been customized for the Windows environment. MS Backup for Windows is extremely user-friendly and flexible. By using standard Windows operations (with either the mouse or the keyboard) you easily can back up all or some of the data on your hard disk—while you're performing other tasks in other open windows!

Starting MS Backup for Windows

As part of the normal DOS 6 installation, MS Backup is installed as an icon in the Microsoft Tools group (see fig. 5.17). You start MS Backup for Windows by simply double-clicking the Backup icon.

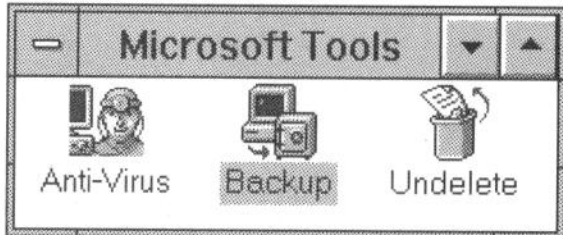

Fig. 5.17

The Microsoft Tools Program group.

Before you can use MS Backup for Windows to back up your data, you must configure the program for your system. On subsequent launches, MS Backup relies on this configuration to perform its backup chores.

NOTE If you install both versions of MS Backup (MS Backup for DOS and MS Backup for Windows) on your system, each version must be configured before it can be used. Although both versions perform the same functions, they use two separate configuration files.

Configuring MS Backup for Windows

MS Backup for Windows configuration and compatibility testing are important procedures. These tests analyze the components of your system to determine the fastest and most reliable method possible to back up data from your hard disk.

When you first start MS Backup for Windows, you see the dialog box shown in figure 5.18. This dialog box informs you that the compatibility tests for floppy disks have not been run, and that backup reliability is not ensured until the tests are completed. Choose OK to continue.

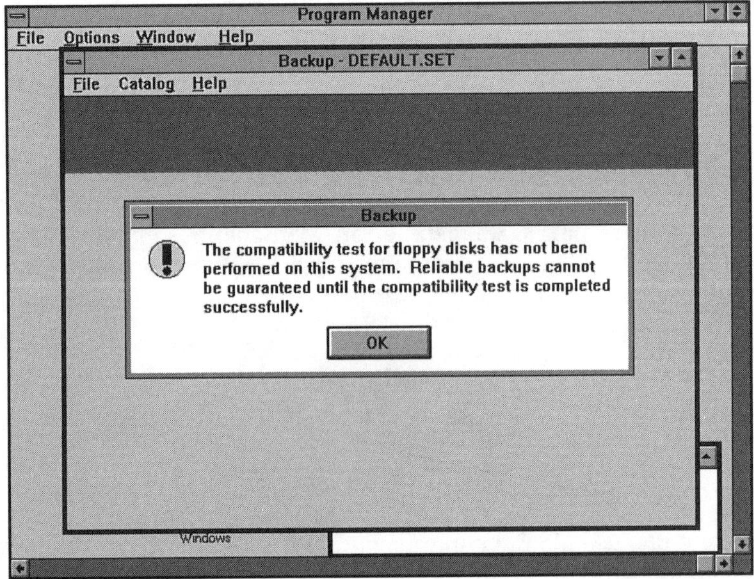

Fig. 5.18

Running the compatibility tests to ensure reliable backups.

Next, MS Backup for Windows asks if you want to configure Backup (see figure 5.19). Click Yes to configure your system.

MS Backup for Windows displays a dialog box telling you to remove any floppy disks and click OK. It then displays the dialog box shown in figure 5.20, asking you to select a drive to test. Select a drive and click Start.

The next dialog box tells you not to use the floppy disk drives during the test. Click OK to continue. The test then begins. Watch the prompts and change disks when prompted. When the backup phase is complete, you are prompted to reinsert disk 1. This begins the compare test. When the compatibility test is complete, MS Backup for Windows displays the dialog box shown in figure 5.21. Choose OK to return to the main MS Backup for Windows screen.

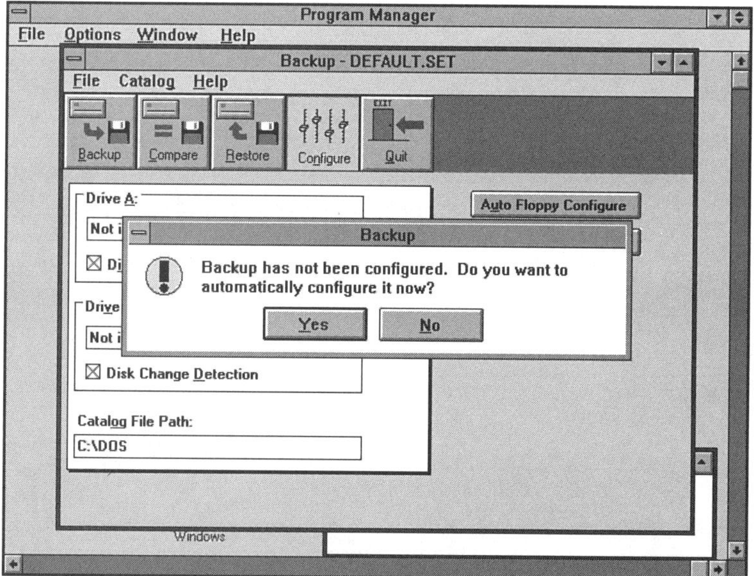

Fig. 5.19

Clicking **Yes** to configure your system.

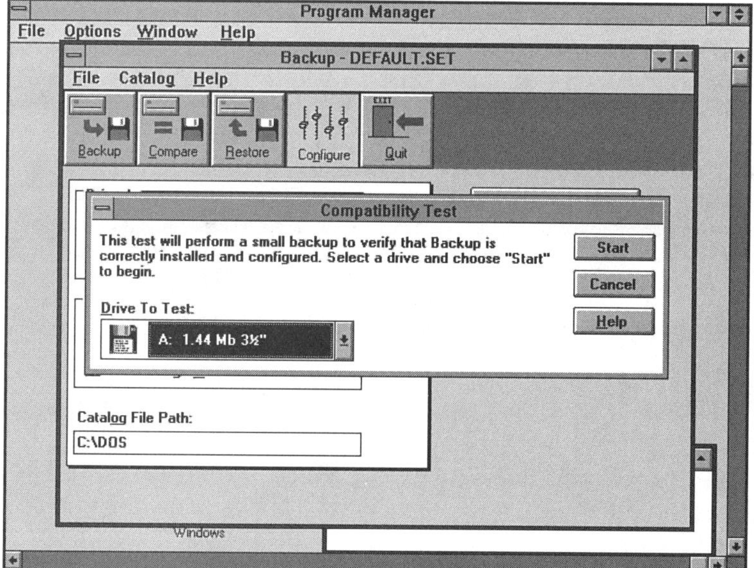

Fig. 5.20

Selecting a drive to test.

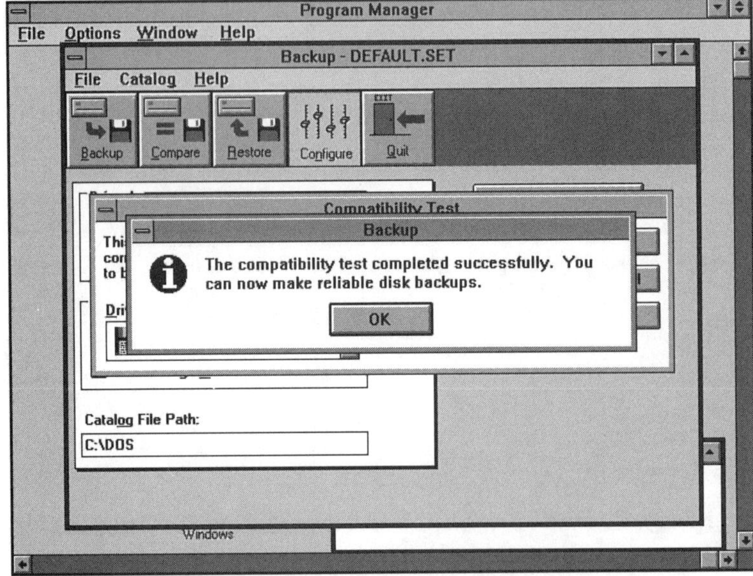

Fig. 5.21

The completion of the compatibility test.

> **CAUTION:** Because MS Backup for Windows can continue with backups even while you are working with other Windows programs, you must remember not to use the floppy disk drives for any other purpose during backups. If you attempt to use the floppy disk drives to read or save a file during backups, it is very possible that some files may be damaged or destroyed.

Backing Up Files with MS Backup for Windows

After you complete the configuration procedure, click the **B**ackup button. This displays the backup options. You can set several options for your backup operation: setup file, drive to back up, destination of backup files, type of backup, and the specific files to back up. For a normal backup, however, follow these general steps:

1. With MS Backup for Windows running, make sure that the **B**ackup option is selected (see fig. 5.22).
2. Select the setup file to use from the pull-down Setu**p** File list box.

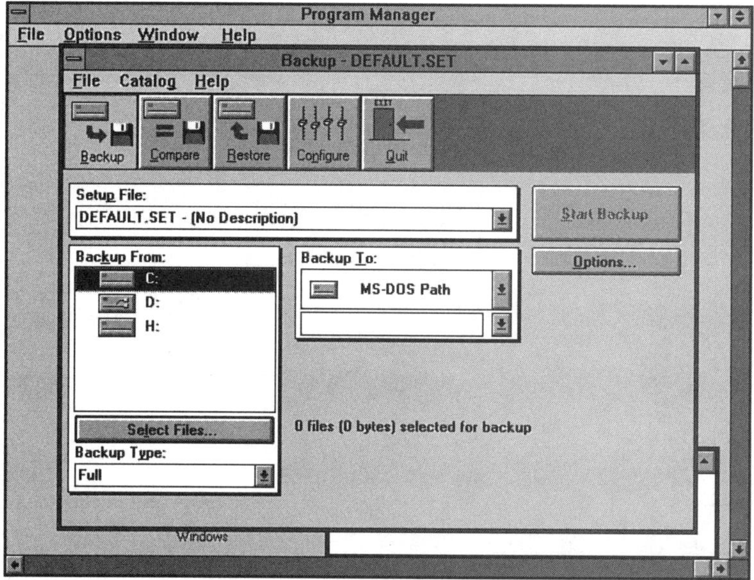

Fig. 5.22

MS Backup for Windows after the Backup option is selected.

3. Select the drive that holds your data from the Backup From list box.
4. Select the drive that will receive your backup data from the pull-down Backup To list box.
5. Choose the Select Files option and select the files you want to back up (see fig 5.23). Click OK after you select the files to back up.
6. Select the type of backup you want from the pull-down Backup Type list box.
7. Choose the Start Backup option to begin the backup.

Selecting a Backup Type

MS Backup for Windows can perform the same three types of backups as MS Backup for DOS—Full, Incremental, and Differential. See "Understanding Backup Types," earlier in this chapter, for a complete description of these three types of backups.

To choose a backup type in MS Backup for Windows, select the type of backup you want from the pull-down Backup Type list box (see fig. 5.24).

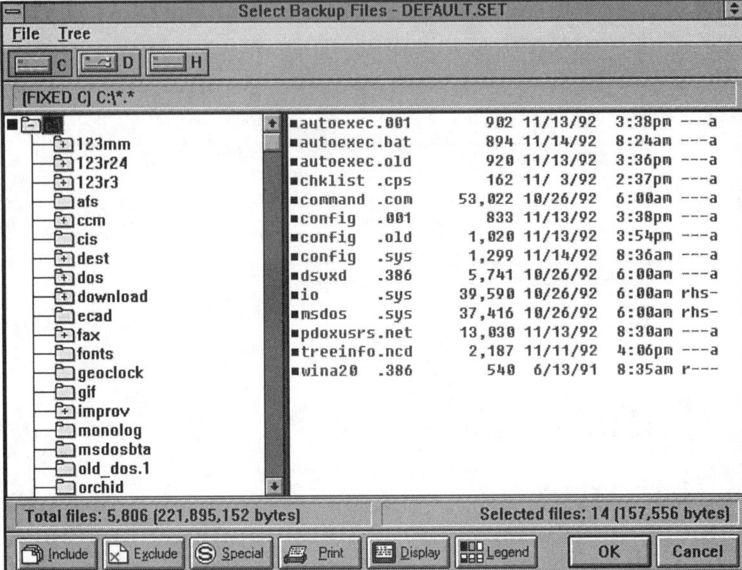

Fig. 5.23

Selecting files for backup.

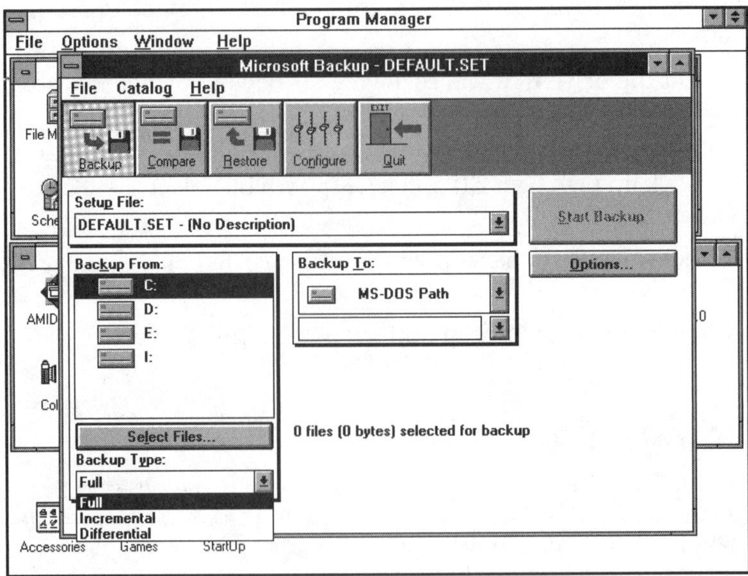

Fig. 5.24

Selecting the type of backup in MS Backup for Windows.

Using Setup Files

Like MS Backup for DOS, MS Backup for Windows also uses setup files to quickly restore an established set of backup options. See "Working with Setup Files," earlier in this chapter, for more information on setup files.

To save a setup file in MS Backup for Windows, select Save Setup **A**s from the **F**ile menu. Once you have saved a setup file, you can reuse thosc samc backup options when you perform future backups.

Using Backup Options

Select the **O**ptions button to display the Backup Options dialog box shown in figure 5.25. See "Choosing Backup Options," earlier in this chapter, for more information on each of the available backup options.

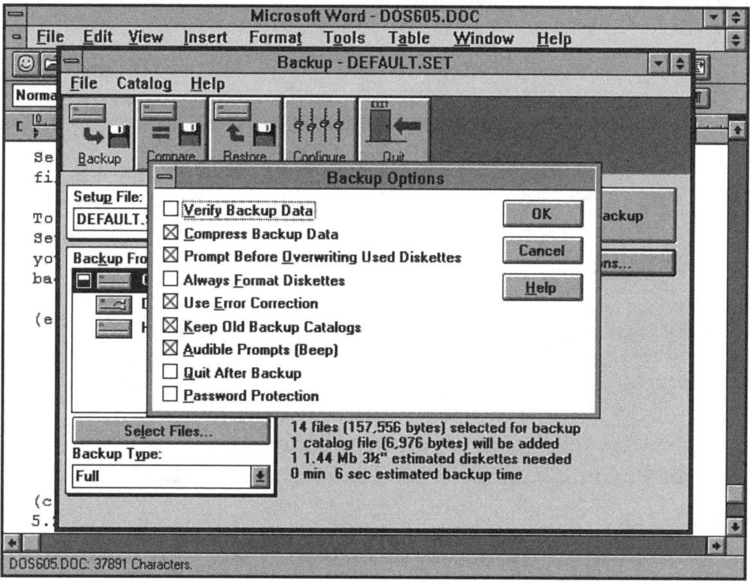

Fig. 5.25

Selecting backup options from the Backup Options dialog box.

Restoring Data with MS Backup for Windows

Select the **R**estore button to display the MS Backup for Windows restore screen (see fig. 5.26).

Restoring data with MS Backup for Windows is very similar to backing up data. You specify the drive containing the files to restore, the destination of the files, and any options you want to use. You then select the **S**tart Restore button and follow the prompts.

For more information on restoring data and the available options, see "Restoring Data," earlier in this chapter.

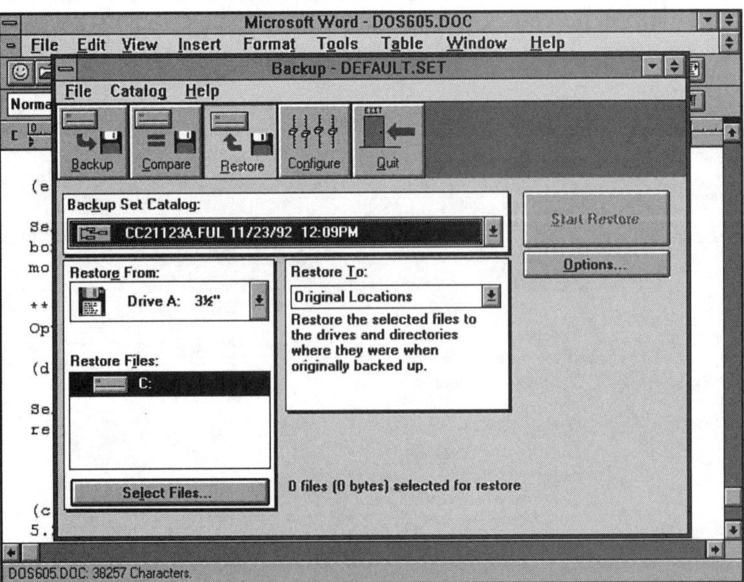

Fig. 5.26

Restoring files with MS Backup for Windows.

Comparing Data with MS Backup for Windows

Comparing data ensures that the data on the backup sets is identical to the data on your hard disk. Essentially, comparing data is identical to restoring data, except that no data is copied from the backup set to the hard disk.

To compare data in MS Backup for Windows, choose the **C**ompare button. See "Using Compare," earlier in this chapter, for more information on comparing data.

Chapter Summary

Few PC users back up their data as often as they should. This lack of backups makes their data files vulnerable to disk failures, accidental erasure, viruses, and many other forms of destruction. The MS Backup for DOS and MS Backup for Windows programs included in DOS 6 make backing up much easier and faster. This chapter showed you how to use these new programs to protect yourself and your data from loss.

You also can keep your data protected by regularly using MS Anti-Virus for DOS or MS Anti-Virus for Windows—programs you learn about in the next chapter. These programs can prevent computer viruses from destroying your program and data files. You also learn how to maintain this protection through continuous checking and periodic updates.

Using Virus Protection

Computer viruses have become big news. Although it's difficult to accurately assess how much of a threat viruses really pose, you can protect yourself from them by using DOS 6's antivirus utilities. In this chapter, you learn what a computer virus is and how to protect your system from the dangers viruses may present.

What Are Viruses?

Computer viruses are programs that become attached to files and are activated when you use the file. Many types of viruses exist: some viruses place themselves in your computer's memory; other viruses attach themselves to the boot-sector or partition table; still other viruses attach themselves to your executable files.

Viruses fall into three general categories. Table 6.1 summarizes these categories.

Table 6.1 Categories of Computer Viruses

Category	Description
Boot sector virus	Infects the *boot sector*—the portion of a disk read whenever you start your system. A boot sector virus is loaded into memory and then can infect every disk you use—floppy disks as well as hard disks.
File infector	Adds virus code to executable files. When the infected file is run, the virus can spread to other program files.
Trojan horse	A virus disguised as a legitimate program. May cause extensive damage including file destruction, low-level disk format, or partition table corruption.

Many viruses are destructive, damaging the files they come into contact with, deleting all the files on your hard disk at a certain day and time, or corrupting the partition table of your hard disk. Other viruses are not damaging, but annoying, issuing random sounds or sending off-color messages to the screen.

No viruses should exist, but unfortunately they do. Creating and releasing computer viruses is a crime, but you still must protect yourself from them. DOS 6 provides important tools to help you protect your system.

Create a Start-up Disk Now

If your system is infected by a virus, it may be difficult or even impossible to remove the virus unless you are prepared in advance. Right now would be a good time to prepare yourself.

Prepare a *start-up disk*—a floppy disk created with the command FORMAT A: /S. Copy the Microsoft Anti-Virus for DOS files (MSAV*.*) to the disk, along with any DOS 6 utility programs you feel may be useful (although you have a choice of either Microsoft Anti-Virus for DOS or Microsoft Anti-Virus for Windows, a floppy disk cannot hold Windows itself, and if a virus infects your system, you must be able to boot from an uninfected disk). Write-protect the disk, label it *Anti-Virus Start-up Disk*, and store the disk in a safe place.

If your system is infected by a virus, use your start-up disk to boot your system. Then use the copy of Microsoft Anti-Virus for DOS on the Anti-Virus Start-up disk to remove the virus infection.

How Do Viruses Spread?

Viruses spread from one computer to another through the sharing of files. If you never communicate with another computer, never add new software, or never use a floppy disk that was used on another computer, your system will remain virus-free.

Many people fear computer bulletin boards because they have read stories about viruses being spread by downloading files. Actually, most computer bulletin boards (also commonly called *BBSs*) test their files rigorously, and pose little real threat. Newly uploaded files that have yet to be checked by the system operator present the greatest danger, but such files are easily avoided.

Most computer bulletin boards only enable files to be uploaded to a "new uploads" directory. If you wait until files have been moved to other directories, rather than downloading them from the new uploads area, you usually can be certain that the files are safe to download.

Computer information services, such as CompuServe and Prodigy, constantly check for viruses. Your PC's chances of contracting a computer virus from one of these services is also minimal.

If on-line services are relatively safe, how do viruses spread? The most common route seems to be through the sharing of illegal copies of software. Someone makes a copy of a program, passes it along to someone else, who passes it along to another person. Along the way, a virus infects the "borrowed" software, and the "free copy" of a program ends up costing you lost data or worse. (Not even software manufacturers are immune to viruses spreading as a result of using copies of software—in the past few years, several major software companies have discovered viruses that resulted from someone spreading around infected software.)

In some cases, programs that claim to be something other than what they really are—*Trojan horses*—spread viruses. Programs have become so complex that few PC users would be able to know for certain that the spreadsheet, word processor, or game program someone gave them wasn't actually modified with added virus code.

It's very difficult to identify or eliminate all possible sources of computer-virus infection. The antivirus programs in DOS 6, however, give you a very large measure of protection.

Installing Antivirus Protection

If you did not choose to install the optional programs when you upgraded to DOS 6, you can add the antivirus programs to your hard disk later. To add the antivirus programs to your hard disk now, follow these steps:

1. Insert the DOS 6 upgrade disk labeled *Disk 1/Setup* into drive A (or B).
2. Make the drive with the setup disk the current drive by typing **A:** (or **B:**) and pressing Enter.
3. Type the command **SETUP /E** and press Enter.
4. Select the program(s) you want to add. You can install MS Anti-Virus for Windows, MS Anti-Virus for DOS, or both.

DOS 6 includes not only MS Anti-Virus for Windows and MS Anti-Virus for DOS (programs that search both your system's memory and disk files for known viruses), but also a memory-resident program, VSafe, that you can install to maintain a constant watch for virus activity. This memory-resident program is copied to your hard disk when you install the Windows or DOS antivirus program. VSafe is covered in detail in the section "Maintaining Virus Protection," later in this chapter.

Using MS Anti-Virus for DOS

Just as DOS 6 includes two very similar versions of MS Backup, it also includes two very similar versions of MS Anti-Virus: MS Anti-Virus for DOS and MS Anti-Virus for Windows. Although the two program versions perform nearly the same functions, there are a few differences between MS Anti-Virus for DOS and MS Anti-Virus for Windows that you should note:

- You can create a high-density, boot floppy disk that contains all the files necessary to run MS Anti-Virus for DOS. MS Anti-Virus for Windows, however, requires Microsoft Windows, which is much too large to fit on a floppy disk. If your system is infected by a virus, you may need Microsoft Anti-Virus for DOS to remove the infection. See "Create a Start-up Disk Now," earlier in this chapter, for more information.
- You can run Microsoft Anti-Virus for DOS from a batch file—such as AUTOEXEC.BAT. If you want to run MS Anti-Virus for Windows automatically, you must start Windows first.

You can use MS Anti-Virus for DOS in two ways. You can use its Windows-like graphical interface, or you can include the necessary parameters when you issue the command to run the program at the DOS prompt. In the next section, you see how to issue DOS commands to run the program at the DOS prompt.

Using the Command-Line Interface

In most cases, you probably will find MS Anti-Virus for DOS' graphical interface easier to use than its command-line interface. MS Anti-Virus for DOS' graphical interface is quite similar to MS Anti-Virus for Windows, which you learn about later in this chapter. If you run MS Anti-Virus for DOS from a batch file—for example, AUTOEXEC.BAT—however, you include the parameters that tell the program how to function. The basic MS Anti-Virus for DOS command line follows:

*d:path***MSAV** *drive: parameters*

Table 6.2 summarizes the optional parameters for MS Anti-Virus for DOS.

Table 6.2 MS Anti-Virus for DOS Optional Parameters

Option	Description
/?	Displays help
/25	Sets screen display to 25 lines (default)
/28	Sets screen display to 28 lines (VGA only)
/43	Sets screen display to 43 lines (VGA & EGA)
/50	Sets screen display to 50 lines (VGA only)
/60	Sets screen display to 60 lines (Video 7 only)
/A	Scans all drives except A and B
/BF	Uses BIOS font (use if graphics don't display properly)
/BT	Enables graphics mouse in Windows, enables graphics fonts with Desqview or UltraVision
/BW	Uses black-and-white color scheme (black-and-white monitor)
/C	Scans and cleans disk and files for viruses

continues

Table 6.2 Continued

Option	Description
/F	Suppresses names of files scanned. Valid only when used with /N or /P
/FF	Speeds up display—causes snow on some monitors (CGA only)
/IN	Runs program in color even if color monitor is not detected
/L	Scans all local (non-network) drives except A and B
/LCD	Uses LCD color scheme (LCD only, usually laptop)
/LE	Enables left-handed mouse—exchanges left and right mouse buttons
/MONO	Uses monochrome color scheme (IBM monochrome)
/N	Suppresses interface information. Displays text in MSAV.TXT file, if any
/NF	Specifies no fonts—don't use graphics characters
/NGM	Specifies no graphics mouse—use default mouse character instead
/P	Displays command-line interface in place of graphic interface
/PS2	Resets mouse hardware (use if mouse disappears or freezes)
/R	Switches the Report option On
/S	Scans disk and files for viruses (On by default)
/VIDEO	Displays the video command-line options

For example, to run MS Anti-Virus for DOS automatically whenever you start your system, scanning memory and drive C for viruses, add the following line to AUTOEXEC.BAT:

```
MSAV C: /N
```

If your system includes more than one hard disk, or has a single disk partitioned to create several logical drives, you probably want to scan all local (non-network) drives. To scan all local drives except A and B, type the following command line:

```
MSAV /N /L
```

Using the Graphical Interface

Because the two versions of MS Anti-Virus—MS Anti-Virus for DOS and MS Anti-Virus for Windows—are two versions of the same program, you will find that once you know how to use either one, the other will seem quite familiar (fig. 6.1 shows the MS Anti-Virus for DOS graphical interface). Because the programs are so similar, you can refer to the next section on using MS Anti-Virus for Windows for more information on using MS Anti-Virus for DOS' graphical interface.

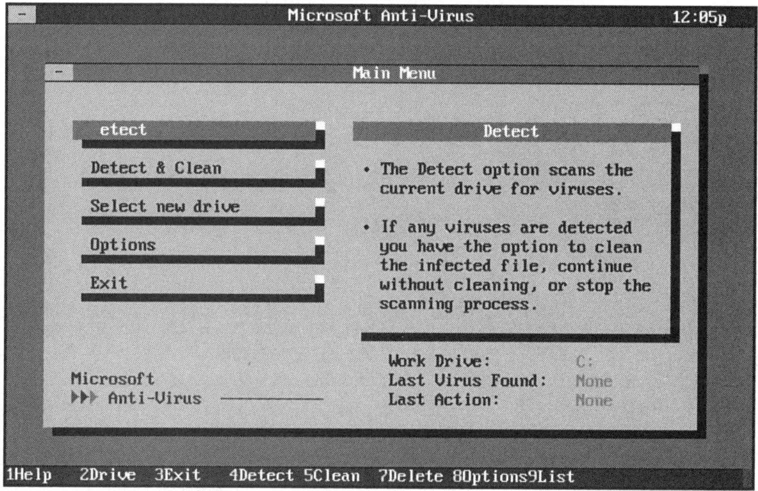

Fig. 6.1

The MS Anti-Virus for DOS graphical interface.

Using Anti-Virus for Windows

Just as you use a backup program to protect your valuable data files from accidents and hardware failures, you use an antivirus program to protect those files from virus-caused modifications or destruction. MS Anti-Virus is a DOS 6 program that you use to search memory and disk files for known viruses.

MS Anti-Virus protects against *known* viruses. Because new viruses released in the future may not be recognized, the program was designed so that you can quickly update it for continued protection. See "Obtaining Periodic Updates," later in this chapter, for more information.

To load MS Anti-Virus for Windows, double-click the program's icon in the Microsoft Tools program group. The program's opening screen appears (see fig. 6.2).

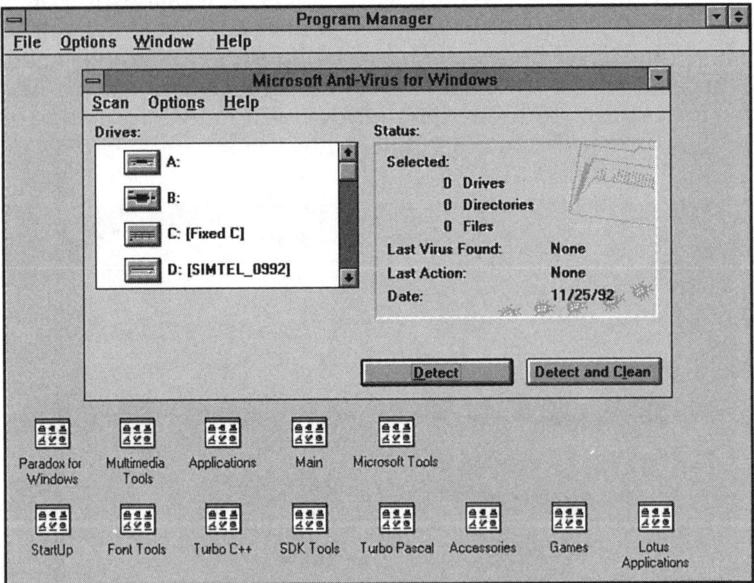

Fig. 6.2

The MS Anti-Virus for Windows opening screen.

The MS Anti-Virus opening screen displays a menu bar with three drop-down menus: **S**can, Optio**n**s, and **H**elp. Table 6.3 summarizes the options on the **S**can menu, and table 6.4 summarizes the options on the Optio**n**s menu. The **H**elp menu is self-explanatory.

Table 6.3 Scan Menu Options

Command	Description
Detect	Displays a warning if it finds a file with a known virus, but does not automatically remove the virus. Also warns about executable files that have changed.
Clean	Removes known viruses automatically. If the **V**erify Integrity option is on, warns if it finds a changed executable file—a possible sign of an unknown virus.
Delete CHKLIST **F**iles	Deletes the checklist files (CHKLIST.MS) used to defend against unknown viruses. The **V**erify Integrity feature will no longer work. Checklist files store each executable file's size, DOS attributes, date, and checksum.

Command	Description
Virus List	Displays a list showing each virus name, alias, type, size, and the number of variants of all the viruses recognized by MS Anti-Virus. For detailed information on specific viruses, double-click the virus name or select the virus name and choose **I**nfo (Alt+I).
E**x**it Anti-Virus	Exits MS Anti-Virus. If you have selected the **S**ave Settings On Exit option, any changes you have made to the program's configuration are saved.

Table 6.4 Options Menu Options

Command	Description
Set **O**ptions	Enables you to configure MS Anti-Virus' options: **V**erify Integrity Prompt **W**hile Detect **C**reate New Checksums Anti-**S**tealth Create Checksu**m**s on Floppies Check **A**ll Files **D**isable Alarm Sound Wipe De**l**eted Files Create **B**ackup These settings are stored in the CPAV.MS file. If password protection has been installed, MS Anti-Virus requires the password to change any settings.
Save Settings on Exit	Saves your settings to the CPAV.MS file when you quit.

Understanding MS Anti-Virus Options

MS Anti-Virus has several options you use to customize the program's operations to suit your needs. When you select Set **O**ptions from the Optio**n**s menu, the Options dialog box shown in figure 6.3 appears.

The following sections describe each of these options. To select an option, click the check box to the left of the option, or press Alt plus the underlined letter in the option. (The letter in the option is underlined on-screen, but appears in bold in this book.) To select Anti-**S**tealth, for example, press Alt+S.

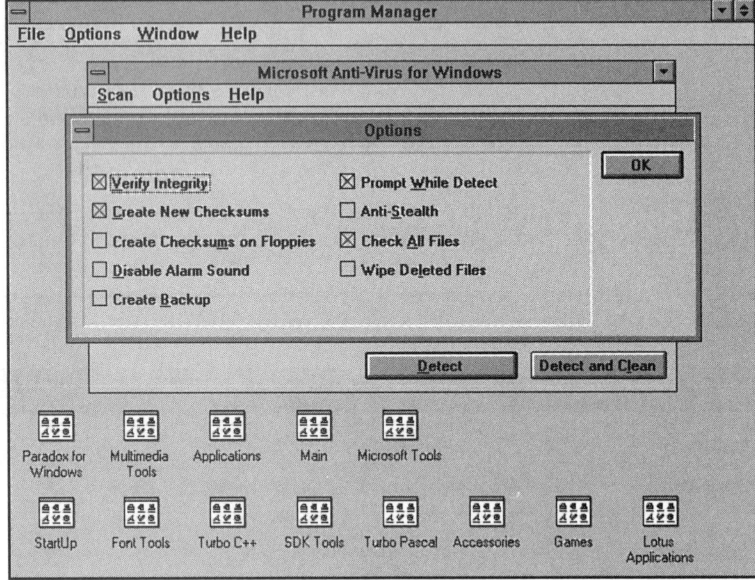

Fig. 6.3

Using the Options dialog box to customize MS Anti-Virus for Windows.

Using the Verify Integrity Option

The Verify Integrity option enables MS Anti-Virus and VSafe to alert you if executable files have been changed. You would not normally expect changes in these types of files, so changes may indicate the presence of a virus.

When Verify Integrity is selected and you perform a Detect scan by clicking the Detect button, MS Anti-Virus displays a warning each time it finds an executable file that has changed. If a virus—known or unknown—makes changes in executable files, this option can detect those changes.

Using the Prompt While Detect Option

When the Prompt While Detect option is selected (it is the default setting), MS Anti-Virus displays the Verify Error and Virus Found warnings during Detect scans. If Prompt While Detect is off, MS Anti-Virus does not provide any warnings during the Detect scan. This option should remain selected.

Using the Create New Checksums Option

When the Create New Checksums option is selected, MS Anti-Virus creates a checklist file (CHKLIST.MS) for each directory it scans. This file contains statistics about each executable file in the directory, including the file's size, date, and DOS attributes. On subsequent scans, MS Anti-Virus can use these statistics to verify that the files have not changed. VSafe also uses the checklist file to defend against unknown viruses.

Select Create New Checksums to take advantage of the Verify Integrity feature, which provides a method of detecting changes made by both known and unknown viruses.

Using the Anti-Stealth Option

Certain viruses, known as *Stealth* viruses, can infect files without appearing to change them. These viruses can evade Verify Integrity option protection. If you select the Anti-Stealth option and make sure that the Verify Integrity option also is selected, MS Anti-Virus uses a low-level verification technique during Detect scans that finds and alerts you to Stealth-infected files.

Selecting Anti-Stealth slows virus detection slightly, but offers the most comprehensive protection possible.

Using the Create Checksums on Floppies Option

The Create Checksums on Floppies option directs MS Anti-Virus to create a checklist file (CHKLIST.MS) for each directory it scans on a floppy disk. This file contains statistics about each executable file in the directory, including the file's size, date, and DOS attributes. On subsequent scans, MS Anti-Virus can use these statistics to verify that the files have not changed.

Using the Check All Files Option

When the Check All Files option is selected, all files are checked for viruses. When this option is deselected, only executable files are checked. Selecting this option provides better protection, but slows virus-checking slightly.

Executable files end with the following extensions:

386	APP	BIN
CMD	COM	DLL
DRV	EXE	FON
ICO	OV*	PGM
PIF	PRG	SYS

Using the Disable Alarm Sound Option

Select the Disable Alarm Sound option if you do not want to hear a beep when a warning message appears or when a virus is located or cleaned. Warning messages still appear, but MS Anti-Virus does not beep to draw your attention.

Using the Wipe Deleted Files Option

When the Wipe Deleted Files option is selected, MS Anti-Virus provides the option to overwrite each cluster of infected files so that every trace of them is eradicated. If this option is not selected, MS Anti-Virus provides the option to delete infected files. Because deleted files remain on the disk, they could be recovered and reinfect your system. The Wipe Deleted files option provides increased security against viruses.

Using the Create Backup Option

When the Create Backup option is selected, MS Anti-Virus makes a backup of any file infected with a virus before cleaning the original file. The backup file is renamed with a VIR extension.

This option can be very dangerous because it allows a virus-infected file to remain on your disk. If the infected file is your only copy of a file, and you would rather use an infected program than not have it at all, select this option with extreme caution.

Scanning for Viruses

After you select the options you want MS Anti-Virus to use, you select the drives you want to scan. Select a drive by pointing and clicking the left mouse button, or by using the arrow keys to highlight a drive's icon and then pressing the space bar. When you select a drive, MS Anti-Virus reads the file and directory information for the drive. You can select additional drives after each drive's file and directory information has been read.

Figure 6.4 shows the MS Anti-Virus for Windows screen after drive C is selected and the file and directory information has been read.

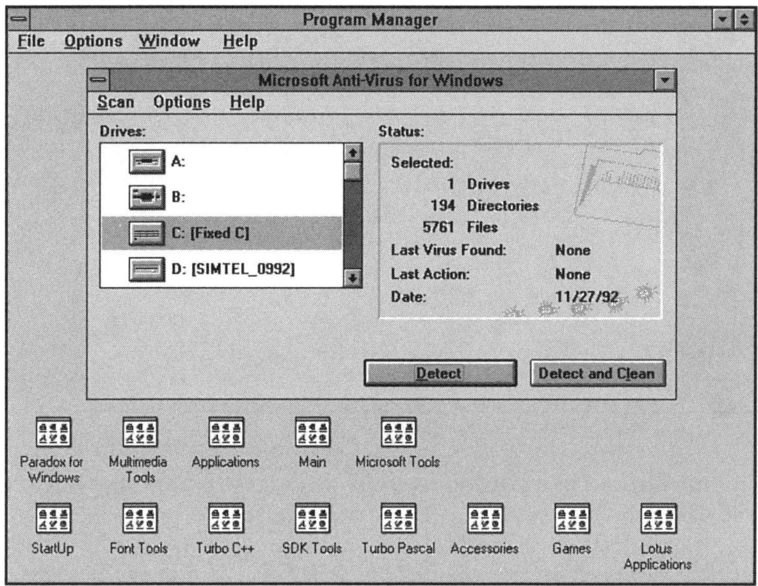

Fig. 6.4

MS Anti-Virus for Windows after drive C is selected.

After you select the drives you want to scan, select **D**etect (Alt+D) or Detect and C**l**ean (Alt+L). If you want MS Anti-Virus to automatically delete any virus-infected files from your disk, select Detect and C**l**ean. If you would rather have MS Anti-Virus inform you of virus-infected files, and direct the disposition of those files yourself, choose **D**etect.

When you select **D**etect or Detect and C**l**ean, MS Anti-Virus first scans memory for any viruses. It then begins scanning the files on the selected disk drives. If you select **D**etect, MS Anti-Virus alerts you and displays the Verify Error dialog box shown in figure 6.5 when it finds an executable file that has changed—whether through a legitimate change or because of a virus.

If you know the change is legitimate, click the **U**pdate button (or press Alt+U) to correct the file's statistics in the checklist file. If the file should not have changed, and you feel a virus may be responsible, click the **D**elete button (or press Alt+D) to remove the file from your disk. To stop the scan so that you can make further checks on whether the change is legitimate, click the **S**top button (or press Alt+S). To continue without taking any action on the current file, click the C**o**ntinue button (or press Alt+O).

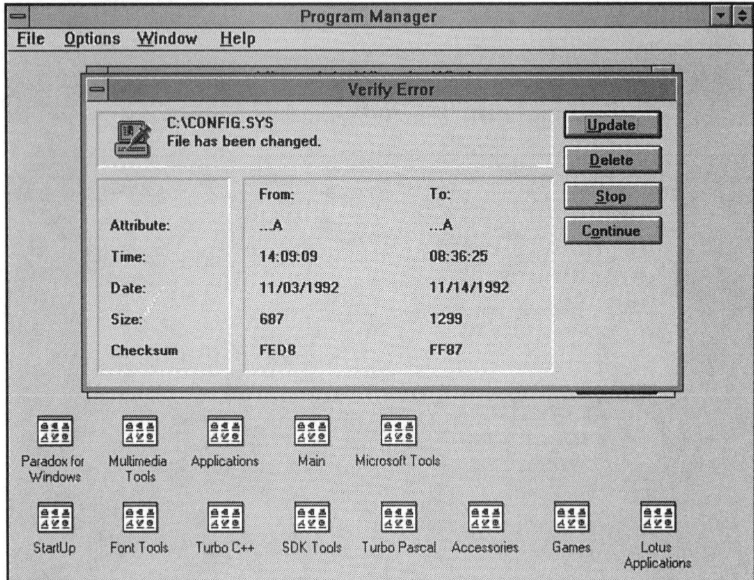

Fig. 6.5

The Verify Error dialog box, informing you that an executable file has changed.

As MS Anti-Virus scans your files, it displays its progress as shown in figure 6.6.

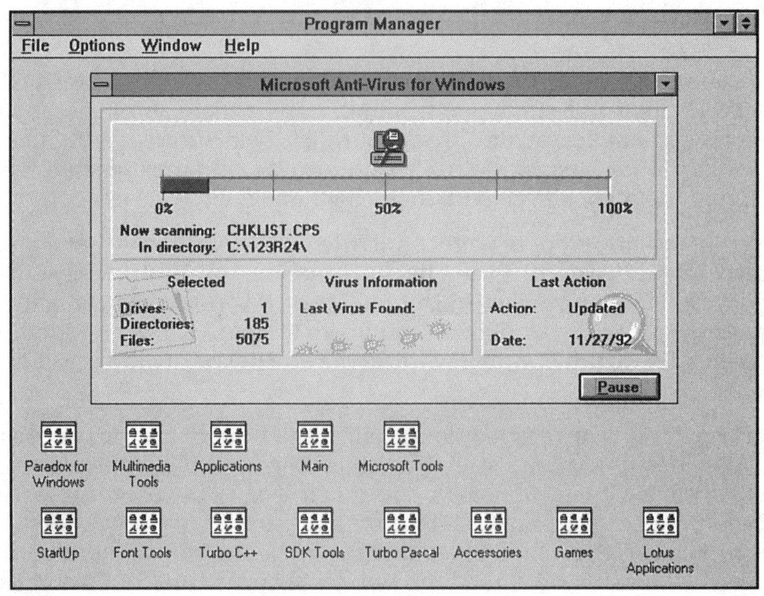

Fig. 6.6

MS Anti-Virus for Windows displaying its progress as it scans your files.

Depending on the number of files on your disk and the speed of your system, scanning for viruses may take several minutes. When the scan is complete, MS Anti-Virus displays a statistics screen as shown in figure 6.7. The Statistics screen shows the number of disks scanned, the number of files scanned, how much time the scan required, statistics on the number of infected files, and statistics on how many files were cleaned.

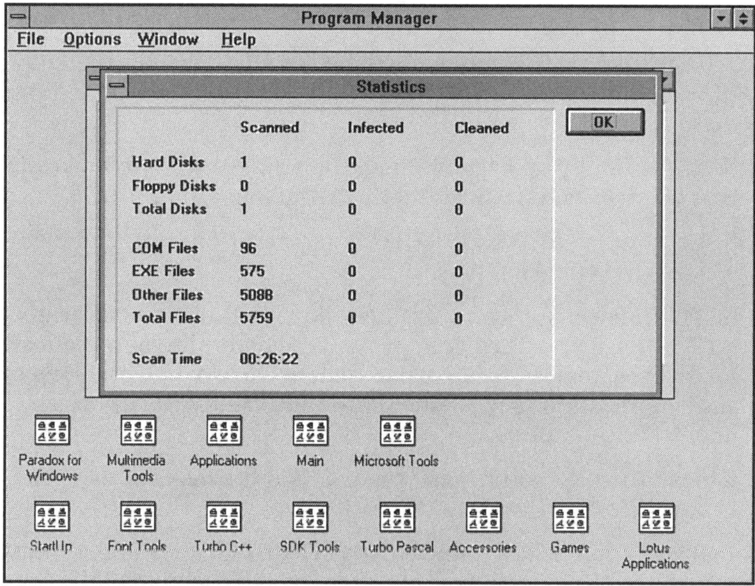

Fig. 6.7

The Statistics dialog box summarizing the virus scan.

Click OK to return to the MS Anti-Virus main screen.

Deleting Checklist Files

MS Anti-Virus uses checklist files (CHKLIST.MS) to store each executable file's size, DOS attributes, date, and checksum. MS Anti-Virus and VSafe use these statistics to defend against unknown viruses. A checklist file is stored in each directory.

To save disk space, you can delete the checklist files by selecting a drive and choosing Delete CHKLIST Files. The **V**erify Integrity feature, however, will no longer work, and you will be unprotected against unknown viruses. To select this option, choose Delete CHKLIST **F**iles from the **S**can menu.

You also may want to delete the checklist files before you install a software upgrade, because new versions of software often use files with the same names as those of older versions of the software. In some cases, such as upgrading to a new version of Windows, an upgrade may replace dozens or even hundreds of files with identical names. Each of these new files will trigger a verify error the next time you perform a virus scan.

If you are installing a software upgrade, you may want to follow this procedure:

1. Scan the drive to which you will be installing the new version of the software to make certain that no viruses have infected the disk.
2. Scan the floppy disks containing the new software to make sure that no viruses have infected the installation disks.
3. Select the Delete CHKLIST **F**iles command from the **S**can menu to remove the checklist files from the drive.
4. Install the new software version following the manufacturer's instructions. If you have your system configured to automatically load VSafe, remove VSafe from memory before you start the software installation (see "Using Continuous Antivirus Checking," later in this chapter).
5. Rescan the drive on which you installed the new software to rebuild the checklist files.

Although you could simply delete the checklist files manually, software-installation programs may modify or replace files in many different directories. It can be difficult for you to identify all the directories that an installation program might modify, and whether a verify error produced by a subsequent virus scan was the result of installing the software or the work of a virus.

Viewing the Virus List

MS Anti-Virus has information on well over 1,000 viruses. This information includes the name of the virus, any known aliases, the type of virus, its size, and how it affects your system. You can view the information in the virus list by selecting Virus List from the **S**can menu. Figure 6.8 shows the MS Anti-Virus for Windows Virus List dialog box.

To view additional information about a virus, highlight the virus and click the **I**nfo button, or double-click the virus. Figure 6.9 shows a typical additional information dialog box. Select OK to return to the Virus List dialog box. Select OK again to return to the MS Anti-Virus for Windows main screen.

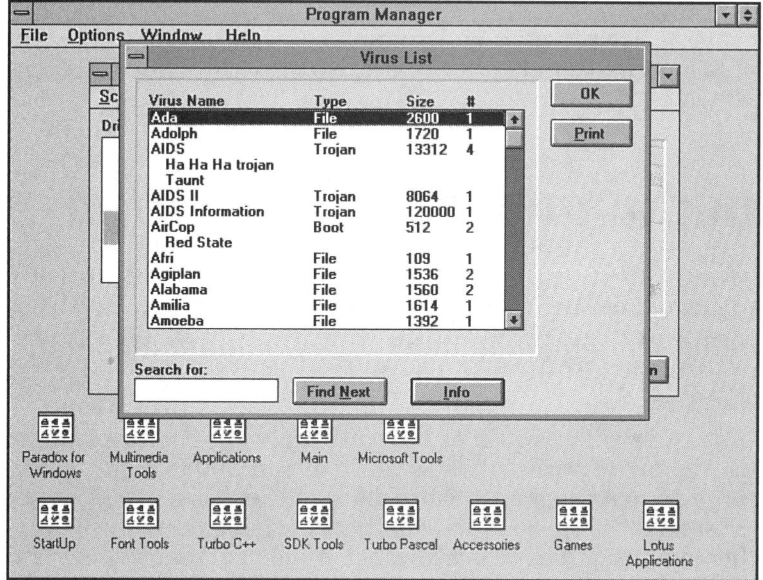

Fig. 6.8

The MS Anti-Virus for Windows Virus List dialog box.

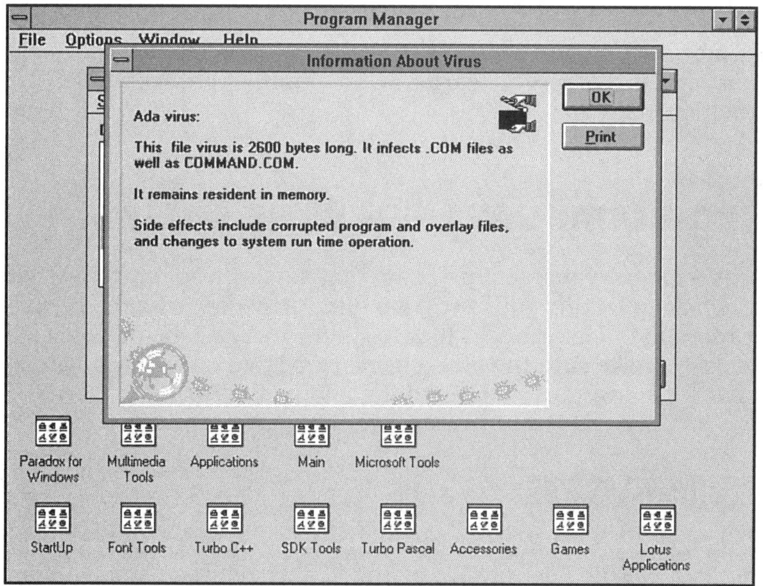

Fig. 6.9

The Information About Virus dialog box showing additional information on a virus.

Although MS Anti-Virus recognizes well over 1,000 viruses, it may not be able to protect you against new viruses that appear in the future. Fortunately, you can take additional steps to protect your system from new, unknown viruses. The next sections show you how to protect against virus-like activities on a continuing basis, as well as how you can obtain periodic updates to your existing virus list for maximum protection.

Maintaining Virus Protection

Protecting your system against computer viruses is not a task you can perform one time and feel that you have a permanent shield. The criminal types who create viruses continue to produce variations intended to thwart such protection. New, unknown viruses may appear at any time.

DOS 6's antivirus strategy goes beyond simply looking for a known group of computer viruses. One important part of this strategy is a memory-resident program, VSafe, which can keep a constant watch on your system for suspicious activity that may indicate a virus at work. Another important part of this strategy is the upgradability of the virus list. As new viruses are discovered, you can add information on these new viruses so that both MS Anti-Virus for Windows and MS Anti-Virus for DOS can identify them.

In the next section, you see how to add continuous antivirus checking to your system. Later, you learn how to obtain upgraded virus list information.

Using Continuous Antivirus Checking

VSafe is a memory-resident program that acts as a sentry to prevent viruses from infecting your program files, providing maximum, continuous protection. VSafe checks files for known viruses before they start, it checks to make sure the file's checksums have not changed, and it watches for suspicious activity that could be the result of a virus.

Installing VSAFE

You can install VSAFE from the command line or by placing a command in your AUTOEXEC.BAT file. To install VSafe from the command line, type **VSAFE** and press Enter.

The VSafe logo appears, as shown in figure 6.10. In addition to informing you that VSafe was loaded successfully, this screen shows the key combination you use to display VSafe (Alt+V is the default), and the amount of memory VSafe is using.

```
          VSafe (tm)

   Copyright (c) 1991-1993
 Central Point Software, Inc.
     Hotkey:    <Alt><V>

VSafe successfully installed.
VSafe is using  7K of conventional memory,
                0K of XMS memory,
               64K of EMS memory.

In Windows C:\SCREENS>
```

Fig. 6.10

The screen showing that VSafe was loaded successfully.

Unloading VSafe from Memory

VSafe uses up to 44K of conventional memory, which may be a problem in some cases. Fortunately, you can remove VSafe from memory without restarting your system.

If you must remove VSafe from memory, first remove any terminate-and-stay-resident (TSR) programs that were installed after VSafe was installed. Remove TSRs in the reverse order of their original installation. If you loaded VSafe and then a TSR called MYTSR, for example, remove MYTSR from memory first, and then remove VSafe. When you are ready to remove VSafe, type **VSAFE /U** at the DOS prompt.

Determining VSafe's Conventional Memory Requirements

When you load VSafe, the program determines what types of memory are available for its use. The amount of conventional memory VSafe uses depends on whether expanded (EMS) or extended (XMS) memory is available.

If VSafe is Using	It Needs This Much Conventional Memory
Expanded (EMS) Memory	7K
Extended (XMS) Memory	23K
Conventional Memory Only	44K

If EMS memory is available, for example, VSafe uses 64K of EMS memory and 7K of conventional memory.

Configuring VSafe

You can access any of VSAFE's eight configurable options from the command line or through a pop-up window. If you are using Windows, you can access VSafe's pop-up window through the TSR manager—an optional program you load to manage TSR programs in Windows.

Loading the TSR Manager

To access TSR programs such as VSafe from Windows, you first must load the TSR Manager. You load the TSR Manager by adding the following command to your WIN.INI file:

```
LOAD=MWAVTSR.EXE
```

This line automatically loads the TSR Manager whenever you start Windows. If you use Windows 3.1, you can load the TSR Manager whenever you start Windows by adding a new program item to the StartUp group. If you would prefer to load the TSR Manager manually, add C:\DOS\MWAVTSR.EXE as a new program item in an existing program group, such as the Microsoft Tools program group. See your Windows documentation for more information on adding new program items to program groups.

Understanding VSafe Options

VSafe has several options that you can configure through a pop-up window or by using command-line parameters. These options control how VSafe monitors activities on your computer. Whether you use the pop-up window or command-line parameters, the main configuration options are the same.

Configuring VSafe Using the Pop-Up Window

After you load VSafe into memory, you can access its pop-up window by pressing Alt+V if you are in DOS. Or, if you are in Windows, you can use the Task List by pressing Ctrl+Esc and selecting TSR Manager. If you use TSR Manager to access VSafe's pop-up window, click the VSafe icon in the TSR Manager window to display the VSafe pop-up window. Figure 6.11 shows the VSafe pop-up window as it appears in Windows.

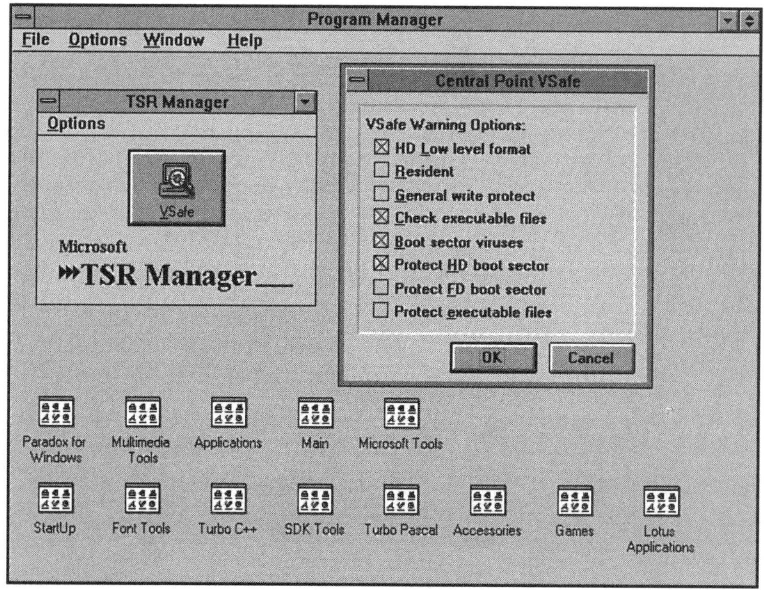

Fig. 6.11

The VSafe pop-up window as it appears in Windows.

To configure VSafe from the DOS command prompt, press the VSafe hot key Alt+V. The VSafe Warning Options pop-up menu, which looks similar to figure 6.11, appears. You can change any of the settings by pressing the number associated with the option. When you are finished making changes, press Esc to exit. Regardless of the method you use to access the VSafe pop-up window, the options are the same. Table 6.5 summarizes the VSafe options.

Table 6.5 VSafe Configuration Options

Option	Action
HD **L**ow-Level Format	Issues a warning when a command is given that would perform a low-level format of your disk and destroy all of the data. Default is On.
Resident	Issues a warning if a program is attempting to use regular DOS methods to terminate and stay resident in the memory. Many programs do this intentionally. Seeing this warning does not necessarily mean that there is a virus. Default is Off.

continues

Table 6.5 Continued

Option	Action
General Write Protect	Makes it impossible to write anything to the hard disk. You may want to use this option if you want to run a program that you suspect has a virus. If a program attempts to write to your hard disk, VSafe displays a screen warning of the attempt. Choose **S**top to prevent the program from writing to the disk, **C**ontinue to allow the program to go on functioning, or **B**oot to reboot your PC.
Check Executable Files	Checks executable files for viruses anytime they are run. Default is On.
Boot Sector Viruses	Checks all disks for boot-sector viruses. Default is On.
Protect **H**D Boot Sector	You see a warning message on your screen if any program attempts to write to the hard disk's boot sector. Default is On.
Protect **F**D Boot Sector	You see a warning message on your screen if any program attempts to write to the floppy disk's boot sector. Default is Off.
Protect **E**xecutable Files	You see a message if any attempt is made to modify an executable file. Default is Off.

Configuring VSafe Using Command-Line Parameters

You also can load VSafe configuration options into memory from the command line. To do so, you specify the parameter number followed by a plus sign (+) to turn on the option or a minus sign (–) to turn off the option. If you normally load VSafe using a command line in a batch file, you probably will want to use command-line parameters to set VSafe's configuration options. Table 6.6 summarizes VSafe's command-line options.

Table 6.6 VSafe Command-Line Options

Parameter	Description
/1	HD low-level format warning
/2	Resident warning
/3	General write protect
/4	Check infected files
/5	Boot sector infection warning
/6	Protect hard disk BOOT area
/7	Protect floppy disk BOOT area
/8	Write-protect executable files
/?	Display Help screen
/Ax	Set hot key as <Alt+x>
/Cx	Set hot key as <Ctrl+x>
/D	Disable checksum creation
/N	Use if a network driver will be loaded after VSafe
/NE	Don't use expanded memory
/NX	Don't use extended memory
/U	Remove VSafe from memory

Suppose that you want to change the *hot key*—the key combination used to access the VSafe pop-up window—to Ctrl+V, you want VSafe to notify you if a program attempted to become memory resident, and you wanted VSafe to use a network driver that will be loaded after VSafe. You can use the following command line to load VSafe:

```
VSAFE /CV /2 /N
```

VSafe is an important part of DOS 6's antivirus protection. VSafe remains in memory monitoring system activities, looking for suspicious actions that could indicate a virus. Unlike Microsoft Anti-Virus for DOS and Microsoft Anti-Virus for Windows, which primarily attempt to find known viruses, VSafe looks for all types of viruses—known or unknown.

Another important part of DOS 6's ongoing antivirus protection is its capability to be upgraded as new viruses appear. The next section explains how you can get these updates.

Obtaining Periodic Updates

Microsoft Anti-Virus for DOS, Microsoft Anti-Virus for Windows, and VSafe were created by Central Point Software, and have been licensed to Microsoft for inclusion in DOS 6. You can obtain periodic updates to the virus list through Central Point Software using the coupon at the back of your MS-DOS User's Guide and Reference.

As new viruses are discovered, Central Point Software creates signature files to define the virus. If you keep your virus signatures up-to-date, then you improve your chances of detecting a virus before it does damage. You can reach Central Point Software through the following methods:

Central Point Software Technical Support
6 a.m. to 5 p.m., Pacific time zone
Monday through Friday
(503) 690-8080

Central Point Software Technical Support fax line
(503) 690-7133

Central Point Software bulletin board
24 hours
8N1 (503) 690-6650

Central Point Software CompuServe forum
Type **GO CENTRAL** after logging onto CompuServe

Mail to:
Central Point Software, Inc.
15220 NW Greenbrier Parkway
Suite 200
Beaverton, OR 97006
Attn: Technical Support

When you call or write Central Point Software, be sure to include a complete description of your system and what type of help you need. Be specific.

Chapter Summary

For the most complete protection, you should use Microsoft Anti-Virus for DOS or Microsoft Anti-Virus for Windows to search for known viruses before they can strike, and VSafe to protect against unknown viruses when they attempt to strike. These important tools make DOS 6 safer to use than any earlier version of DOS. Their widespread use could drastically reduce the spread of computer viruses, and may even discourage the creation of new viruses. In this chapter, you learned how to use these tools to protect your system from the destructive effects of virus infection.

The next chapter introduces another enhancement to DOS 6—increased protection against accidental file deletion. In that chapter, you learn how to absolutely protect against the loss of files caused by accidental deletions.

7

CHAPTER

Recovering Deleted Files

It's pretty easy to lose an important file by accidentally deleting it. Everyone makes mistakes, of course, but losing valuable data or program files because you had a momentary lapse seems like a high price to pay for a small error.

DOS versions prior to DOS 5 did not provide a means of recovering accidentally deleted files. If you deleted a file in error, you accepted that the file was gone forever, hoped that you had a recent copy of the file, or went out and purchased a separate utility program such as the Norton Utilities. In fact, more people bought early versions of the Norton Utilities for one feature—its ability to "undelete" files—than for all the rest of its features combined.

Even though DOS 5 enabled you to recover accidentally deleted files, you had to be very lucky if the file you wanted to recover was deleted more than a few moments earlier. In addition, if you undeleted files in the wrong order, you could easily destroy any chance of recovering other deleted files. Clearly, there was room for improvement.

Deleted-file recovery in DOS 6 has been improved greatly. Not only is it easier to use—with both DOS and Windows versions of the software—but you can easily configure your system so that deleted files always can be recovered completely and in perfect condition! In this chapter, you learn how to use Undelete for DOS and Undelete for Windows to prevent simple errors from causing major problems.

How Can I Recover Lost Files?

It's certainly reasonable to wonder how a deleted file can be recovered. After all, if a file is erased, shouldn't it be completely removed from the disk? When you erase words written on a piece of paper, they disappear, after all.

Deleted files are not really erased from the disk. Truly erasing a file would require writing over all of the disk space occupied by the file. To save time, DOS takes a simpler and more pragmatic approach. Instead of erasing files, DOS simply marks the file's directory entry to show the file as deleted, and then marks the disk space occupied by the file as available for use.

This simple approach to file deletion makes recovering accidentally deleted files fairly simple. As long as no other file has used the deleted file's disk space, the deleted file probably is intact. You simply remove the directory entry mark that shows the file as deleted, and reallocate its file space.

As with most things in life, recovering deleted files is seldom as simple as it should be, however. Because DOS uses the first character of the file name to mark files as deleted, there's no record of the original first character of deleted file names. Usually that isn't a big problem, but finding all of a file's data may be. Because files are not always stored in contiguous areas on a disk, and only the address of the first piece is recorded in the file's directory entry, it can be difficult to find all of a file's pieces. Fortunately, you can overcome some of these problems with *delete tracking*—a method you can specify that keeps track of the first character of the file name and the location of all the pieces of deleted files.

For total security, however, you cannot rely on simply tracking the first character of the file name and the location of all the pieces of deleted files. Remember that DOS marks a deleted file's disk space as available for reuse. As soon as you delete a file, its disk space is ready to be overwritten by saving another file. Whether your deleted file will be overwritten very soon depends on several factors, including the amount and location of available disk space (and, it seems, the importance of the deleted file).

DOS 6 offers a new approach to ensuring the recovery of deleted files. You can configure DOS 6 to use *delete sentry*—saving deleted files in a special, hidden directory. If a deleted file has been saved using the delete-sentry method, recovery is guaranteed.

DOS 6's undelete tools also include another new feature—the capability to recover accidentally deleted directories. Directories are special types of files that hold the information necessary to find your files on your disk. If a directory is deleted, none of the files it contained can be recovered unless you first can recover the directory.

In the following sections, you learn to use DOS 6's tools for recovering accidentally deleted files.

Using Undelete for DOS

Undelete for DOS is similar to the UNDELETE command in DOS 5, but it has some significant changes. In DOS 5, for example, you used the separate MIRROR command to load deletion tracking—the feature that keeps track of the first character and the disk sectors used by deleted files. In DOS 6, deletion tracking is built into Undelete for DOS and Undelete for Windows.

Another important change in Undelete for DOS 6 is delete sentry—the built-in feature that saves deleted files in a special, hidden directory. The delete sentry feature is covered in detail in the section "Installing the Delete Sentry," later in this chapter.

Quickly Undeleting Files

Using Undelete for DOS to quickly undelete a file is simple. The following line shows the syntax for the command:

d:path\UNDELETE *drive:path\filename options*

To recover deleted files with an SYS extension in the current directory, for example, you would use the following form of the command:

UNDELETE *.SYS

Figure 7.1 shows an example of this command.

In figure 7.1, Undelete for DOS found one deleted file with an SYS extension. Because neither the delete-sentry control file nor the deletion-tracking file were found, Undelete for DOS did not know the first character of the file name for the deleted file it found. As a result, the first prompt it displayed looked like this:

```
?NSI     SYS     9029 10-26-92  6:00a  ...A  Undelete (Y/N)?
```

To undelete the file, press Y. Undelete for DOS then prompts you for the first character of the file name:

```
Please type the first character for ?NSI    .SYS:
```

Type the first character, in this case **A**, and Undelete for DOS recovers the file.

```
UNDELETE - A delete protection facility
Copyright (C) 1987-1993 Central Point Software, Inc.
All rights reserved.

Directory: C:\SAMPLES
File Specifications: *.SYS

    Delete Sentry control file not found.

    Deletion-tracking file not found.

    MS-DOS directory contains    1 deleted files.
    Of those,    1 files may be recovered.

Using the MS-DOS directory method.

      ?NSI     SYS     9029 10-26-92  6:00a  ...A  Undelete (Y/N)?Y
      Please type the first character for ?NSI    .SYS: A

File successfully undeleted.

C:\SAMPLES>
```

Fig. 7.1

Recovering files with Undelete for DOS.

NOTE If you have not installed the memory-resident delete-sentry or deletion-tracking features, it is very important to attempt to recover accidentally deleted files as soon as possible. If you wait too long, the chances of the deleted file's space or directory entry being overwritten increases greatly.

Understanding Undelete for DOS Options

Undelete for DOS has several command-line options you can use to modify how the program functions. Table 7.1 summarizes these options.

Table 7.1 Undelete for DOS Command-Line Options

Option	Description
/?	Displays help on the UNDELETE command.
/ALL	Undeletes all specified files automatically without prompting. If no delete-sentry or deletion-tracking file is available, Undelete for DOS supplies a substitute first file name character.
/DOS	Uses only the DOS directory information to undelete files.
/DS	Uses only the deletion-sentry files to undelete files.
/DT	Uses only the deletion-tracking files to undelete files.
/LIST	Lists the deleted files available to be recovered without actually undeleting them.
/LOAD	Loads undelete using the UNDELETE.INI options.
/PURGE*d:*	Purges contents of the delete-sentry directory on drive *d:*.
/S*d:*	Enables the delete-sentry method of undelete protection on drive *d:*.
/STATUS	Displays the status of Undelete for DOS.
/T*d:-ENTRIES*	Enables the delete-tracking method of undelete protection on drive *d:*, optionally tracking the specified number of entries.
/UNLOAD	Unloads Undelete for DOS from memory.

If you use the /ALL option, Undelete for DOS undeletes all the specified files without pausing to ask whether a file should be undeleted, and without requesting an initial character for the file name. If the delete-sentry or deletion-tracking feature is in use, the correct first character is used. If Undelete for DOS must rely on the information in the DOS directory listing, the program substitutes a character (#, %, &, 0-9, or A-Z) to produce a unique file name. In this case, you probably will want to rename the recovered files later.

The /DOS option tells Undelete for DOS to ignore any delete-sentry or deletion-tracking files it finds, and instead use the DOS directory-listing information when undeleting files. The /DOS option method is the most unreliable method of recovering deleted files.

The /DS option tells Undelete for DOS to recover only files found in delete-sentry control files. This results in complete recovery of files contained in the \SENTRY directory, but ignores any files that may have been deleted before delete-sentry protection was loaded.

The /DT option tells Undelete for DOS to recover only files found in deletion-tracking files. This method is more reliable than using the DOS directory-listing information, but it does not guarantee recovery of deleted files that have been overwritten by files saved later.

The /LIST option tells Undelete for DOS to display a list of the deleted files that it can recover without actually recovering those files. You can combine this option with other options, such as /DOS, /DS, or /DT, to see how effective each method may be before you select a recovery method.

The /LOAD option loads Undelete for DOS as a memory-resident program using the settings in the UNDELETE.INI file. These settings install the delete-sentry method of protecting deleted files, enable the \SENTRY directory to use up to 20 percent of the disk space, keep deleted files for seven days, and track all files except those with the following file extensions:

DOV	SPL	TMP
IMG	SWP	VM?
RMG	THM	WOA

The /PURGE option instructs Undelete for DOS to *purge* (remove) the files from the \SENTRY directory on the current drive or the specified drive. Because Undelete for DOS automatically deletes files from the \SENTRY directory after a specified length of time or if disk space is becoming low, you generally can ignore this option.

The /S option instructs Undelete for DOS to enable the delete-sentry method of protecting deleted files on the specified drive. This is the surest method of ensuring that deleted files can be recovered.

The /STATUS option displays the current settings for memory-resident file-deletion protection. If memory-resident file-deletion protection has not been installed, this option displays the message `UNDELETE not loaded`.

The /T option tells Undelete for DOS to enable the deletion-tracking method of protecting deleted files on the specified drive. Optionally, you can specify the number of files to track. Deletion tracking is not as secure as the delete-sentry method. If you are going to install memory-resident file-deletion protection, the /S option is a better choice than the /T option.

The /UNLOAD option instructs Undelete for DOS to remove memory-resident file-deletion protection from memory. If you want to change the method used to track deleted files, or if you simply need to free up memory, use this option. Unless you reinstall memory-resident file-deletion protection, however, only the DOS directory information will be available for recovering accidentally deleted files.

TIP

You may want to use the /U option before you use a program such as a database manager that creates and deletes a large number of temporary files. By using the /U option, you prevent the deleted temporary files from purging your \SENTRY directory or the deletion-tracking file.

Using Undelete for Windows

Undelete for Windows performs the same functions as Undelete for DOS, but uses a graphical interface for easier operation. Figure 7.2 shows the Undelete for Windows main screen. To load Undelete for Windows, first start Windows. When the Windows Program Manager is displayed, point to the Undelete icon in the Microsoft Tools program group and double-click the left mouse button (the Undelete icon looks like a trash can with a printed document being removed). If the Microsoft Tools Program group is not visible, you can use the Program Manager File Run command, and type **MWUNDEL.EXE** in the Command Line text box.

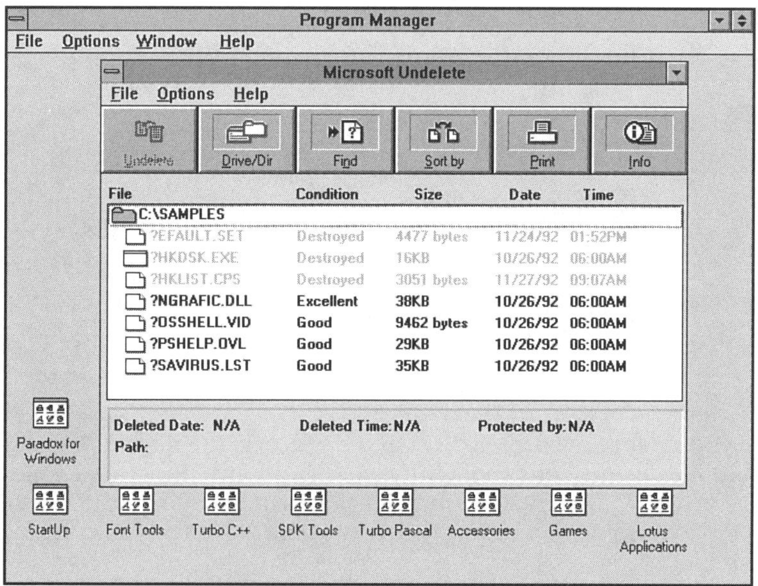

Fig. 7.2

The Undelete for Windows main screen.

When you load Undelete for Windows, the program reads the directory information for all deleted files in the current directory—which is usually the directory from which you started Windows. In figure 7.2, the current directory is C:\SAMPLES.

Selecting a Different Drive or Directory

If the deleted files you want to recover are not in the selected directory, select the correct directory first. To select a different directory, click the **D**rive/Dir button (Alt+D) to display the Change Drive and Directory dialog box shown in figure 7.3. Select the correct drive or directory and choose OK. If you want the recovered files to be created on a different drive or directory, select the destination drive and directory, and click the **D**irectory button.

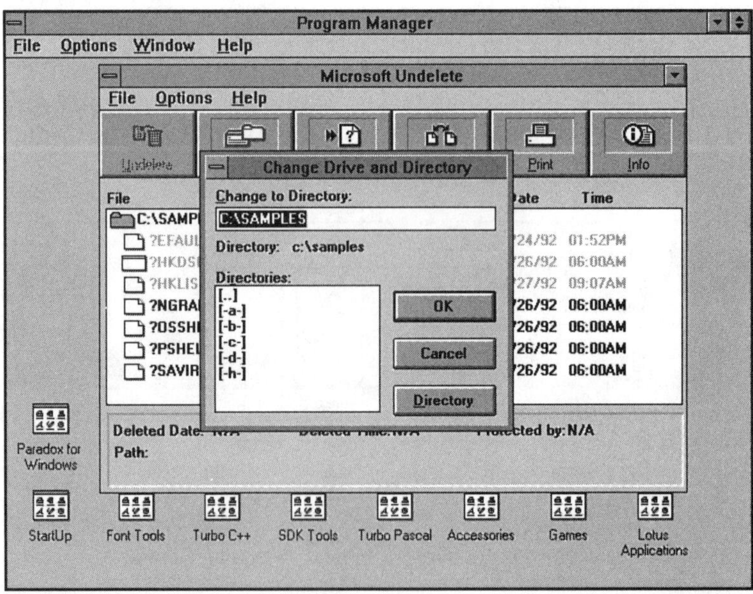

Fig. 7.3

The Change Drive and Directory dialog box.

After you select the correct drive and directory, the file list displays the deleted files using icons to identify each entry as a directory or file. A question mark (?) at the beginning of the file name indicates that the deletion was not protected by the delete-sentry or deletion-tracking method.

Understanding Deleted File Conditions

The Condition column tells you the likelihood of successful recovery for each listed file. Table 7.2 summarizes the possible conditions.

Table 7.2 Undeletion File Conditions

Condition	Description
Perfect	The file can be completely undeleted. Only files protected by Delete Sentry are perfect.
Excellent	All the file's clusters are available and unfragmented, but there is a chance that some data was overwritten. This condition is the best you can expect for files protected by Delete Tracker and for small files not protected by Delete Sentry or Delete Tracker.
Good	All the file's clusters are available, but the file is fragmented and there is a chance that some data was overwritten. This condition is the best you can expect for most files not protected by Delete Sentry or Delete Tracker.
Poor	The file's first cluster and probably more are not available. Use one of the Undelete methods offered by Undelete for DOS.
Destroyed	This file cannot be undeleted because all of its known clusters have been overwritten. You may be able to recover some data from a destroyed file by using Undelete methods offered by Undelete for DOS.
Recovered	This file was undeleted during the current session.

Recovering Files with Undelete for Windows

When you select a file, the status panel at the bottom of the Undelete for Windows screen shows you the date and time the highlighted file was deleted, the delete-protection method used (Delete Sentry, Delete Tracker, or DOS), and the location of the file on the disk (see fig. 7.4).

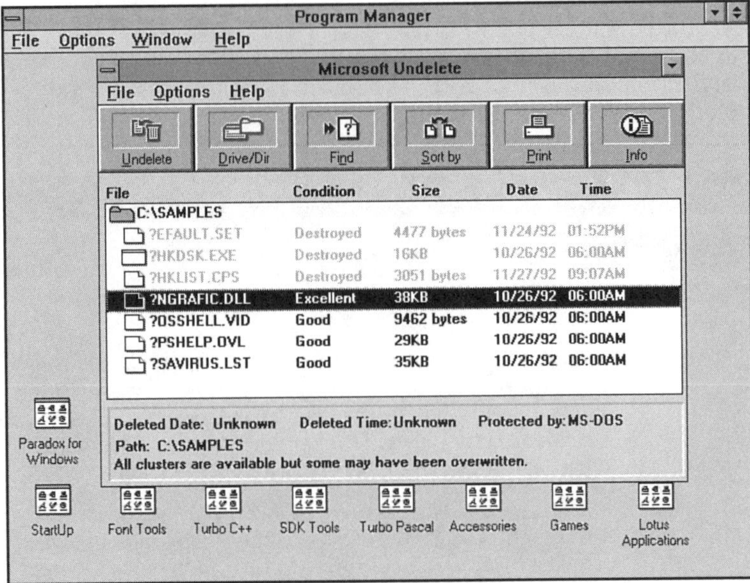

Fig. 7.4

The status panel showing information on the selected file.

If the highlighted file is one that Undelete for Windows can recover, the **U**ndelete button (Alt+U) becomes available. If the file's condition is listed as Perfect, Excellent, or Good, you probably can recover the file with Undelete for Windows. If the file's condition is listed as Poor or Destroyed, you may be able to recover portions of the file using Undelete for DOS, but you probably will not find the recovered portions of much use.

After you select a deleted file to recover, the next step depends on whether memory-resident file-deletion protection was in place when the file was deleted. If not, Undelete for Windows displays the Enter First Character dialog box shown in figure 7.5. If this dialog box is displayed, enter a first character for the file name. Undelete for Windows then undeletes the file and changes its condition to Recovered.

If you cannot decide whether the highlighted file is really the file you want to recover, click the **I**nfo button (Alt+I). Undelete for Windows displays the File Information dialog box shown in figure 7.6. This dialog box shows additional information about the file to help you determine whether the highlighted file is the one you want. If several deleted files have the same file names and extensions, for example, knowing when the file was deleted may help you choose the correct file.

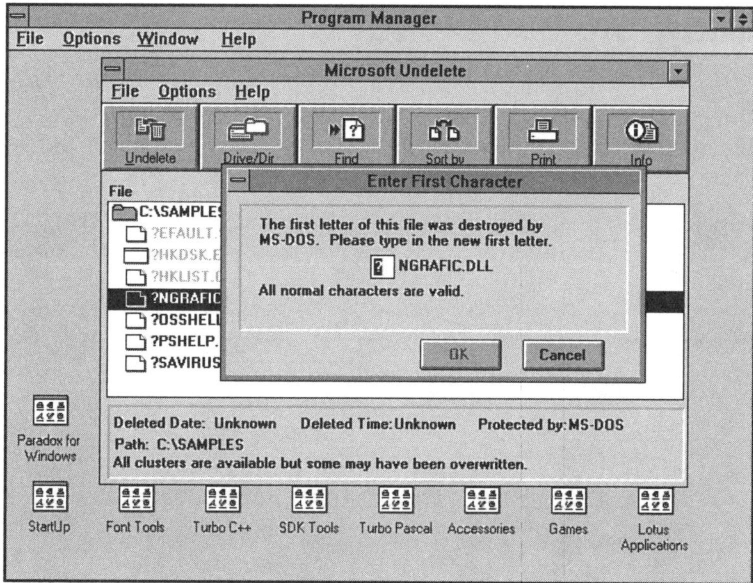

Fig. 7.5

The Enter First Character dialog box.

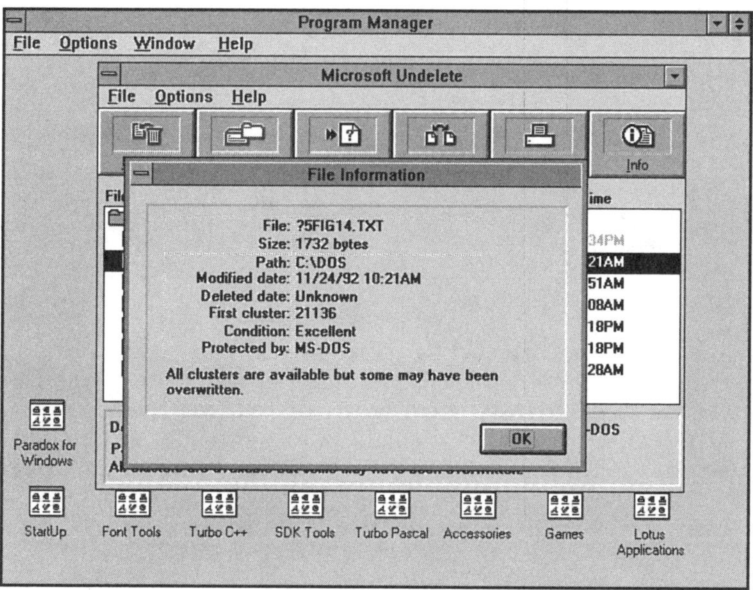

Fig. 7.6

The File Information dialog box showing additional information about the file.

Sorting the File Display

Just as sorting a normal directory listing may help you locate specific files more easily, sorting a long list of deleted files may help you locate the files you want to recover. Undelete for Windows can sort deleted files according to several different criteria.

To select the sort order used to display the deleted files, click the **S**ort button (Alt+S). Undelete for Windows displays the Sort By dialog box (see fig. 7.7).

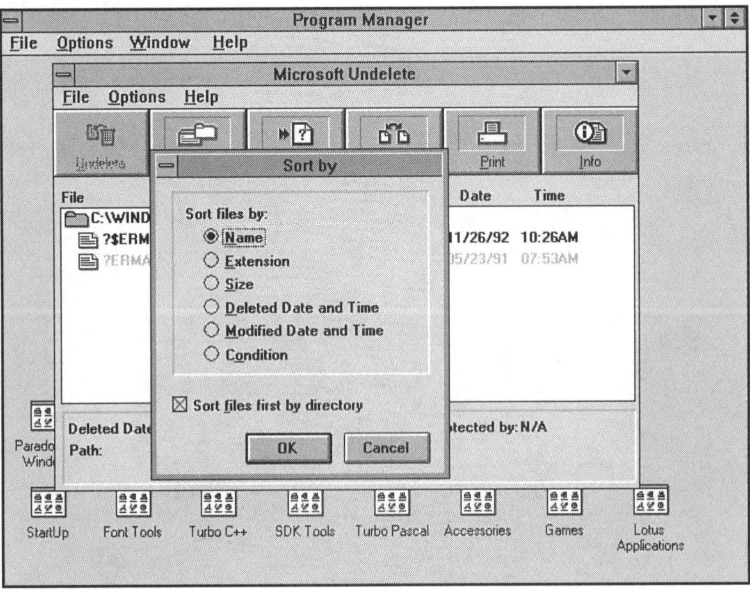

Fig. 7.7

Using the Sort By dialog box to change the display order.

In addition to the normal sorting options—sort by name, extension, size, or modified date—Undelete for Windows can sort deleted files by when they were deleted (if Delete Sentry or deletion tracking is installed) or by their condition. Each sorting option offers a different way of looking at the list of deleted files, and one view may help you locate just the file you need.

Locating Files by Content

Sometimes it may be difficult to know exactly which deleted file is the one you need. With the DOS eight-character limitation on file names, it can be difficult enough to remember which active file contains the particular data you need. After files have been deleted, it may be even more difficult—if not impossible—to locate the file you want.

Undelete for Windows can search through the deleted files on the disk to find specific text. You can search for text such as *1993 Budget* or *Dear Grandma Darlene*, for example. You can search through all deleted files on the disk or narrow your search. To search for files containing specific text, click the Fi**n**d button (Alt+N). Undelete for Windows displays the Find Deleted Files dialog box (see fig. 7.8).

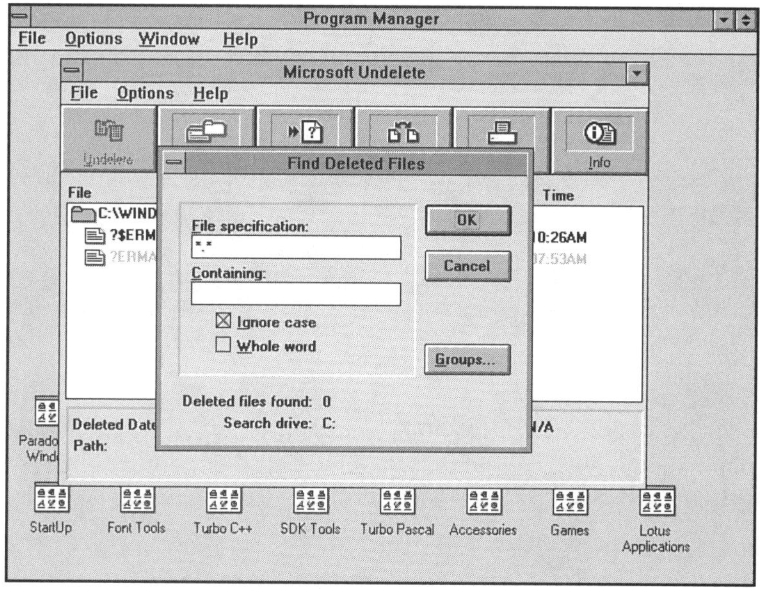

Fig. 7.8

The Find Deleted Files dialog box.

Type the text you want to find in the **C**ontaining text box. The text you type here must exactly match the text in the deleted file. If the deleted file contains the text *1993-Budget*, for example, you will not find the file if you type **1993 Budget**. Select the **I**gnore Case check box to find text regardless of whether the case matches the text you typed, and select **W**hole word if you want to find an entire word rather than a word contained within another word.

If the deleted file you want to find was created by a specific application, click the **G**roups button to display the Search Groups dialog box (see fig. 7.9). Undelete for Windows can search for the typical file extensions used by specific application programs. Selecting C:\123MM\123W, for example, places several file extensions (*.wrk +*.wks +*.wk1 +*.wk3 +*.wr1) in the **F**ile Specification text box. These file extensions include all the data file types that an application might normally produce, and therefore narrow the search to files from a single application.

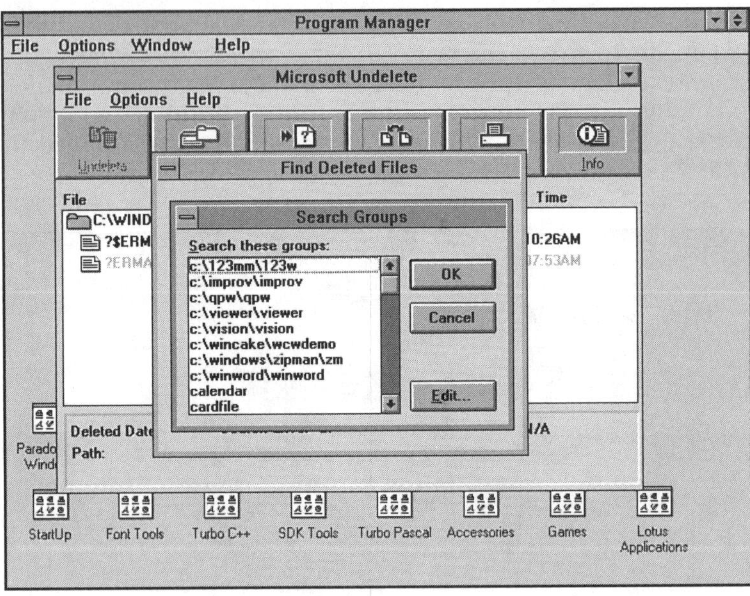

Fig. 7.9

Using the Search Groups dialog box to select files from one application.

You also can use the **F**ile Specification text box by typing specific file extensions manually. To find text within deleted document files, you might type ***.DOS**, for example.

Selecting and Unselecting Files

If your deleted file list is quite long, you may want to narrow the list further by using the **O**ptions Select **by** Name and **O**ptions **U**nselect by Name commands. These two commands enable you to restrict the display of deleted files using wild-card file specifications.

To display only deleted files that match a particular file specification, use the **O**ptions Select **by** Name command. To see only deleted files with an EXE extension, for example, select **O**ptions Select **by** Name and type ***.EXE** in the **F**ile Specification text box. Press Enter or click OK to confirm your selection.

To suppress the display of files that match a particular file specification, use the **O**ptions **U**nselect by Name command. To prevent files beginning with the letter *C* from appearing in the list of deleted files, for example, select **O**ptions **U**nselect by Name and type **C*.*** in the **F**ile Specification text box. Press Enter or click OK to confirm your selection.

You can use both of these commands together for maximum utility. For example, if you issue the two commands listed in these examples, your deleted file list will include all files that do not begin with *C* and that have an EXE extension.

Printing the Deleted File List

You may find it easier to locate specific deleted files if you have a printed list, rather than trying to scroll through a long list on-screen. If, for example, your search options have resulted in many different files that seem to match, a printed list may help you narrow the search.

To print a list of the deleted files, specify any necessary options such as the drive and directory, files containing specific text, or files produced by a specific application. Once you have the file list displayed on-screen, click the **P**rint button (Alt+P). If necessary, use the Printer **S**etup command on the **F**ile menu to select and set up your printer before printing.

Installing Memory-Resident File-Deletion Protection

Whether you use Undelete for Windows or Undelete for DOS, your deleted files are only partially protected unless you install one of the two types of memory-resident file-deletion protection. If you rely on DOS, your chances of recovering accidentally deleted files are fairly poor, especially if you wait very long to attempt to recover a file or if your files are fragmented.

DOS 5 introduced a method of tracking deleted files called the Delete Tracker. This method retained information about deleted files including the complete file name, its location on disk, and when the file was deleted. The primary advantages of this method were that the first character of the file name was not lost, overwriting the file's directory listing did not prevent the file from being recovered, and fragmented files could be recovered. This method did not, however, protect against the file's disk space being overwritten. The sooner you attempted to recover accidentally deleted files, the more likely your success.

DOS 6 has an even better method of ensuring that deleted files can be recovered—the Delete Sentry. The Delete Sentry leaves deleted files in the same physical location on disk, but moves their directory entries to a special hidden directory called \SENTRY. Unless your system needs to use some of the disk space used by the files in the \SENTRY directory, Delete Sentry guarantees perfect deleted-file recovery. To prevent the \SENTRY directory from growing too large, deleted files are retained for a specific length of time and then are purged. Older deleted files also are purged if Delete Sentry needs room for newer deleted files.

You can install either type of memory-resident file-deletion protection using a DOS command (see "Understanding Undelete for DOS Options," earlier in this chapter), or by using Undelete for Windows. The following sections show how to install these optional forms of protection using Undelete for Windows and Undelete for DOS.

Installing the Delete Sentry

To begin installing either type of memory-resident file-deletion protection using Undelete for Windows, from the **O**ptions menu (Alt+O), choose **C**onfigure Delete Protection (Alt+C). This displays the Configure Delete Protection dialog box shown in figure 7.10.

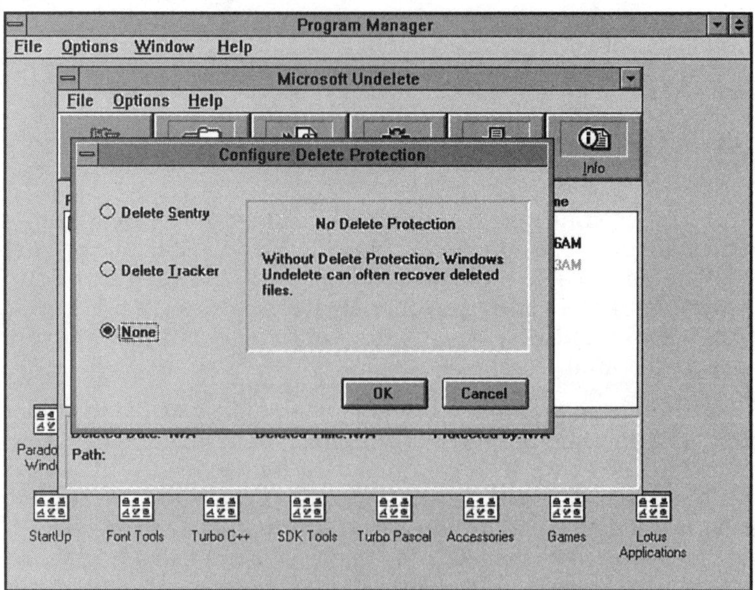

Fig. 7.10

The Configure Delete Protection dialog box.

Select the radio button for the type of delete protection you want to use. Select Delete **S**entry (Alt+S) and choose OK to display the Configure Delete Sentry dialog box shown in figure 7.11. The options you choose in this dialog box determine how the memory-resident Delete Sentry protects your deleted files.

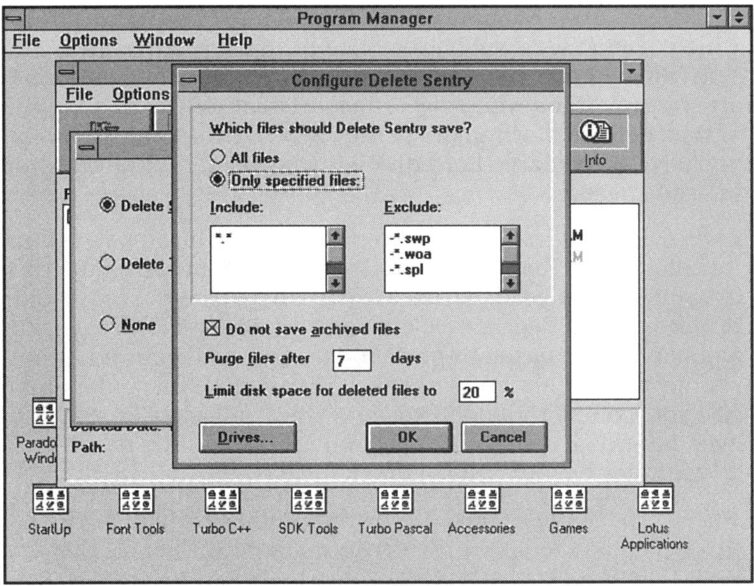

Fig. 7.11

The Configure Delete Sentry dialog box.

The following options are available in the Configure Delete Sentry dialog box:

- *All Files:* Protects all files on the current drive. This option may not be the best choice because temporary files created and then deleted by application programs may cause more important files to be purged from the \SENTRY directory.

- *Only Specified Files:* Includes the names of files you want Delete Sentry to protect. Your specifications can include wild cards and plus (+) and minus (-) signs in front of the file specification. Use minus signs to indicate files that you do not want protected. By default, several types of temporary files are excluded from protection. Do not use path names—included and excluded files apply to all protected drives and all directories on those drives. If you select the Only Specified Files option, use the **I**nclude list box to specify groups of files you want to include. Use the **E**xclude list box to specify groups of files you want to exclude.

- *Do Not Save Archived files:* Disables Delete Sentry protection of files that have not changed since the last backup, as indicated by their archive bits. If a file has been backed up and is unchanged, you can use your backups to restore the file if it is accidentally deleted. This saves room in the \SENTRY directory for files that have not been backed up.
- *Purge Files After:* Enables you to enter a number of days after which deleted files will be removed from the hidden directory. You can manually purge files at any time. By default, deleted files are purged after seven days. You may want to increase the length of time deleted files remain in the \SENTRY directory, especially if you have a very large hard disk with a considerable amount of unused space.
- *Limit Disk Space for Deleted Files To:* Sets the maximum amount of free disk space that can be used for Delete Sentry files. When this percentage is exceeded, Delete Sentry begins to purge the oldest protected files. Because Delete Sentry automatically reduces the amount of space used to protect deleted files if your other applications require hard disk space, you can make this number any size you want. If too much space is used for Delete Sentry, however, hard disk operations probably will run a little more slowly as your files become fragmented.
- *Drives:* Opens the Choose Drives for Sentry dialog box. You use this dialog box to select the drives containing the files that you want Delete Sentry to protect.

After you make your selections, choose OK to display the Update Autoexec.bat dialog box (see fig. 7.12). You can choose to save the necessary changes in AUTOEXEC.BAT or in AUTOEXEC.SAV.

If you elect to save the changes in AUTOEXEC.SAV, you can review those changes and modify AUTOEXEC.BAT manually. Before Delete Sentry file-deletion protection is installed, you must close any Windows applications, exit from Windows, and reboot your system. If you saved the changes in AUTOEXEC.SAV, you also must modify AUTOEXEC.BAT to include the new command line loading Delete Sentry file-deletion protection before rebooting.

Installing the Delete Tracker

Although both Delete Sentry and Delete Tracker require the same amount of memory, Delete Sentry provides much better protection than Delete Tracker. Unless reduced disk performance due to file fragmentation caused by Delete Sentry's retention of deleted files becomes a problem, you should use Delete Sentry if you want memory-resident file-deletion protection.

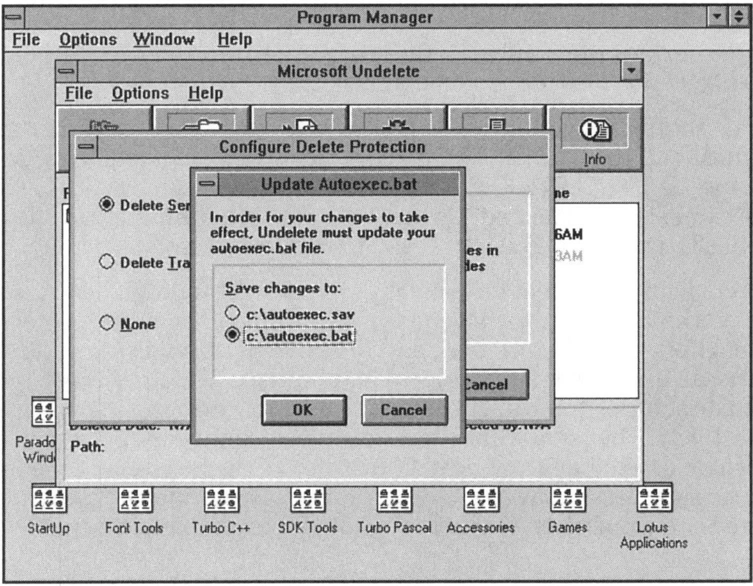

Fig. 7.12

The Update Autoexec.bat dialog box.

If you do decide to try Delete Tracker instead of Delete Sentry, select the Delete Tracker radio button in the Configure Delete Protection dialog box. Respond to the prompts to select the Delete Tracker options appropriate for your system. As with Delete Sentry, Delete Tracker memory-resident file-deletion protection takes effect only after you have selected all options, AUTOEXEC.BAT is modified, and your system is rebooted.

Installing Delete Protection from DOS

You also can install the Delete Sentry or Delete Tracker from the DOS command line, or by adding a command to AUTOEXEC.BAT. The command you use to add Delete Sentry follows:

UNDELETE /S*drive*

Drive is the optional drive letter of the drive containing the files that you want to protect. If you do not specify a drive, the current drive is protected.

The command you use to add Delete Tracker follows:

UNDELETE /Tdrive*entries*

Drive is the drive letter for the drive whose files you want to protect. If you specify Delete Tracker file protection, you must specify a drive.

Entries specifies the number of files to track. By default, Delete Tracker tracks 25 to 303 files, depending on disk size.

If you want to change the Delete Sentry or Delete Tracker configuration, you must edit the UNDELETE.INI file, which will be located in the same directory as UNDELETE.EXE—usually C:\DOS. You can use EDIT, EDLIN, or any other text editor that does not add formatting to the file. UNDELETE.INI includes several easy-to-understand sections.

The [configuration] section typically includes the following entries to specify whether files that have not been modified should be protected, the length of time to store files, and the percentage of disk space Delete Sentry can use. The [sentry.drives] and [mirror.drives] sections specify which directories to protect using Delete Sentry or Delete Tracker, respectively. The [sentry.files] section specifies the file specifications to include or exclude from protection (file specifications preceded with a minus sign are not saved). The [defaults] section specifies whether Delete Sentry or Delete Tracker is enabled (only one can be enabled).

Undeleting Directories

DOS is a file-oriented disk operating system. That is, anything you store on a disk must be stored as a file. Directories are special types of files that have certain attributes and characteristics that enable them to track other files.

If you delete a directory, you cannot recover either the files or any directories it contained, unless you first undelete the directory (unless, of course, you use Delete Sentry memory-resident file-deletion protection). Also, you must use Undelete for Windows to recover deleted directories; you cannot recover deleted directories using Undelete for DOS.

Before you can undelete a directory, you must select the deleted directory's parent directory. If you delete all the files in C:\SAMPLES, and then delete the directory C:\SAMPLES, for example, you must select the deleted directory's parent directory, C:\, if you want to undelete C:\SAMPLES. Figure 7.13 shows the Undelete for Windows main screen in this example.

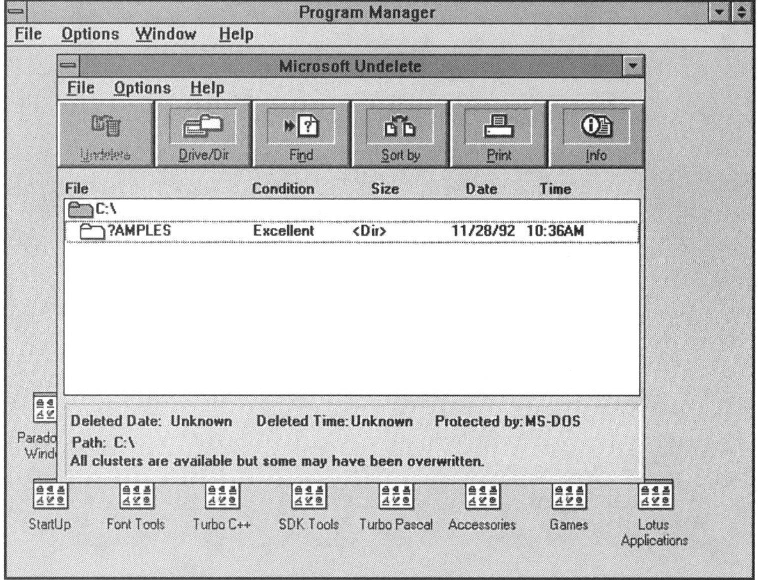

Fig. 7.13
Selecting a deleted directory to undelete.

Because the deleted directory's condition is listed as Excellent, the chances of recovering this directory are quite good. To undelete the C:\SAMPLES directory, use the same procedure as you use to undelete any other file. Select the deleted directory and click the Undelete button. Figure 7.14 shows that the directory's condition has been changed to Recovered.

After you undelete the directory, you can change to that directory and undelete files in the directory. Figure 7.15 shows how Undelete for Windows displays the deleted files in the recovered directory.

Remember that all files contained in a directory must be deleted before the directory can be deleted. Whenever you delete directories, you therefore are faced with at least a two-step project if you want to recover files that were in the directory. If you configure your system to use Delete Sentry memory-resident file-deletion protection, however, you are much more likely to be able to recover files from the deleted directory. In fact, if you use Delete Sentry, you can recover deleted files without first recovering the directory that contained them. Simply use the **D**irectory button in the Change Drive and Directory dialog box to specify a new directory in which to restore the deleted files.

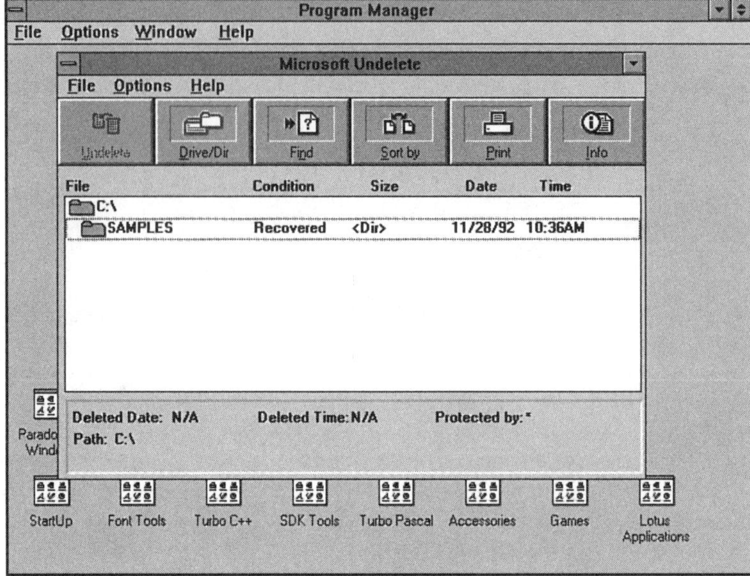

Fig. 7.14

The deleted directory's condition changed to Recovered.

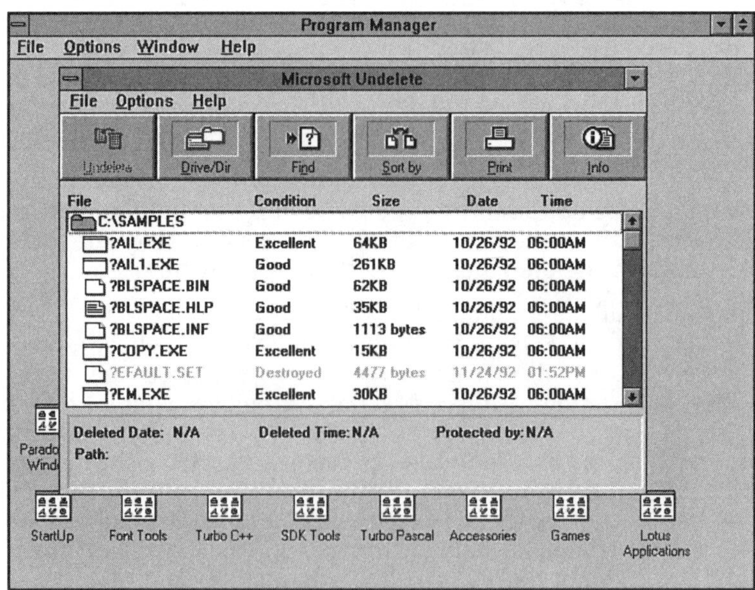

Fig. 7.15

Deleted files in the recovered directory ready for undeletion.

Chapter Summary

DOS 6 adds powerful new tools and methods to help you recover files and directories that have been deleted accidentally. Because every PC user occasionally makes a mistake and deletes a file in error, the coverage of DOS 6's file-undeletion capabilities in this chapter is important to all upgraders to DOS 6.

Networks are becoming more important to PC users every day. If you aren't connected to a network yet, you may be soon. If you don't have a network, but you have two PCs—such as a desktop system and a laptop, DOS 6 has built-in file- and printer-sharing capabilities you can use without the complications or expense of a network. Chapter 8 shows you how to use DOS 6's capabilities to connect PCs without a network.

8

CHAPTER

Connecting PCs with Interlnk

Connectivity is fast becoming a major topic of interest in the PC world. As computers become faster and more powerful, the capability to share data seamlessly and the option of sharing expensive printers and other peripherals are becoming more important every day.

Whether or not you have access to a network, you probably have many reasons to share information between two or more PCs. If you use computers in a business environment, you probably have more than one computer processing the same types of data. Using floppy disks to carry information between those computers quickly becomes tiresome—especially if you must share files on a regular basis.

Although a network offers powerful features that many PC users need, there are many times that you may not want to connect your PC to a network. Few PC users, for example, want to go to the expense and complexity of networking their home PCs—even if they own two or more systems.

DOS 6 has a program called Interlnk, which provides many of the features of a simple network, but without requiring you to have a network. Interlnk enables you to share files and use printers attached to another computer, and does not require any additional hardware except for a simple cable you use to connect the two computers (see "Making the Right Hardware Connection," later in this chapter).

Connecting Two PCs Without a Network

Although Interlnk provides many of the features of a simple network, it is not really a network. When you use Interlnk, you can use only one of the two connected computers as long as Interlnk is active. The computer that you use is called the *client.* The other computer, which cannot be used for anything else as long as you are using Interlnk, is called the *server.*

Sharing Files and Printers

When you connect two PCs using Interlnk, the disk drives on the server appear as extra disk drives on the client. If, for example, you connect two PCs that each have two floppy disk drives and a single hard disk, the client system appears to have six disk drives. Its own drives are A, B, and C. The three new drives are D (drive A on the server), E (drive B on the server), and F (drive C on the server). In addition, any standard parallel printer ports on the server appear as additional printer ports on the client.

Figure 8.1 shows how Interlnk *remaps* (assigns new drive letters) the drives on the server. When Interlnk remaps physical hard drives, such as server drives C, D, and I, it displays their capacities. Logical drives, such as server drives E through H, do not list a size because they are not actual disk drives (they are usually drive letters assigned on a network). To display the server drive remappings, type the command **INTERLNK** and press Enter.

```
In Windows C:\>INTERLNK

   Port=COM1

   This Computer          Other Computer
     (Client)                (Server)
   -------------      ------------------------
     D:      equals     A:
     E:      equals     B:
     F:      equals     C: (129Mb) FIXED C
     G:      equals     D: (65Mb)  Fixed D
     H:      equals     E:
     I:      equals     F:
     J:      equals     G:
     K:      equals     H:
     L:      equals     I: (499Kb) Fixed C
     LPT2:   equals     LPT1:

In Windows C:\>
```

Fig. 8.1

Interlnk remapping server drives to new drive letters.

In figure 8.1, drive C on the server is mapped to drive F on the client. Once you know which drive letters are assigned to each server drive, you can use those drives as if they were physically attached to the client system. To copy a file called MEMO1.DOC from the \DOCUMENT directory on server drive C to the \DOCUMENT directory on client drive C, for example, you can use the following command:

```
COPY F:\DOCUMENT\MEMO1.DOC C:\DOCUMENT\MEMO1.DOC
```

Loading Interlnk

To use Interlnk, you must load a device driver on the client system and the Interlnk server application on the server system. You also must connect the two systems through their serial or parallel ports (see "Making the Right Hardware Connection," later in this chapter).

On the client system, you must include a directive line in CONFIG.SYS that loads INTERLNK.EXE as a device driver. If INTERLNK.EXE is in C:\DOS, you can add the following line to CONFIG.SYS:

```
DEVICE=C:\DOS\INTERLNK.EXE
```

By default, Interlnk remaps three disk drives and all available printer ports on the server. Interlnk also scans the serial and parallel ports on the client PC as it attempts to find the server. If upper memory is available, Interlnk automatically loads into an upper memory block, thus saving approximately 8K of conventional memory.

In some instances, you may want Interlnk to remap additional drives. If the server has two hard disks, for example, you must remap at least four drives if the client system is to access drive D on the server. Another Interlnk option you may want to include in CONFIG.SYS tells Interlnk on which serial or parallel port it will find the server. Using this option prevents Interlnk from resetting any printers actually connected to the client system as it scans the ports. Table 8.1 summarizes the options you can use when you load INTERLNK.EXE in CONFIG.SYS.

Table 8.1 INTERLNK.EXE Options

Option	Description
/AUTO	Installs the INTERLNK.EXE device driver in memory only if a connection with the server can be established. By default, Interlnk is installed in memory even if a connection cannot be established.

continues

Table 8.1 Continued

Option	Description
/BAUD:rate	Sets a maximum baud rate for serial communication. Valid values for rate are 9600, 19200, 38400, 57600, and 115200. Use a lower rate if one of the PCs cannot reliably support the default—115200.
/COM:*x*	Specifies a serial port to use for data transfer. The *x* parameter specifies the number or address of the serial port. If you omit *x*, Interlnk searches all serial ports and uses the first one it finds connected to the server. If you specify /COM and omit /LPT, Interlnk searches only for serial ports. By default, Interlnk scans all serial and parallel ports.
/DRIVES:#	Specifies the number of redirected drives. By default, the number is 3. To redirect printers only, specify 0.
/LOW	Loads the INTERLNK.EXE device driver into conventional memory, even if UMBs are available. By default, INTERLNK.EXE is loaded into a UMB, if available.
/LPT:*x*	Specifies a parallel port to use for data transfer. The *x* parameter specifies the number or address of the LPT port. If you omit *x*, Interlnk uses the first parallel port that it finds connected to the server. If you specify /LPT and omit /COM, Interlnk searches for parallel ports only. By default, Interlnk scans all serial and parallel ports.
/NOPRINTER	Prevents Interlnk from redirecting printers. By default, Interlnk redirects all available printer ports.
/NOSCAN	Installs the INTERLNK.EXE device driver in memory, but prevents establishing a connection between client and server during setup. By default, the client tries to establish a connection with the server as soon as you install INTERLNK.EXE.
/V	Prevents conflicts with a computer's timer. Specify this switch if you have a serial connection between computers and one of them stops running when you use Interlnk to access a drive or printer port.

For example, to load the Interlnk device driver, connect to the server through serial port 2, and allow the client system access to four disk drives on the server, you can use the following CONFIG.SYS directive:

```
DEVICE=C:\DOS\INTERLNK.EXE /COM:2 /DRIVES:4
```

If you occasionally connect to a server, but don't want to change CONFIG.SYS to load the Interlnk device driver each time, include the /AUTO parameter in the directive. Whenever you boot your system, Interlnk looks for a connection to the server. If the server is connected and ready to use, Interlnk loads into memory on the client system. If the server is not connected, or if it does not have the server software loaded, Interlnk does not load on the client, and does not use any memory.

Loading Intersvr

Start INTERSVR on the server system before you boot or reboot the client system. This enables the client PC to successfully access the server when the INTERLNK.EXE device driver is loaded.

Before you can use Interlnk to access the drives or printers on the server, you must load the server software. To load the Interlnk server software, type the following command on the PC whose files or printers you want to access:

```
INTERSVR
```

This command starts the Interlnk server, which provides serial or parallel file-transfer capability through redirected drives, and printing through redirected printer ports. You can connect a laptop computer to a desktop computer and share files, for example. You can use either system as the server, and the other system as the client—remember, the *client* is the system whose keyboard you use, and the *server* is the system providing extra disk drives or printers to the client. When you start the Interlnk server, a screen similar to figure 8.2 is displayed on the server.

The screen in figure 8.2 is displayed until you stop the Interlnk server by pressing Alt+F4. When you stop the Interlnk server, the client system loses access to the server's drives and printers.

The INTERSVR command has similar options to those you use on the Interlnk device driver line. In fact, four of the options—/LPT:*x*, /COM:*x*, /BAUD:rate, and /V—are identical to the same options for the Interlnk device driver. You also can optionally specify a drive to redirect, to prevent the client from accessing, or to display the server screen in monochrome. The complete INTERSVR syntax follows:

d:path\INTERSVR *drives:/x:drive: /LPT:x/COM:x/BAUD: rate/B/V*

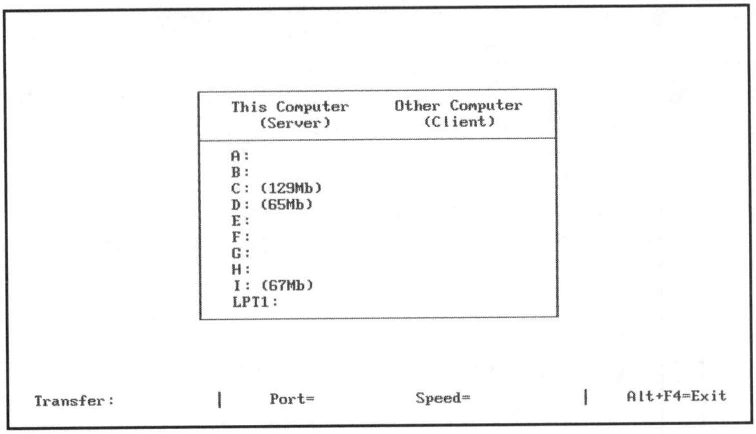

```
This Computer      Other Computer
  (Server)            (Client)

A:
B:
C: (129Mb)
D: (65Mb)
E:
F:
G:
H:
I: (67Mb)
LPT1:

Transfer:       |   Port=        Speed=        |   Alt+F4=Exit
```

Fig. 8.2
The Interlnk server display.

To specify a specific drive, include its drive letter and a colon in the command line. To exclude a drive, precede the drive letter with /X=, as in /X=D: to prevent the client PC from accessing files on drive D. If you cannot read the display, include the /B switch to display the server screen in monochrome.

Copying Interlnk Remotely

Even if one of the computers you want to connect does not have the correct size of floppy disk drive, or maybe even lacks floppy disk drives altogether, you still can install Interlnk as long as you have the correct cable connecting the two systems. You must have a seven-wire, null-modem cable connection to perform a remote copy and install the Interlnk files on the system that cannot read the files from the floppy disk (cables are discussed in the next section). In addition, the MODE command must be available on the remote system.

To copy Interlnk files from one computer to another, use the following syntax:

```
INTERSVR /RCOPY
```

This command displays the Interlnk Remote Installation screen shown in figure 8.3.

Use the up- or down-arrow to highlight the serial port connected to the remote computer, and press Enter. The next screen instructs you to type two commands on the remote computer (see fig. 8.4). The first command—MODE COM1:2400,N,8,1,P—sets the serial port to the correct configuration so that the two computers can communicate (if the remote computer has the serial cable connected to serial port 2, replace COM1: with COM2:). The next command—CTTY COM1—directs the remote system to accept commands through the serial port instead of the keyboard.

```
Interlnk Remote Installation

Interlnk will copy its program files to another computer that is connected
to this one by a 7-wire null-modem cable.

Before continuing, make sure the cable connects the two computers' serial
ports.

Specify the serial port of the other computer, and then press ENTER:

COM1
COM2

Enter=Continue   F3=Exit   |
```

Fig. 8.3

The Interlnk Remote Installation screen.

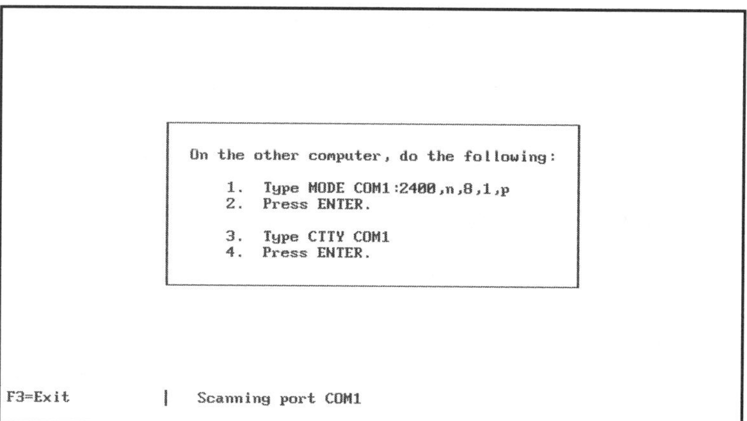

On the other computer, do the following:
1. Type MODE COM1:2400,n,8,1,p
2. Press ENTER.
3. Type CTTY COM1
4. Press ENTER.
F3=Exit
Scanning port COM1

Fig. 8.4

Typing two commands on the remote PC.

After you enter the commands on the remote system, the Interlnk files are transferred automatically. You then can choose one system as the server, and the other as the client. Install the Interlnk device drive on the client, reboot the system, and start the Interlnk server.

Making the Right Hardware Connection

Earlier, you learned that to use the Workgroup Connection, you must have a network adapter card installed in your PC, and you must be properly connected to the network cabling. Interlnk also requires a proper connection, but its needs are much simpler and less costly than those of the Workgroup Connection.

Interlnk can use serial or parallel ports to connect two PCs. Both systems must use the same type of port, however. You cannot use a serial port on one system and a parallel port on the other.

Connecting Via Parallel Ports

Parallel ports commonly are used to connect to printers. Data is transmitted eight bits in parallel at a time—thus the name *parallel port.* PC parallel ports typically use a female, 25-pin, "D" connector. A parallel cable usually is intended for connecting a PC to a printer, and has a male, 25-pin, "D" connector on the end that plugs into the PC, and a 36-pin printer connector on the other end. To connect two PCs by their parallel ports, you probably will have to buy a special cable made for that purpose.

Because parallel data travels eight bits at a time instead of one bit at a time, data transmission over a parallel cable usually is faster than over a serial cable. Unfortunately, the design of parallel cables restricts their length to around 10 feet. Serial cables easily can be 50 to 100 feet without any problems.

If you choose to connect your two systems with a parallel cable, be certain that it has the proper connectors so that each end can plug into one of your PCs. The following list shows the proper connections for the two connectors.

Connector 1 Pin	Connector 2 Pin
2	15
3	13
4	12
5	10
6	11

Connector 1 Pin	Connector 2 Pin
10	5
11	6
12	4
13	3
15	2
25	25

CAUTION: Parallel cables for connecting two PCs may look similar to serial cables, but require low-capacitance cable, the correct connectors, and proper internal connections. To prevent damage to your systems, make certain that you have the correct cable before you try to connect your PCs.

Connecting Via Serial Ports

Serial ports commonly are used to connect to modems or for a serial mouse. These ports transmit data one bit at a time, and usually are much slower than parallel ports. Serial ports on PCs usually use a male, 25-pin or 9-pin, "D" connector.

Serial cables can have between 3 and 25 wires, and may have male or female connectors, depending on their intended connection. Serial cables do not have the same length restrictions as parallel cables, and usually are much less expensive than parallel cables of the same length.

Using a Three-Wire Cable

Serial data transmission requires as few as three wires connecting the two systems. Three-wire cables offer several advantages over other types of cables: they are cheaper, lighter, and easier to make.

Unfortunately, three-wire cables generally support the lowest data-transmission rate, because the two PCs must use the data lines to tell each other whether data is being received properly.

To connect two PCs using a three-wire serial cable, you connect the two connectors as follows:

If Connector 1 Has 9 Pins	If Connector 1 Has 25 Pins		If Connector 2 Has 9 Pins	If Connector 2 Has 25 Pins
3	2	Connect	2	3
2	3	To:	3	2
5	7		5	7

If the first PC has a 9-pin serial port, for example, and the second PC has a 25-pin serial port, pin 3 of the 9-pin connector should be wired to pin 3 of the 25-pin connector.

Using a Seven-Wire Cable

Seven-wire serial cables use the extra wires to connect *handshaking lines*—electronic signals that enable the two computers to tell each other when more data can be sent successfully. Serial data-transmission over a seven-wire cable usually is faster and more reliable than over a three-wire cable.

A seven-wire serial cable often is called a *null-modem* cable, because the cable takes the place of a modem between the two PCs. Use the following diagram to connect a seven-wire, null-modem cable:

If Connector 1 Has 9 Pins	If Connector 1 Has 25 Pins		If Connector 2 Has 9 Pins	If Connector 2 Has 25 Pins
2	3		3	2
3	2		2	3
4	20	Connect	6	6
5	7	To:	5	7
6	6		4	20
7	4		8	5
8	5		7	4

TIP

Rather than purchasing or building a seven-wire, null-modem cable, you may find that it is easier and less expensive to buy a seven-wire, straight-through cable and a seven-wire, null-modem adapter. Such adapters and cables should be easy to find—probably much easier to find than null-modem cables.

Chapter Summary

As computers become faster and more powerful, the capability to connect PCs so that they can share data and peripherals is becoming very important. This chapter introduced you to Interlnk, the very powerful connectivity system that is part of DOS 6. You learned how to connect your PC to another PC using Interlnk. You also learned about the types of cables you can use to make the connection.

The next chapter shows you how to easily configure your PC for different purposes, and even create interactive menus that enable you to select configuration options when you start your system. You also learn about the new features in DOS 6 that greatly reduce the dangers and worries that can be associated with customizing your system's configuration.

9

CHAPTER

Controlling Configurations

New hardware and software often comes with device drivers or memory-resident programs that must be loaded when you boot your system. In addition, some programs require other changes to your system's operating configuration, as well. In some cases, the changes required by one piccc of hardware or software may even conflict with the settings required by another piece of hardware or software.

These conflicts often lead PC users to develop multiple system configurations, perhaps even starting the system from a floppy disk for certain special situations. These multiple configurations lead to one result—confusion. When you start your system, for example, are you properly configured for program A or program B? Will your scanner work, or is the network adapter card using the same interrupt as the scanner? Is there enough expanded memory for your favorite game, or is memory still configured for maximum extended memory for your spreadsheet program?

As confusing as all this sounds, consider what may happen when you add another new piece of equipment and its device drivers. If you are lucky, your system will start and run normally. But if a conflict develops between device drivers, your system may even refuse to start. Unless you have a boot floppy disk, you may not be able to start your PC and correct the problem. Even if you do succeed in booting your system, will you remember to add the new commands to every copy of CONFIG.SYS and AUTOEXEC.BAT?

Fortunately, DOS 6 offers solutions to both the confusion of maintaining multiple configurations and device driver conflicts. With these new improvements, you easily can manage multiple configurations in a single copy of CONFIG.SYS and make intelligent choices in AUTOEXEC.BAT. If a device driver conflict occurs, DOS 6 even offers you new ways to boot the system without resorting to a boot floppy disk.

This chapter shows you how to finally bring some sense into managing your computer's multiple configuration options by using the following new features in DOS 6:

- *Clean boot:* Enables you to bypass CONFIG.SYS and AUTOEXEC.BAT completely.
- *Interactive boot:* Enables you to selectively process CONFIG.SYS directives and decide whether to bypass AUTOEXEC.BAT.
- *Directive confirmation at boot:* Enables you to select individual CONFIG.SYS directives each time you boot your system.
- *Configuration menus in CONFIG.SYS:* Enable you to select sets of configuration options when you boot your system.
- *New CONFIG environment variable:* Enables you to make choices in AUTOEXEC.BAT or other batch files based on system configuration.
- *CHOICE command:* Enables you to create interactive menus in AUTOEXEC.BAT and other batch files.

These new features make configuring your system easier and safer. Whether you want to make a simple change occasionally, or whether you require a full-blown menu containing many different optional settings, you will find the information you need in this chapter.

Using Clean Boot

Clean boot is the name of one of DOS 6's emergency tools. The name results from what this tool does, which is to enable your PC to boot without processing any of the commands in CONFIG.SYS or AUTOEXEC.BAT.

In other words, your system boots and loads DOS just as if there were no CONFIG.SYS or AUTOEXEC.BAT files on your hard disk. None of the device drivers are loaded, none of the CONFIG.SYS directives are executed, and none of the commands in AUTOEXEC.BAT are executed.

If you are a relatively cautious PC user, and haven't made any changes to CONFIG.SYS or AUTOEXEC.BAT, you may wonder why clean boot exists. What is accomplished by bypassing CONFIG.SYS and AUTOEXEC.BAT? Aren't the commands in these two files important?

The reason for clean boot is simple—sometimes what seems like a simple change to CONFIG.SYS or AUTOEXEC.BAT can have disastrous effects. Including the wrong range of memory addresses may cause EMM386 to lock up your system, for example. A new device driver command line may accidentally cause two adapter cards to try and use the same DMA address or the same IRQ number—again with the potential to prevent your system from completing booting. Many more such hazards may await you as you attempt to add new hardware to your PC or as you install new software.

Sometimes you don't even have to make any changes yourself to have these sorts of problems. If you purchase a new software package, its installation program may make changes to CONFIG.SYS or AUTOEXEC.BAT without even telling you what it is doing. The next time you try to start your PC, you receive a big surprise when your system doesn't function.

When you upgrade to DOS 6, you probably will notice the new message `Starting MS-DOS ...`, which appears as your system is booting. This message appears shortly after your PC completes its memory test, and usually after any system ROM messages are displayed. The `Starting MS-DOS ...` message is your clue to when you can invoke the clean boot process. As soon as you see this message, press the F5 key (or hold down one of the Shift keys). This is your signal to DOS to bypass both CONFIG.SYS and AUTOEXEC.BAT.

The two-second pause while the `Starting MS-DOS ...` message is displayed enables you to invoke the clean boot or the interactive boot process (see the next section, "Using Interactive Boot"). You can prevent a user from invoking clean boot or interactive boot by adding the line SWITCHES=/N /F to CONFIG.SYS. Make certain that you have a boot floppy disk if you add this line, however.

Your system may not function properly after a clean boot. If your hard disk requires a device driver, for example, you may not be able to access your hard disk. Also, because AUTOEXEC.BAT is skipped, none of your DOSKEY macros will be available and your PATH command will not be executed—which may result in the `Bad command or file name` message when you try to use external DOS commands or run applications programs. Extended memory, expanded memory, upper memory blocks, and the high memory area will be unavailable as well. Usually, it is a better idea to try the interactive boot process (discussed in the next section) instead of using clean boot.

Using Interactive Boot

The clean boot process discussed in the preceding section totally bypasses everything in both CONFIG.SYS and AUTOEXEC.BAT. Although this prevents device drivers, CONFIG.SYS directives, and AUTOEXEC.BAT commands from conflicting with each other, it is usually not the best choice for dealing with these conflicts. Instead, consider trying the *interactive boot.*

The interactive boot process enables you to decide whether each executable line in CONFIG.SYS is processed, and whether AUTOEXEC.BAT is bypassed. If you have a problem with your system locking up at start up, the reason it could not boot properly can probably be traced to one line, or at the most, a few lines in CONFIG.SYS. Less commonly, a change in AUTOEXEC.BAT has caused the problem. By using interactive boot, you choose which commands are executed.

To use the interactive boot process, boot your system and wait until the `Starting MS-DOS ...` message is displayed. Press the F8 key. Instead of processing the commands in CONFIG.SYS without delay, DOS displays each command on your screen along with a prompt similar to this:

```
DEVICE=C:\DOS\INTERLNK.EXE /AUTO /COM [Y,N]?
```

If you want DOS to execute the displayed command, press Y. To skip the line, press N. If you are having problems because of a new command just added to CONFIG.SYS, you probably will find that you can skip the one new line and execute all the others.

After DOS processes the commands in CONFIG.SYS, it displays the following prompt:

```
Process AUTOEXEC.BAT [Y,N]?
```

If you suspect that a command in AUTOEXEC.BAT has caused the problem booting, press N to bypass AUTOEXEC.BAT. Otherwise, press Y to execute its commands.

After your system has booted successfully, edit the problem-causing command lines in CONFIG.SYS or AUTOEXEC.BAT and try rebooting your PC normally. If you still experience a problem, you may have made more changes than you realize, and you will have to edit additional lines.

TIP

If you aren't sure whether a particular line in CONFIG.SYS or AUTOEXEC.BAT is causing a problem, add **REM** followed by a space to the beginning of the line. DOS considers lines that begin with REM and a space to be *remark* (or *comment*) lines, and bypasses them when the system boots. You also can use a semicolon (;) and a space to indicate a remark line in CONFIG.SYS but not in AUTOEXEC.BAT.

Changing a line to a remark enables the line to remain otherwise unchanged, and makes restoring the line later much easier than if you had to retype the entire line.

To change the line

```
DEVICE=C:\DOS\HIMEM.SYS
```

to a remark and prevent loading the HIMEM.SYS device driver, change the line to

```
REM DEVICE=C:\DOS\HIMEM.SYS
```

or

```
; DEVICE=C:\DOS\HIMEM.SYS
```

Using Directive Confirmation at Boot

You can use 22 CONFIG.SYS directives in DOS 6:

BREAK	DRIVPARM	MENUCOLOR	SET
BUFFERS	FCBS	MENUDEFAULT	SHELL
COUNTRY	FILES	MENUITEM	STACKS
DEVICE	INCLUDE	NUMLOCK	SUBMENU
DEVICEHIGH	INSTALL	REM	SWITCHES
DOS	LASTDRIVE		

In addition, DOS 6 includes 12 installable device drivers:

ANSI.SYS	DRIVER.SYS	HIMEM.SYS	RAMDRIVE.SYS
DBLSPACE.SYS	EGA.SYS	INTERLNK.EXE	SETVER.EXE
DISPLAY.SYS	EMM386.EXE	POWER.EXE	SMARTDRV.EXE

Add to this the many device drivers specific to various pieces of hardware or software that you may have installed, and the possible combinations are almost endless.

With all these possibilities, you may have one or two lines in CONFIG.SYS that you sometimes want to execute, but at other times you do not. Carefully watching for the `Starting MS-DOS ...` message each time you boot your system, and then quickly pressing the F8 key during the two second pause can be difficult. If you are a little too slow, you must reboot the system. In addition, you probably don't want to confirm each line every time you boot your PC; nor do you want to confirm whether to process AUTOEXEC.BAT every time.

You can use an easier method to tell DOS to ask you to confirm whether to process CONFIG.SYS directives. Instead of pressing the F8 key and using interactive boot, place a question mark (?) between the directive and the equal sign (=). For example, to have DOS ask for confirmation before carrying out the command

```
DEVICE=C:\DOS\INTERLNK.EXE /AUTO /COM
```

You can change the command to read

```
DEVICE?=C:\DOS\INTERLNK.EXE /AUTO /COM
```

When DOS encounters this modified line, it displays the same prompt as if you pressed F8 and were using interactive boot:

```
DEVICE=C:\DOS\INTERLNK.EXE /AUTO /COM [Y,N]?
```

Press Y to execute the directive or N to skip it.

This method of specifying whether to execute certain CONFIG.SYS directives is easier than using interactive boot, but it does have disadvantages. Each time DOS encounters the line—that is, every time you boot your system—the PC stops booting and waits for you to decide whether to execute the line. If you have several related lines, you not only have to remember which ones to execute together, but you also must confirm each line. In the next section, you learn about an easier way to manage multiple configurations.

Using Multiple Configurations

Multiple system configurations are often the only way to accommodate all the different ways people use PCs. If you use Windows, for example, it is best to use configuration commands that provide the maximum amount of extended (XMS) memory. Some game programs, however, cannot use this type of memory, but instead require expanded (EMS) memory. You may need to load the Workgroup Connection drivers when you want to use the network's laser printer, and you may use Interlnk to share files with your laptop PC. Although you may be able to find one standard configuration that accommodates all of these needs, it's more likely that custom configurations will provide better performance or at least more of the types of memory each type of use demands.

DOS 6 has several new CONFIG.SYS directives that you can use to manage multiple configurations. These commands enable you to create menus within CONFIG.SYS of optional configurations. After you boot your system, DOS displays your menu and enables you to select exactly which configuration to use.

Creating CONFIG.SYS Menus

DOS 6 has five new CONFIG.SYS directives you use to create configuration menus; INCLUDE, MENUCOLOR, MENUDEFAULT, MENUITEM, and SUBMENU. Each menu can have up to nine choices, but you can define submenus if you need additional options. Table 9.1 summarizes each of these directives.

Table 9.1 DOS 6 CONFIG.SYS Menu Directives

Directive	Description
INCLUDE	Includes the contents of a named configuration block in the selected configuration.
MENUCOLOR	Sets the text and background colors for the start-up menu. Can be used only in a menu block.
MENUDEFAULT	Specifies the default menu item on the start-up menu, and, optionally, sets a time-out value. If you do not use MENUDEFAULT, the default is item 1. Can be used only within a menu block.
MENUITEM	Defines one (of up to nine) menu item on the start-up menu. Can be used only in a menu block.
SUBMENU	Defines an item on the start-up menu that displays another set of choices. Can be used only in a menu block.

Understanding Blocks

To control how DOS executes the commands in CONFIG.SYS, you separate different groups of directives into *blocks*. Each block has a *block heading*—a label identifying the block. Block headings consist of a block name contained within square brackets ([]).

A block name can contain up to 70 characters. It cannot contain spaces, backslashes (\), forward slashes (/), commas (,), semicolons (;), equal signs (=), or square brackets ([]). Two block names, [MENU] and [COMMON], have special meanings. [MENU] can be used to define only the start-up menu block, and [COMMON] defines a block of commands that always are executed regardless of your selection in the start-up menu. Each block name must be unique, but multiple [COMMON] blocks are permitted.

Defining a Menu Block

To create a *start-up* menu (the menu used to select configuration options), you must define a menu block. You use the block heading [MENU] to begin defining the start-up menu's menu block. You can include only one [MENU] block heading in CONFIG.SYS; submenus must use other block headings.

The MENUCOLOR, MENUDEFAULT, MENUITEM, and SUBMENU commands can be used only within a menu block. Of these, only MENUITEM is required—the other commands are optional.

The MENUCOLOR command uses the following syntax:

MENUCOLOR=text_color,*background_color*

Text_color specifies the color of the menu text. You can specify a value from 0 to 15, as follows:

0=Black	8=Gray
1=Blue	9=Bright blue
2=Green	10=Bright green
3=Cyan	11=Bright cyan
4=Red	12=Bright red
5=Magenta	13=Bright magenta
6=Brown	14=Yellow
7=White	15=Bright white

Background_color specifies the color of the screen background using the same color numbers as text_color. If you do not specify a value, DOS displays the text on a black background. Be sure to specify different values for text_color and *background_color*, or the text will not be readable.

To display yellow text on a blue background, for example, use the following command:

MENUCOLOR=14,1

The MENUDEFAULT command uses the following syntax:

MENUDEFAULT=blockname,*timeout*

Blockname specifies the block name of the default menu item. When DOS displays the start-up menu, the default menu item is highlighted and its number appears after the `Enter a choice` prompt.

Timeout specifies how many seconds DOS waits before starting the computer with the default configuration. If you don't specify a time-out value, DOS waits until you press Enter. Valid time-out values range from 0 to 90 seconds. A time-out of 0 seconds forces automatic selection of the default, bypassing the menu display.

To set the block named WIN_NET as the default menu item, and select it automatically after displaying the menu for three seconds, for example, use the following command:

MENUDEFAULT=WIN_NET,3

The MENUITEM command uses the following syntax:

MENUITEM=blockname,*menu_text*

Blockname specifies the name of a configuration block. If the menu item is selected from the start-up menu, DOS carries out the commands in the named configuration block, as well as any commands before the menu block in CONFIG.SYS and any commands in [COMMON] configuration blocks. If DOS cannot find a block with the specified name, the item does not appear on the start-up menu.

Menu_text is optional text displayed for this menu item. If no *menu_text* is specified, DOS displays the block name as the menu item.

The SUBMENU command uses the same format as the MENUITEM command. Instead of referring to a configuration block, however, blockname refers to another menu block.

Figure 9.1 shows a typical start-up menu block. In this example, DOS displays three configuration choices. If the user does not make a selection within three seconds, the default item, WIN_NET, is selected automatically.

```
[MENU]
MENUCOLOR=14,1
MENUITEM=WIN_NET        Load Network drivers
MENUITEM=INTERLINK      Load Interlink driver
MENUITEM=NO_DRIVERS     Don't load drivers
MENUDEFAULT=WIN_NET,3
```

Fig. 9.1

A start-up menu block enabling you to select a configuration.

Defining a Configuration Block

Configuration blocks are named groups of related configuration directives. In figure 9.1, three configuration blocks are named: WIN_NET, INTERLINK, and NO_DRIVERS. Each configuration block contains the necessary directives to load a specific set of device drivers and set other configuration options.

Often, the same set of options are used in more than one configuration block. In some cases, the same options are common to all configuration blocks. Rather than duplicating these options in each configuration block, you can reuse the directives by using the INCLUDE command and [COMMON] blocks.

Directives in [COMMON] blocks are always executed. Create as many blocks labeled [COMMON] as you want, and place in them the directives that always must be executed, regardless of which configuration is selected from the start-up menu.

TIP Always include a [COMMON] block as the last block in CONFIG.SYS (you do not have to include any directives in this block). When you follow this procedure, if a software installation program adds commands to the end of CONFIG.SYS, those commands will be added to the [COMMON] block and executed regardless of the start-up menu selection chosen. You may want to edit CONFIG.SYS and move the new commands to their own configuration block later.

To execute a set of directives needed in more than one, but not in all, possible configuration selections, place those directives in their own named configuration block. Use the INCLUDE command to execute those directives.

The three choices on the start-up menu shown in figure 9.1 each require a different combination of directives, for example. In some cases, those directives must be executed in a specific order. Three configuration blocks—named NORMAL, MIDDLE, and FINAL—each contain a group of directives used by the selections on the start-up menu. In each case, however, the order in which the directives are executed is slightly different. Also, two of the start-up menu options load additional device drivers. Figure 9.2 shows how the INTERLINK, NO_DRIVERS, and WIN_NET configuration blocks appear in CONFIG.SYS.

```
[INTERLINK]
INCLUDE NORMAL
INCLUDE MIDDLE
DEVICE=C:\DOS\INTERLNK.EXE /DRIVES:10 /AUTO /COM
INCLUDE FINAL
[NO_DRIVERS]
INCLUDE NORMAL
INCLUDE MIDDLE
INCLUDE FINAL
[WIN_NET]
INCLUDE NORMAL
DEVICE=C:\WINDOWS\PROTMAN.DOS /I:C:\WINDOWS
DEVICEHIGH=/L:2 C:\WINDOWS\WORKGRP.SYS
DEVICE C:\WINDOWS\EXP16.DOS
INCLUDE MIDDLE
INCLUDE FINAL
```

Fig. 9.2
Configuration blocks enabling different system configurations.

Note that all three configuration blocks start by executing the directives in the NORMAL configuration block, and end by executing the directives in the FINAL configuration block. Another way to accomplish this same result is to place the directives in the NORMAL configuration block at the beginning of CONFIG.SYS, before the start-up MENU block, and to place the directives in the FINAL configuration block in a COMMON configuration block at the end of CONFIG.SYS. Both methods produce the same results, but the method used in the example provides slightly more versatility, especially in adding new configuration options in the future.

Using the CONFIG Environment Variable

When you include a start-up menu in CONFIG.SYS, DOS 6 creates a new *environment variable* called CONFIG. Environment variables are values that DOS stores in memory and then makes available to any program that needs to use that value. Some common environment variables include the following:

COMSPEC	Specifies location of command interpreter COMMAND.COM
DIRCMD	Sets defaults for DIR command
PATH	Specifies set of directories DOS searches for program files
PROMPT	Specifies characters DOS uses to display its command prompt
WINPMT	An alternative command prompt you can specify for use in a Windows DOS Prompt window

The CONFIG environment variable contains the name of the configuration block selected from the start-up menu. For example, if the default WIN_NET configuration block is selected in figure 9.2, the CONFIG environment variable contains the value WIN_NET.

You can use the value of the CONFIG environment variable to control the operation of batch files, such as AUTOEXEC.BAT, by using the IF batch command. You may include the lines shown in figure 9.3 in AUTOEXEC.BAT, for example, to execute different sets of commands depending on which start-up menu configuration option was selected.

If you use the CONFIG environment variable in this way, you can make a single menu selection in CONFIG.SYS and control both the configuration options selected in CONFIG.SYS and the commands executed in AUTOEXEC.BAT. You also can use this method to load device drivers in CONFIG.SYS and then load their related TSR programs in AUTOEXEC.BAT. If you choose a configuration option that does not load the device driver, use the IF command to check the value of the CONFIG environment variable and determine whether to load the TSR.

In the next section, you learn how to add even more flexibility by creating interactive menus in batch files using the new CHOICE command.

```
GOTO %CONFIG%
GOTO END
:INTERLINK
a group of commands for using Interlnk
GOTO END
:WIN_NET
a group of commands for using Windows for Workgroups
GOTO END
:NO_DRIVERS
another group of commands
:END
```

Fig. 9.3

Using the CONFIG variable to make selections in AUTOEXEC.BAT.

Creating Menus in Batch Files

The new menu commands for CONFIG.SYS make managing multiple configurations much easier. Now a single copy of CONFIG.SYS can hold all the options you need. The CHOICE command, also new to DOS 6, provides a similar capability for batch files such as AUTOEXEC.BAT.

DOS' batch language always has lacked a good, easy method of interacting with the PC user. True, you could test the user's input to see what arguments are typed on the command line following the batch file's name, but there really wasn't an easy way within DOS to display a menu of options and then wait for the user to make a selection. If you wanted to create interactive menus, you had to use another program like the Batch Enhancer in the Norton Utilities.

Understanding the CHOICE Command

You use the CHOICE command to make batch files interactive by accepting user responses to prompts. You can display a menu of application programs, for example, and run the program the user selects. You also can use the CHOICE command to allow the user to select additional configuration options not available in CONFIG.SYS.

When you use the CHOICE command to create a batch-file menu, you can display a prompt, wait as the user selects from a set of keys, and return a value to the batch program that indicates the key which was pressed. You can specify a default key to use if the user does not make a selection, and you can specify that the batch file delay up to 99 seconds waiting for the user's response.

The CHOICE command uses the following syntax:

CHOICE */C:keys /N /S /T:c,nn text*

/C:keys specifies the group of keys the user can press. If you specify a group of keys, they are displayed within square brackets ([ ]), and are followed by a question mark (?). If you don't specify the /C switch, [YN]? is the default. The colon (:) is optional.

/N specifies that the group of keys the user can press are not displayed (but they are still the valid set of choices). Any *text* you specify is still displayed, however.

/S causes the group of keys the user can press to be case-sensitive. If */S* is not specified, CHOICE accepts upper- or lowercase characters.

/T:c,nn specifies the number of seconds to pause before defaulting to a specified key. Use *c* to specify the default key to select if the user does not press another key within the allotted time. Use *nn* to specify the number of seconds to pause. You can use pause values between 0 and 99. If you specify 0, CHOICE waits indefinitely.

Text is optional text you want to be displayed before the key prompt. Quotation marks are necessary only if you include a switch character (\) as part of the text before the prompt. If you don't specify optional text, only the key prompt is displayed.

Understanding ERRORLEVEL

The CHOICE command returns the user's response as an *ERRORLEVEL*—a number that indicates which key was pressed. You then use the IF ERRORLEVEL batch command to determine which key was pressed.

The ERRORLEVEL number that CHOICE returns corresponds to the position of the indicated character in the list of acceptable keys. If the user presses the first key in your list, CHOICE returns an ERRORLEVEL value of 1. If the user presses the fifth key in your list, CHOICE returns an ERRORLEVEL value of 5.

For example, if you enter

CHOICE /C:BRIAN

in a batch file, CHOICE displays the following prompt:

```
[B,R,I,A,N]?
```

If the user presses the letter A, CHOICE returns an ERRORLEVEL value of 4.

Understanding the IF ERRORLEVEL Command

You use the IF ERRORLEVEL batch command to determine which key was pressed, but you must understand how this command functions. When the IF ERRORLEVEL batch command tests an ERRORLEVEL value, it is testing to see if the value is *at least as high* as the specified value. Higher values are accepted as true.

Suppose that you want to know which character the user pressed in response to the `[B,R,I,A,N]?` prompt. Because N is the fifth character, CHOICE returns an ERRORLEVEL value of 5 if the user presses N. The following batch command tests to see whether the ERRORLEVEL value is 5 or higher, and therefore whether N was pressed:

IF ERRORLEVEL 5 ECHO You pressed N

You may conclude that you could add the following batch command to tell you whether A was pressed:

IF ERRORLEVEL 4 ECHO You pressed A

Unfortunately, if the user pressed N, the following result would be displayed:

```
You pressed N

You pressed A
```

Because the ERRORLEVEL value produced when the user presses N is 5, both IF ERRORLEVEL tests are true because the actual ERRORLEVEL value is equal to or higher than the test value. Because you probably only want one test to succeed, you must structure your batch file to prevent a lower ERRORLEVEL test from being performed once a higher ERRORLEVEL test has succeeded. Figure 9.4 shows one method of structuring your batch file to accomplish this goal.

```
@ECHO OFF
CHOICE /C:BRIAN
IF ERRORLEVEL 5 GOTO NPRESS
IF ERRORLEVEL 4 GOTO APRESS
IF ERRORLEVEL 3 GOTO IPRESS
IF ERRORLEVEL 2 GOTO RPRESS
ECHO You pressed B
GOTO END
:RPRESS
ECHO You pressed R
GOTO END
:IPRESS
ECHO You pressed I
GOTO END
:APRESS
ECHO You pressed A
GOTO END
:NPRESS
ECHO You pressed N
:END
```

Fig. 9.4

Using CHOICE to determine user input.

In this batch file, the CHOICE command displays the `[B,R,I,A,N]?` prompt and waits for the user's response. The first IF ERRORLEVEL command line tests to see whether the ERRORLEVEL value is 5 or greater. If it is, program control branches to the section labeled `:NPRESS`, where the line `You pressed N` is displayed and the batch file ends.

If the user presses I, the ERRORLEVEL value is 3, so the first two IF ERRORLEVEL tests fail. The third test is successful, and program control branches to the section labeled `:IPRESS`, where the line `You pressed I` is displayed. Following this, the command line `GOTO END` is executed, and the batch file ends.

If the user presses B, all of the IF ERRORLEVEL tests fail. The batch file continues to the next line, which displays the line `You pressed B`. Following this, the command line `GOTO END` is executed, and the batch file ends.

Figure 9.4 shows one way to use the CHOICE command. You also can use CHOICE to create menus in a batch file by preceding the CHOICE command with several lines that use the ECHO command to display menu options and descriptions. If you want, you can specify a default selection that is selected if the user does not press a key within a specified time.

TIP

If you use the CHOICE command to create a menu of applications programs, create the menu in a separate batch file—not AUTOEXEC.BAT. With this method, you can return to your menu batch file after you complete your work in an application by typing the name of the menu batch file at the DOS prompt, or by including its name as the last command in an application's batch file.

Chapter Summary

Managing multiple system configurations, dealing with incompatible configuration options, and creating batch-file menus are all much easier in DOS 6 than in any earlier version of DOS. This chapter showed you how to take advantage of these new features and greatly simplify the tasks involved in maintaining and upgrading your PC.

The final chapter shows you how to use DOS 6 on your portable PC. Although most portable systems are quite capable, they are often less powerful than desktop systems, and usually have fewer resources that you can afford to waste.

10

CHAPTER

Using DOS 6 on Your Portable PC

Portable PCs are fast becoming an important part of the PC arena. Portables are becoming faster and more powerful, and often have fairly large capacity disk storage and bright displays. Still, the majority of the available portable systems are much more expensive than equally powerful desktop systems. Hardware upgrades, such as larger hard disks, are also more expensive—if even available—on portables.

Many types of portable PCs are available. Some are true laptop systems that you can use while sitting on an airplane, for example. Other portables are larger and heavier, and may even require access to an electrical outlet. Still others are small enough to fit in one hand. Because of this broad range of systems, it would be impossible to mention how each specific feature of DOS 6 may apply to every type of portable PC. As a generic term, therefore, this book simply refers to portable PCs.

If you use a portable PC, you probably are very careful about what types of software you install on your system. Hard disk space—if your portable even has a hard disk—may be at a premium. You probably don't want to use up your disk space storing programs that you will never use. If you upgrade your portable to DOS 6, you probably will want to install only the features you can use.

Another precious commodity on most portables is battery power. The longer the battery's charge lasts, the more work you can get done between recharging. If you can save enough power to stretch out the battery life another half hour, you may be able to finish a report or proposal that enables you to beat your competition.

Finally, if you have a desktop system, you probably have to share data between your portable and your desktop systems. Regardless of whether the two PCs can share floppy disks, exchanging very much data via floppy disks takes too much time.

This chapter addresses these issues and shows you how to make the best use of the DOS 6 upgrade on your portable PC.

Installing DOS 6 on Your Portable PC

Installing DOS 6 on your portable PC is easy—if your portable has plenty of room to spare on its hard disk and the right size of floppy disk drive. If your hard disk doesn't have enough available space, if your DOS 6 upgrade package has the wrong size floppy disks, or if your portable lacks floppy disk drives, the task isn't nearly as easy.

If your portable PC has a large hard disk and the correct floppy disk size, and if you don't care about whether you are wasting disk space on files you don't need, simply install the DOS 6 upgrade as discussed in Chapter 2, "Upgrading to DOS 6." If you want a more efficient DOS 6 setup tuned to your portable system, however, read the following sections in this chapter.

Using Setup

The DOS 6 Setup program has two options that may make more sense than the default setup for those upgrading a portable PC to DOS 6. The first option is to install DOS 6 on floppy disks instead of installing it on the hard disk. The second option you may want to consider is the minimal setup, which installs only the DOS 6 files necessary to boot the system using DOS 6.

If your portable does not have a hard disk, your only option is to install DOS 6 on floppy disks. This also may be your best option if your hard disk lacks the space necessary to hold both DOS 6 and your old DOS version's files.

On the other hand, using the minimal setup option enables you to install DOS 6 one piece at a time. If hard disk space on your portable is really scarce, you can use the minimal setup option to select each of the DOS 6 features you want and skip the ones for which you don't have enough room.

Installing DOS 6 on Floppy Disks

By installing DOS 6 first to floppy disks, you not only create a set of disks that you can use later to install DOS 6 on your hard disk, but you also create a working set of DOS 6 disks. Because these disks will contain most of the DOS 6 files (but not MS Anti-Virus, MS Backup, or MS Undelete), you can try out the new features before you upgrade your portable's hard disk to DOS 6.

If you want to install DOS 6 on floppy disks using the Setup program, your drive A must be a 1.44M 3 1/2-inch drive or a 1.2M 5 1/4-inch drive. You also must have three high-density floppy disks that are compatible with drive A. If drive A is not a high-density drive, you can order 720K or 360K setup disks from Microsoft, or you can use the minimal setup option discussed in the next section.

To install DOS 6 on floppy disks using the Setup program, follow these steps:

1. Insert the DOS 6 Setup Disk 1 into drive A or drive B.
2. Type **A:SETUP /F** (or **B:SETUP /F**) and press Enter.
3. Follow the screen instructions to create the three floppy disks containing DOS 6. Label these disks *Startup/Support*, *Help/BASIC/ Edit/Utility*, and *Supplemental*.

After you complete the setup to floppy disks, you can insert the Startup/Support disk you just created into drive A and press Ctrl+Alt+Del to start DOS 6. You can use DOS 6 for a time to make certain that it functions properly on your system, or you can use the three floppy disks now to install DOS 6 on your hard disk.

Installing DOS 6 from Floppy Disks

One advantage of installing DOS 6 on floppy disks first, and then using those new disks to install DOS 6 on your hard disk, is that you do not need as much room on your hard disk. When you use the DOS 6 Setup program to install DOS 6 on a hard disk, the program saves your old version of DOS in a new directory. Depending on which version is currently on your hard disk, this new directory may require almost 2M of disk space.

Although the Setup program's method enables you to return to your old version of DOS, it is very unlikely that you will ever use this option. If you install DOS 6 on your hard disk using the three floppy disks you created when you installed DOS 6 on floppy disks, you easily can bypass the step of saving your existing DOS version.

If you want to install DOS 6 on your hard disk using the three DOS 6 floppy disks, skipping the step of saving your existing DOS version, follow these steps:

1. Insert the Startup/Support disk into drive A.
2. Press Ctrl+Alt+Del to start DOS 6.
3. Type the command **SYS C:** and press Enter.
4. After you see the message `System transferred`, copy the DOS 6 files from the floppy disk to your DOS directory on the hard disk by typing the command **COPY A:*.* C:\DOS** and pressing Enter.

If your DOS directory on your hard disk has a different name, substitute the correct name in the command.

5. Remove the Startup/Support disk, and insert the Help/BASIC/Edit/Utility disk into drive A.
6. Copy the files from this disk to your DOS directory on the hard disk by typing the command **COPY A:*.* C:\DOS** and pressing Enter.
7. Remove the Help/BASIC/Edit/Utility disk, and insert the Supplemental disk into drive A.
8. Copy the files from this disk to your DOS directory on the hard disk by typing the command **COPY A:*.* C:\DOS** and pressing Enter.
9. Remove the Supplemental disk from drive A.
10. Press Ctrl+Alt+Del to start DOS 6 from the hard disk.

If you install DOS 6 using this procedure, MS Anti-Virus, MS Backup, and MS Undelete will not be installed on your hard disk. If you choose to install either the DOS or Windows versions of any of these optional utilities, you can add them at any time after DOS 6 has been installed. To install one or more of these programs, insert the DOS 6 Setup Disk 1 into drive A, type the command **A:SETUP /E**, and press Enter. Follow the instructions on your screen to select the program versions you want to install.

Installing DOS 6 Minimally

The DOS 6 Setup program also offers the minimal setup option. This option places only the three DOS 6 files necessary to boot the system on the hard disk. You then can use the EXPAND command to copy and expand exactly the DOS 6 files you want on your hard disk. You must use the EXPAND command because most of the DOS 6 files on the Setup disks are compressed to save disk space. Compressed files have the last character of their file extension converted to an underbar (__), such as ATTRIB.EX__. You cannot use the compressed files until they have been expanded.

> **CAUTION:** After you use the minimal setup option to enable your hard disk to boot DOS 6, the external commands (such as FORMAT) from your current DOS version will no longer function. You must replace those programs with their DOS 6 equivalents before you can use the external DOS commands.

To perform a minimal DOS 6 setup, follow these steps:

1. Insert the Startup/Support disk into drive A.
2. Type the command **A:SETUP /M** and press Enter.
3. Follow the instructions on your screen.
4. When minimal setup is complete, press Ctrl+Alt+Del to restart your system and boot DOS 6.
5. Copy EXPAND.EXE to your DOS directory. Type the command **COPY A:EXPAND.EXE C:\DOS** and press Enter.

After you perform the minimal setup and boot DOS 6, use the EXPAND command to copy and expand the DOS 6 files. If you do not have the C:\DOS directory specified in the PATH environment variable, type the command **PATH C:\DOS** and press Enter. This command enables you to access the EXPAND command. The syntax of the EXPAND command follows:

EXPAND *drive:\path*\filename destination

Drive:\path\filename specifies the location or name of a file or set of files to be expanded. You cannot use wild cards, but you can specify more than one source file name.

Destination specifies the new location or name of an expanded file or set of files. Destination can be a drive letter and colon, directory name, file name, or a combination. Destination can be a file name only if you have specified a single file name for the source file name.

If you want to expand the ATTRIB program file, for example, you will find it on Setup Disk 1 as ATTRIB.EX_. Use the following command line to expand this file and place it in the DOS directory on drive C:

```
EXPAND A:ATTRIB.EXE C:\DOS
```

You must specify the correct file extension for the expanded program file—not the file extension that ends with an underbar.

Determining Which Files To Expand

If hard disk space is very limited, you may want to be quite selective in deciding which DOS 6 files to expand. DOS 6 includes a large number of optional files; you need to copy only those files necessary to perform the tasks you feel are necessary.

The following list provides a general idea of some of the files on the Setup disks that you may decide not to copy to your hard disk:

- Files with 386 in their names or extensions are not used unless your system has at least an 80386 processor.
- Files with a BAT extension are batch files that are used only by the Setup program. Do not copy these files to your hard disk.
- Program files have COM or EXE extensions. You can recognize the program by the file name, and then decide whether you want to copy the file. In order to be able to format floppy disks, for example, you must copy FORMAT.COM.
- Files with DLL extensions are Windows files. Also, files with names starting with MW are Windows files. If you do not use Windows on your portable, don't copy any of these files.
- Files with DOS extensions are network drivers for the Workgroup Connection. If you do not intend to connect to a network, do not copy any of these files.
- Files with GRB extensions are DOS Shell "Grabber" files. If you do not use the DOS Shell, do not copy any of these files.
- Files with HLP extensions are Help files. If you do not need on-line help, do not copy any of these files.

Using Interlnk To Install DOS 6

If you have a laptop PC and a desktop system, you can use Interlnk to install most of the DOS 6 files on your laptop. You first must install

DOS 6 on your desktop system. You then can use Interlnk to copy some of the DOS 6 files to your laptop.

Before you begin, connect the correct cable between the two systems. See "Making the Right Hardware Connection" in Chapter 8.

If the Setup disks are not compatible with the disk drives on the laptop, exchange the DOS 6 Upgrade package for one with the correct size disks, or use the desktop system to create a start-up disk compatible with the laptop. If drive B on the desktop system is a 1.44M 3 1/2-inch drive and your laptop uses this size disk, for example, follow these steps to set up DOS 6 on the laptop. Start with these steps on the desktop system:

1. Insert a blank, 1.44M disk into drive B of the desktop system.
2. Type the command **FORMAT B: /S** and press Enter.
3. Follow the prompts, and when DOS asks if you want to format another disk, press N.
4. Type the command **COPY C:\DOS\SYS.COM B:** and press Enter (if necessary, substitute the correct name for your DOS directory on drive C).
5. Type the command **COPY C:\DOS\INTERLNK.EXE B:** and press Enter (if necessary, substitute the correct name for your DOS directory on drive C).
6. Type the command **COPY CON B:CONFIG.SYS** and press Enter.
7. Type **DEVICE=INTERLNK.EXE**, press the space bar, and press the F6 function key. This copies a new CONFIG.SYS file to drive B.
8. Remove the floppy disk from drive B and insert it into drive A on the laptop PC.
9. Type the command **INTERSVR** and press Enter. This starts the Interlnk server program.

Now follow these steps on the laptop system:

1. Press Ctrl+Alt+Del to boot the laptop from the floppy disk.
2. When the DOS prompt appears, type the command **SYS C:** and press Enter. This places the DOS 6 boot files on the laptop's hard disk.

3. Type the command **INTERLNK** and press Enter. This confirms that the Interlnk program has started, and shows the drives on both systems.
4. Copy the DOS 6 files from the desktop system to the laptop's C:\DOS directory. You can copy all the files, or selected files, depending on the amount of disk space you want to use.
5. Remove the floppy disk and press Ctrl+Alt+Del to boot the laptop from the hard disk.

DOS 6 now is installed on the laptop. Use the same techniques covered earlier to configure the laptop's memory and other DOS 6 options. If your laptop supports Advanced Power Management, see the next section for another feature you can use.

Using Power Conservation

Your computer spends most of its time waiting. When you ask it to perform a task, it quickly does what is necessary, and then sits idle waiting for your next input. Usually, however, your PC continues to use the same amount of power whether it is working or idling.

Because portable PCs normally depend on battery power, reducing power consumption is important. If your portable can use less power when it is just idling, your battery probably will be able to deliver a usable charge for a longer period of time, and you will be able to use your system longer between recharging.

DOS 6 has a program, POWER.EXE, that helps reduce power consumption on portable PCs—especially those that conform to the new Advanced Power Management (APM) specification. This program loads as a device driver and reduces power consumption up to 25 percent. Even if your PC does not conform to the APM specification, you may see approximately a 5 percent reduction in power consumption.

To load the POWER.EXE device driver, you add a directive to CONFIG.SYS. Use the following syntax to load and configure the device driver (assuming that POWER.EXE is located in C:\DOS):

DEVICE=C:\DOS\POWER.EXE *ADV:MAX|REG|MIN|STD|OFF /LOW*

If you specify the *ADV* argument, follow it with *MAX*, *REG*, *MIN*, *STD*, or *OFF*. This specifies the type of power conservation POWER.EXE should use.

Descriptions of the arguments follow:

Argument	Description
ADV:MAX	Provides maximum power conservation, but may adversely affect performance.
ADV:REG	Balances power conservation with performance (default setting).
ADV:MIN	Provides a smaller power savings, but higher performance.
ADV:STD	Conserves power by using only the power-management features of your computer's hardware. If your computer does not support the APM specification, STD turns off power management.
ADV:OFF	Turns off power management and simply loads the POWER.EXE device driver into memory. You then can control power management from the command line.
/LOW	Loads the POWER.EXE device driver into conventional memory, even if the upper memory area is available. By default, POWER.EXE is loaded into a UMB if one is available.

After you load the POWER.EXE device driver into memory, you can control the level of power management by typing the command **POWER** followed by **ADV:** and the type of power management to use. To change to maximum power conservation, for example, enter the following command:

```
POWER ADV:MAX
```

To see the current power-conservation setting, enter the POWER command without any arguments.

Chapter Summary

Whether you depend on a laptop as your sole PC, or whether you use a laptop along with a desktop system, DOS 6 offers many advantages. You can create more disk space using DoubleSpace, share files using Interlnk, and save power using POWER.EXE. In this chapter you learned how to easily install DOS 6 on your laptop, even if your DOS 6 Setup disks are incompatible with the disk drives on that system.

DOS 6 is a very important step forward in the evolution of DOS—the most compatible and useful operating system for the majority of computer users. *Upgrading to MS-DOS 6* is intended to help you make a quick step up to this latest and best DOS version available.

A

APPENDIX

Connecting PCs with Workgroup Connection

The Workgroup Connection, a stand-alone product sold separately by Microsoft, enables you to connect to a network, share files and printers, and use electronic mail—all from the DOS command line or from within your favorite application programs. You don't have to learn complicated network procedures, either!

This appendix shows you how to use the Workgroup Connection to connect your PC to other PCs via a network.

Connecting to a Network

A computer network usually uses cables or wires to connect two or more PCs so that they can quickly share information over the network. Many types of networks exist, and they may vary in such details as the type of network adapter card required, the physical means used to connect each of the networked systems, and the type of software that controls the network. Regardless of their differences, networks all serve a similar purpose—they enable computer systems to cooperate by making access to data and peripherals easier.

Because there are so many types of networks, it's difficult to suggest the best type of network for each situation. The Workgroup Connection, however, does have certain requirements. If you want to connect to a network and use the Workgroup Connection, all of the following pieces must be in place:

- You must have a network adapter card installed in or attached to your computer. This network adapter card must be compatible with both your computer and the network.
- The network must be controlled by Microsoft LAN Manager or LAN Manager compatible networking software. Or, it must include at least one PC running Microsoft Windows for Workgroups.

Understanding the Workgroup Connection

The Workgroup Connection is sold separately from DOS 6. The Workgroup Connection enables you to access shared directories and printers on a compatible network. You don't even have to remember complicated commands, because shared directories simply function as additional disk drives that you can use with any standard DOS program. Shared printers are just as easy to use, because they function exactly as if they were connected directly to your PC.

TIP One of the easiest ways to network two PCs is to purchase the Microsoft Windows for Workgroups starter kit. This kit includes two network adapter cards, 25 feet of cable, all the connectors you need to connect two PCs, and the Windows for Workgroups software. The kit even includes a video tape that shows you how to install everything yourself—without requiring you to hire a technician. The Windows for Workgroups user kit includes everything you need to add another PC to your Windows for Workgroups network. Both the Windows for Workgroups starter kit and the Windows for Workgroups user kit require an 80386 PC or higher.

Although it enables you to access shared network resources, the Workgroup Connection is a one-way connection in terms of resource sharing—other users on the network cannot access your system and see your files or use any printers attached to your PC. This does not mean, however, that you cannot share files with others on the network. If you want to share files, you can simply copy them across the network to a shared directory on another computer. With the Workgroup Connection, you have control over who can see or use your files.

The Workgroup Connection also has *Microsoft Mail*—a network electronic mail service—built in. Using Microsoft Mail, you can easily send messages to other users on your network, and they can send messages to you. Your system can alert you when someone sends you a message even if you are using your favorite application program.

If you have access to a compatible network, the Workgroup Connection expands your PC's resources and makes sharing information much easier. You remain in control of your system, but you gain a whole new level of access.

Installing the Workgroup Connection

Before you can install the Workgroup Connection, you must install an appropriate network adapter card. Some network adapter cards have switches or jumpers you must set to configure the board for proper operation in your system. Other network adapter cards, like those in the Windows for Workgroups starter kit mentioned earlier, are simply installed into your PC and then configured later using simple command options. Regardless of the type of network adapter card you use, it must be installed, configured, and connected to the network before you install the Workgroup Connection.

When you connect to a network, there must be a way for each computer and person on the network to be uniquely identified. Otherwise, you cannot be certain that you are accessing the correct computer system or sending mail to the intended recipient. The Workgroup Connection uses three pieces of information to create this unique identification:

- *User name:* Identifies each individual user—regardless of the actual computer being used. On a very small network, you probably can use your first or last name as your user name, but on larger networks you may need to use a combination of your initials and last name, your first name and the first character of your last name, or some other designation.
- *Computer name:* Identifies each computer on the network—regardless of which user is actually using the PC. Here again, the names of the different computers on the network must be unique. Often the computer is given the same name as its primary user.
- *Workgroup name:* Identifies all components that make up the workgroup. The workgroup is basically all of the people and computers that work together.

Before you can install the Workgroup Connection, you must decide what user name and computer name you want to use, and you must know the name of your workgroup. You also must know whether your workgroup uses Microsoft Mail, because the Mail files are optional.

To install the Workgroup Connection, follow these steps:

1. If you have not installed and configured your network adapter card, do so before installing the Workgroup Connection.
2. Insert the Workgroup Connection disk into drive A (or B).
3. Type **A:SETUP** and press Enter to begin the installation. (If you inserted the disk into drive B, type the command **B:SETUP**.)

   The Setup for Workgroup Connection screen shown in figure A.1 appears.

```
Setup for Workgroup Connection

        Welcome to Setup for Workgroup Connection.

        Setup prepares Workgroup Connection to run on your computer.

        *  To get additional information about a Setup screen, press F1.

        *  To set up Workgroup Connection now, press ENTER.

        *  To quit Setup without installing Workgroup Connection, press F3.

ENTER=Continue  F1=Help  F3=Exit  F5=Remove Color
```

Fig. A.1

The first Setup for Workgroup Connection screen.

4. Press Enter to continue. Setup attempts to determine where your DOS files are located, and offers to install the Workgroup Connection files in the same directory (see fig. A.2).
5. If necessary, type the name of the directory in which you want to install the Workgroup Connection files. Press Enter to continue.
6. Setup examines your system and determines as much of the system configuration information as possible. Follow the prompts and type the additional information necessary, such as your computer's name, your user name, the workgroup name, and so on. After you have entered all the information, your screen should appear similar to that shown in figure A.3. Press Enter to continue.

```
Setup for Workgroup Connection

        Setup will place your Workgroup Connection files in the
        following directory.

        If this is where you want these files, press ENTER.

        If you want Setup to place the files in a different
        directory, type the full path of that directory, and
        then press ENTER.


        C:\DOS






ENTER=Continue  F1=Help  F3=Exit
```

Fig. A.2

Installing the Workgroup Connection files in your DOS 6 directory.

```
Setup for Workgroup Connection

        If all the options are correct, select 'The listed options
        are correct,' and then press ENTER. If you want to change
        an option, use the UP or DOWN arrow key to select it. Then
        press ENTER to see alternatives for that option.

         Computer name    : BRIAN
         User name        : BRIAN
         Workgroup name   : UNDERDAHL'S
         Install Mail     : Install Mail files.
         Redirector       : Use the basic redirector.
         Pop-up key       : N
         Startup option   : Run Workgroup Connection and log on.
         Path             : C:\DOS
         Network Card     : Intel EtherExpress 16 or 16TP
         Protocol Driver  : Microsoft NetBEUI

         The listed options are correct.

ENTER=Continue  F1=Help  F3=Exit
```

Fig. A.3

Verifying Setup options.

After Setup finishes configuring the Workgroup Connection files for your system, you must reboot your PC in order for the changes to take effect. Remove any floppy disk from drive A and press Ctrl+Alt+Del.

TIP

Installing a new board, such as a network adapter card, in your PC can result in conflicts with existing system components. If your system locks up, or cards such as modem/fax boards refuse to work after you install a network adapter card, the problem is most likely a conflict between the network adapter card and the board that no longer works.

TIP One of the most common conflicts occurs in setting the IRQ (or interrupt) setting of the network adapter card to the same IRQ as an existing system component. Most PC adapter cards use at least one IRQ setting, and some cards use two. With rare exceptions, system components cannot share IRQs. If selecting a different IRQ setting does not solve the conflict, you also may have to select a different DMA (Direct Memory Access) setting, or even a different base memory address for one of the adapter cards. See your adapter board documentation for information on configuring the board.

Starting the Workgroup Connection

The Workgroup Connection loads as a memory-resident program. During setup, you are given the option to automatically load the Workgroup Connection every time you start DOS. Whether you choose this option depends on how important it is to always have the Workgroup Connection services available.

If you always want the electronic mail services available, or if you frequently must access network drives or printers, you probably should load the Workgroup Connection automatically every time you start DOS. On the other hand, if you seldom need these services, but often use programs that perform best when they have the maximum amount of memory available, you probably will want to load the Workgroup Connection only when you need its services. You can unload the memory-resident portion of the Workgroup Connection when you no longer need it.

Logging On to the Network

When you want to use network resources, you must log on to your workgroup. To log on, follow these steps:

1. Type **NET LOGON** and press Enter.
2. If the memory-resident Workgroup Connection has not already been loaded, the following prompt appears:

   ```
   The WORKSTATION service is not started.
   Is it OK to start it? (Y/N) [Y]:
   ```

3. Press Enter to load the memory-resident Workgroup Connection. The following prompt appears:

```
Type your user name, or press Enter if it is <xxxx>:
```

4. If the correct name is displayed, press Enter. Otherwise, type your correct user name and press Enter. The following prompt appears:

```
Type your password:
```

5. Type your password and press Enter.

If this is your first logon, type any password up to 14 characters and press Enter. Type the same password again to verify the password. Once you select a password, you must always type it to log on to the workgroup. *Don't forget your password!*

Using the Workgroup Connection

After you have the Workgroup Connection installed and have logged on to your workgroup, you can access the network's shared resources. You access these resources by using the NET command, followed by any optional parameters you want to use. If you enter the NET command without any optional parameters, the pop-up Workgroup Connection interface appears (see "Using the Pop-Up Interface," later in this chapter). Table A.1 summarizes the NET command's optional parameters. The following sections describe these options in greater detail.

Table A.1 NET Optional Parameters

Parameter	Description
CONFIG	Displays information about your workgroup settings, such as the computer name, your user name, and software version numbers.
HELP	Provides information about Workgroup Connection commands and error messages.
LOGOFF	Removes the existing connection between your computer and the network.
LOGON	Creates a new connection between your computer and the network.
PASSWORD	Changes your logon password. If you establish a password, you must enter the password to log on.

continues

Table A.1 Continued

Parameter	Description
PRINT	Controls print jobs and displays information about print jobs in progress.
START	Starts Workgroup Connection or loads the pop-up Workgroup Connection interface.
STOP	Stops Workgroup Connection or unloads the pop-up Workgroup Connection interface.
TIME	Synchronizes your computer's clock with that of a network time server.
USE	Connects or disconnects from a shared drive or printer, or displays information about connections.
VER	Displays the type and version number of the workgroup redirector you are using.
VIEW	Displays information on shared resources.

Using NET CONFIG

The NET CONFIG command displays your current workgroup settings (see fig. A.4).

```
C:\>NET CONFIG
Computer name                  \\BRIAN
User name                      BRIAN

Software version               3.1
Redirector version             2.50
Workstation root directory     C:\WINDOWS

Workgroup                      UNDERDAHL'S
The command completed successfully.

C:\>
```

Fig. A.4

Using NET CONFIG to display your current workgroup settings.

You can use the NET CONFIG command to confirm that you are properly logged on to the network. You also can identify the name of the computer and the software versions you are using.

Using NET HELP

The NET HELP command displays a summary of the NET command options. To see information about a specific parameter, include the parameter after the NET HELP command. You can type the following, for example:

```
NET HELP CONFIG
```

Using NET LOGOFF

When you are finished using the shared resources on the network, use the NET LOGOFF command to break the connections between your computer and those shared resources. If you do not log off the network, the system whose resources you are sharing will produce an error message if the user attempts to close the network support software.

When you use the NET LOGOFF command, you see prompts informing you that this will disconnect you from the shared resources. To log off without seeing the prompts or confirming your actions use the following command format:

```
NET LOGOFF /YES
```

Using NET LOGON

The NET LOGON command identifies you as a member of a workgroup and reestablishes your *persistent connections*—drives, directories, and printers to which you automatically connect whenever you log on.

If you use the NET LOGON command without any additional parameters, you are prompted for your user name and password. You can, however, include both items on the command line:

NET LOGON *user password*

If you prefer, you can substitute a question mark (?) for *password*, and add /YES to the end of the command line. This command logs you on to the network and bypasses all prompts except the password prompt.

Using NET PASSWORD

The NET PASSWORD command enables you to change your logon password. When you enter the command, you can follow it with your old password and then the new password, or you simply can respond to the prompts as shown in figure A.5.

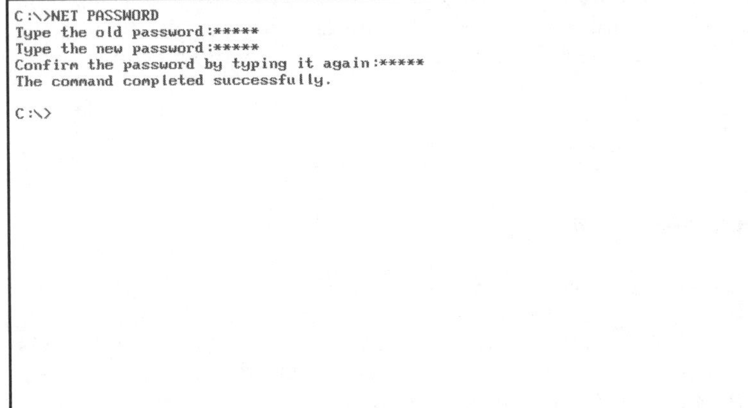

C:\>NET PASSWORD
Type the old password:*****
Type the new password:*****
Confirm the password by typing it again:*****
The command completed successfully.
C:\>

Fig. A.5

Changing your password with NET PASSWORD.

If you choose to respond to the prompts rather than to enter the old and new passwords as command-line arguments, you are given the opportunity to retype your new password. Because you must use the correct password to successfully log on to the network, this chance to verify your new password is valuable.

TIP If you do not require the security of passwords on your network, simply press Enter to create an empty new password. You then can log on to the network without remembering a password. Of course, this allows anyone to log on to your network using your user name, so if you have a need for security, be sure to use passwords.

Using NET PRINT

The NET PRINT command displays information about the print queue on a shared printer or controls your print jobs on the shared printer. NET PRINT has no effect on printers connected directly to your PC.

The NET PRINT command has several options that determine how the command functions. The format of the NET PRINT command follows:

NET PRINT *computer* *queue port job# /PAUSE /RESUME /DELETE /YES*

Table A.2 summarizes the NET PRINT command options.

Table A.2 NET PRINT Options

Option	Description
\\computer	The name of the computer about whose print queue you want information.
\queue	The name of the printer about whose queue you want information.
port	The name of the parallel (LPT) port you use to connect to the shared printer.
job#	The number assigned to a queued print job. You can specify the following options with job#: /PAUSE, /RESUME, and /DELETE.
/PAUSE	Pauses a print job.
/RESUME	Reactivates a print job that has been paused.
/DELETE	Cancels a print job.
/YES	Carries out the NET PRINT command without first prompting you or asking for confirmation.

Using NET START

The NET START command starts the Workgroup Connection or loads the pop-up Workgroup Connection interface into memory. After the pop-up interface is loaded into memory, you can access it by pressing Alt+N (see "Using the Pop-Up Interface," later in this chapter).

The NET START command has several optional parameters you can use. The following syntax shows these options:

NET START *POPUP BASIC FULL WORKSTATION NETBIND NETBEUI /LIST /YES*

Table A.3 summarizes the NET START options.

Table A.3 NET START Options

Option	Description
POPUP	Loads the pop-up Workgroup Connection interface into memory.
BASIC	Starts the basic redirector—the network software.
FULL	Starts the full redirector.
WORKSTATION	Starts the default redirector.
NETBIND	Binds protocols and network card drivers.
NETBEUI	Starts the NetBIOS interface.
/LIST	Displays the components that have been started.
/YES	Carries out the NET START command without prompting you or asking for confirmation.

Using NET TIME

The NET TIME command synchronizes your computer's clock with the shared clock on a Microsoft LAN Manager time server. Usually you will want to set all computers on the network to the same date and time. This command sets your PC's internal clock to match that of the network server. The general syntax of this command follows:

NET TIME *computer /WORKGROUP:wgname /SET /YES*

Table A.4 summarizes the NET TIME command options.

Table A.4 NET TIME Options

Option	Description
\\computer	Specifies the name of the computer whose time you want to synchronize your computer's clock with.
/WORKGROUP	Specifies that you want to use the clock on a computer in another workgroup.
wgname	Specifies the name of the workgroup containing a computer whose clock you want to synchronize your computer's clock with. If there are multiple time servers in that workgroup, NET TIME uses the first time server it finds.

Option	Description
/SET	Synchronizes your computer's clock with the clock on the specified computer or workgroup.
/YES	Carries out the NET TIME command without prompting you or asking for confirmation.

Using NET USE

The NET USE command connects or disconnects your computer from a shared drive, directory, or printer. It also displays information about your current network connections. This command has a large number of options, which are shown in the following syntax line and table A.5:

NET USE *port: drive:* * *\\computer\queue \\computer\directory password ? /PERSISTENT:YES NO LIST SAVE CLEAR /SAVEPW:NO /DELETE /YES*

Table A.5 NET USE Options

Option	Description
*	If used with /DELETE, specifies to disconnect all of your connections. If not used with /DELETE, specifies the next available drive letter.
/DELETE	Breaks the specified connection.
/PERSISTENT	Specifies which connections should be automatically restored the next time you log on. Must be followed by one of these values: YES, NO, SAVE, LIST, or CLEAR.
/SAVEPW:NO	Specifies that the password you enter should not be saved, and will need to be reentered the next time you connect to this resource.
/YES	Carries out the NET USE command without prompting you or asking for confirmation.
?	Specifies to prompt for the password of the shared resource—the default unless the password is optional.
CLEAR	Clears your persistent connections.
computer	Specifies the name of the computer sharing the resource.

continues

Table A.5 Continued

Option	Description
directory	Specifies the name of the shared directory.
drive	The drive letter assigned to a shared directory.
LIST	Lists persistent connections.
NO	Specifies that new connections should not be persistent.
password	Specifies the password for the shared resource, if any.
port	Specifies the parallel port assigned to a shared printer.
queue	Specifies the name of the shared printer.
SAVE	Makes all current connections persistent.
YES	Specifies that new connections should be persistent.

Using NET VER

The NET VER command displays the version number and type of the network software you are using. This command has no options, and displays a screen similar to figure A.6.

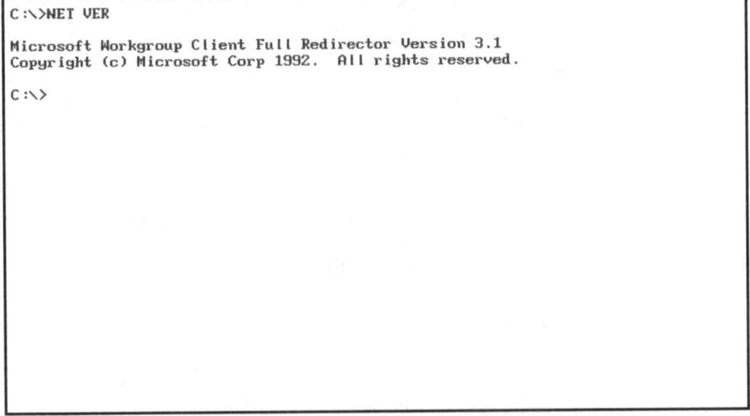

C:\>NET VER
Microsoft Workgroup Client Full Redirector Version 3.1
Copyright (c) Microsoft Corp 1992. All rights reserved.
C:\>

Fig. A.6

Using NET VER to see which network software you are using.

Using NET VIEW

The NET VIEW command provides a list of the computers in a workgroup. If you include the name of a specific computer as a parameter, the command shows all the shared drives, directories, and printers attached to that computer. This command uses the following syntax:

NET VIEW */WORKGROUP:wgname \\computer /YES*

You can use either the */WORKGROUP* and *:wgname* arguments, or the *\\computer* argument. */WORKGROUP* specifies that you want to view the names of the computers that share resources in another workgroup. *:wgname* specifies the name of the workgroup whose computer names you want to view. *\\computer* specifies the name of the computer whose shared resources you want to see listed. */YES* carries out the command without prompting you or asking you for confirmation.

To display a list of computers in your workgroup that share resources, type the NET VIEW command without options (see fig. A.7). Once you know the names of the computers in the workgroup, you can add the computer name as a parameter and display the shared resources on that computer (see fig. A.8).

```
C:\>NET VIEW
Server Name            Remark
-------------------------------------------------------------------
\\BRIAN
\\DARLENE
The command completed successfully.

C:\>
```

Fig. A.7

Using NET VIEW to display the names of the computers in a workgroup.

Using the Pop-Up Interface

Although you can use the Workgroup Connection by typing NET commands at the DOS prompt, many of the functions, such as connecting, disconnecting, or browsing shared resources, are more easily accomplished by using the pop-up Workgroup Connection interface (see fig. A.9).

```
C:\>NET VIEW \\BRIAN
Shared resources at \\BRIAN
Sharename     Type          Comment
-----------------------------------------------------------
C             Disk
FAXABILITY    Print
NEC P9XL      Print
WGPO          Disk
The command completed successfully.

C:\>
```

Fig. A.8

Using NET VIEW to display a computer's shared resources.

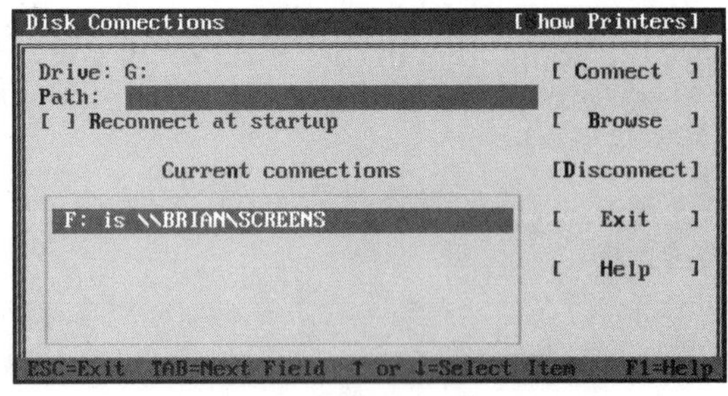

Fig. A.9

The pop-up Workgroup Connection interface.

You can display the pop-up Workgroup Connection interface in one of two ways. You can load the pop-up interface, use it to make or to break connections, and then leave the interface. Or, you can load the pop-up interface as a memory-resident program, and call it whenever necessary—even from within your application programs. Making the pop-up interface memory-resident uses approximately 29K of memory, but it makes controlling network connections much easier because you don't have to leave your applications when you want to make a change.

To load the pop-up interface and display it immediately, but not have it remain memory-resident, use the following command:

```
NET
```

To load the pop-up interface as a memory-resident program, use the following command:

```
NET START POPUP
```

After the pop-up interface is loaded as a memory-resident program, press Alt+N to display the pop-up interface.

If you load the pop-up interface as a memory-resident program, you can use the following command to remove it from memory:

NET STOP POPUP

Once the pop-up interface is displayed, regardless of whether it is memory-resident, you use the same commands to control network connections:

- To connect to a different computer, press Alt+B to display the Browse screen. Use the up- or down-arrow to select a computer, press Tab, use the up- or down-arrow to select a directory, and press Enter.
- To connect to a shared directory whose path you know, press Alt+P, type the path of the shared directory, and then press Enter.
- To disconnect from a shared directory, press Alt+N, use the up- or down-arrow to select the directory, and then press Alt+D.
- To use a different drive letter for a shared directory, press Alt+V, and then type the drive letter you want to use.
- To toggle a connection between persistent and nonpersistent, press Alt+R to select or to clear the Reconnect at Startup box. Persistent connections are automatically reestablished when you restart the Workgroup Connection.
- To control shared printer connections, press Alt+S to display the Printer Connections screen where you select shared printers. To return to the Disk Connections screen, press Alt+S again.
- To quit the pop-up interface, press Esc.

The Workgroup Connection enables you to easily share files and printers on a network. It also enables you to share electronic mail with other users on the network. The next section gives you a quick introduction to the main features of Microsoft Mail, the electronic mail system.

Using Mail

Although file- and printer-sharing are probably the most important uses of the Workgroup Connection, electronic mail offers yet another productivity enhancement for networked systems. People in an office communicate using many different means—meetings, telephone conversations, interoffice mail, and so on.

Making the connection with other people in the office isn't always easy, however. If you walk down to someone's office only to find that they have just stepped out, you have a wasted trip. If you phone someone who spends a great amount of time on the telephone, you may never reach that person when the line is not busy. Interoffice mail may get the message to someone, but will it arrive in time?

Electronic mail provides the means for your network to help solve these types of communications problems. If the recipient has just stepped out, the message will be waiting when the person returns. Because electronic mail doesn't depend on getting past a busy telephone line, that problem is eliminated, too. Electronic mail is also fast—there's no delay waiting for messages to be routed through the mail room.

Installing and Configuring Mail

When you install the Workgroup Connection, you are given the option of installing Mail at the same time. If you did not choose to install Mail at that time, you must do so before you can use Mail. See "Installing the Workgroup Connection," earlier in this chapter, for instructions.

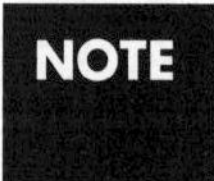

You must be logged on to the network before you can configure or use Mail. If you are not already logged on, type **NET LOGON** to start the Workgroup Connection.

After Mail is installed, type the command **MAIL** and press Enter to start Mail. The first time you start Mail, you must configure the program (see fig. A.10).

```
Setup for Microsoft Mail

        Welcome to Setup for Microsoft Mail.

        Setup will create a new mailbox in a workgroup
        post office for you.

        Before you set up Microsoft Mail, you must know the
        name of the workgroup post office in which you want
        a mailbox.

        To continue, press ENTER.

        To exit without setting up a mailbox, press F3.

        For help during Setup, press F1.

ENTER=Continue  F1=Help  F3=Exit  F5=Remove Color
```

Fig. A.10

The screen that appears the first time you start Mail.

Mail uses a *post office*—a mail server created on one of the computers on the network. You cannot create a post office using Mail, however. You must use a post office created by Windows for Workgroups or LAN Manager. See your Windows for Workgroups or LAN Manager documentation for information on creating a post office.

You must know the name of the post office in order to configure Mail for your PC. The post office name consists of the name of the computer that administers the post office and the shared post office directory name. If you are unsure of the post office name, use the NET VIEW command to find the correct name. In figure A.11, for example, the post office name is \\BRIAN\WGPO.

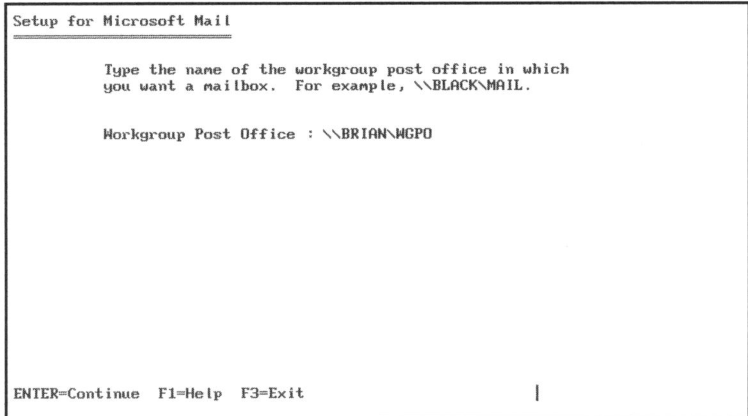

Setup for Microsoft Mail
Type the name of the workgroup post office in which
you want a mailbox. For example, \\BLACK\MAIL.
Workgroup Post Office : \\BRIAN\WGPO
ENTER=Continue F1=Help F3=Exit

Fig. A.11

Entering the name of the post office.

If your mailbox name (your network address) is already in use, Mail displays an advisory message. If this happens, press C to use your current mailbox name, or press Enter to select a new name.

Mail then establishes your mailbox at the network post office and informs you that it is ready to use (see fig. A.12). The next time you start Mail, you are not prompted for the setup information.

Sending Mail

After you install and configure Mail, you are ready to send and receive electronic mail over the network. Type the command **MAIL** and press Enter to load Mail. Then type your mailbox name and press Enter (see fig. A.13).

```
Setup for Microsoft Mail

          Your mailbox is now ready for you to use.

          The next time you start Mail, you will be connected
          to the post office that your mailbox is in.

            - To check your mailbox, press ENTER.

            - To quit Setup and return to the command prompt, press F3.

ENTER=Continue  F1=Help  F3=Exit                    |Setup Complete
```

Fig. A.12

The screen telling you that your mailbox is ready to use.

```
                Microsoft (R) Mail for PC Networks V3.0b
                       MS-DOS Workstation Version

                          Mailbox:  DARLENE

     Copyright 1991-1992 Microsoft Corporation.  All rights reserved.
```

Fig. A.13

Entering your mailbox name when you start Mail.

After you enter your mailbox name, the main Mail screen appears (see fig. A.14). This screen has menu options that enable you to create, read, and manage your electronic mail.

You use the first menu option, Address, to create an electronic mail address list. After you select this option, another menu appears, as shown in figure A.15. Use the options on this menu to manage your personal address list and to make it easier to send mail to the people you correspond with most often.

You can browse the mailbox list to select those mailboxes you want to add to your list (see fig. A.16). Press Enter to select a mailbox you want to add to your personal address list. Press Esc when you are ready to return to the main Mail screen.

```
Address  Read  Compose  Delete  Storage  Print  Options  Update
Select items of mail to read, or read all unread mail if none selected

FROM         SUBJECT                                    DATE      TIME    PRI

                                                                  NUM
```

Fig. A.14

The main Mail screen.

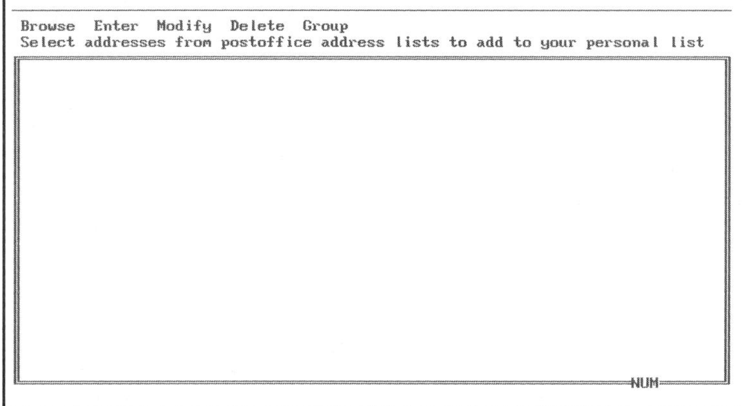
Browse Enter Modify Delete Group
Select addresses from postoffice address lists to add to your personal list
NUM

Fig. A.15

A personal address list to simplify sending mail.

You use the Compose option when you want to send electronic mail to someone else on the network. The Compose screen has several options (see fig. A.17). First, enter the name of the person you are sending mail to in the TO field. If you want copies sent to other people, enter their names in the CC field. The PRIORITY field is used to indicate the message's importance. You can enter numbers 1 (low) to 4 (high), or R (for registered mail—you automatically receive a return message telling you whether the message was received). Use the down-arrow to move the highlight into the message area, and then type your message.

When your message is complete, press Esc to return to the menu. Choose **T**ransmit (press T) and then **Y**es (press Y) to send the message.

```
Browse  Enter  Modify  Delete  Group
Cursor to name to add, Enter to select, Esc to abort

  Postoffice Address List
  Brian Underdahl
  Darlene

                                                        NUM
```

Fig. A.16

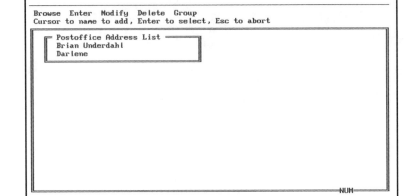

Browsing the mailbox list to select additions for your address list.

```
Edit  Print  Transmit  Storage  View  Clear
F1=Help   F2=Format   F4=Highlight   F5=Include   F6=Mark   F8=Paste

TO:  Brian Underdahl                                  DATE:  12-01-92
                                                      TIME:  11:17
CC:
SUBJECT:
PRIORITY:
ATTACHMENTS:

Hello there, this is DOS 6 electronic mail in action!

                                                        NUM
```

Fig. A.17

Creating a Mail message.

Receiving Mail

You also use Mail to read your incoming mail from other network users. If you have Mail running on your system, you see a message telling you that mail has been received (see fig. A.18).

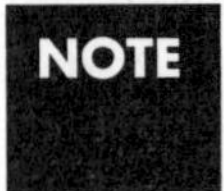

You can still be notified of incoming messages even if you do not have Mail running. See “Using Micro,” later in this chapter.

To read an incoming message, select **R**ead (press R), select the message using the arrow keys, and press Enter. The message then appears on your screen as shown in figure A.19.

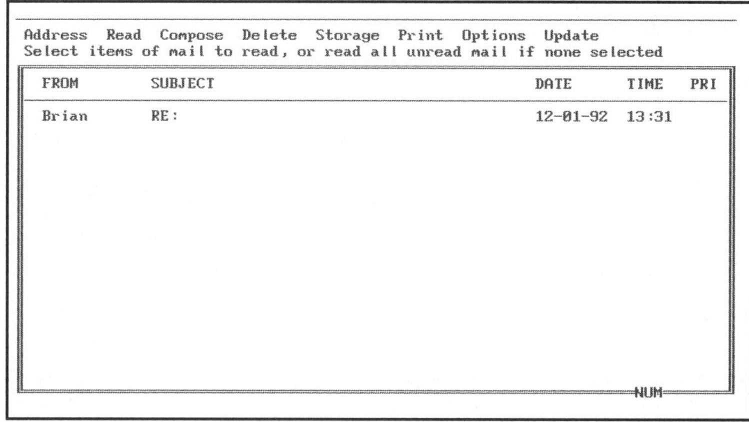

```
Address  Read  Compose  Delete  Storage  Print  Options  Update
Select items of mail to read, or read all unread mail if none selected

FROM          SUBJECT                                     DATE       TIME   PRI
Brian         RE:                                         12-01-92   13:31

                                                                        NUM
```

Fig. A.18 Mail telling you that an incoming message was received.

```
Delete  Hold  Forward  Print  Reply  Storage  Attachments
Get the next toggled message, or exit if none.  F4 = Monochrome

Microsoft Mail v3.0 IPM.Microsoft Mail.Note
From: Brian Underdahl
To:  Darlene
Subject:  RE:
Date: 1992-12-01 13:31
Priority:
Message ID: DE8C5352
Conversation ID: DE8C5352

Hi! Thanks for the message. Our Workgroup Connection and Microsoft Mail are
working just fine.
----------
From: Darlene
To: Brian Underdahl
Date: Tuesday, December 01, 1992 11:20AM

Hello there, this is DOS 6 electronic mail in action!
                                                                        NUM
```

Fig. A.19 Reading an incoming message.

After you read the message, you can choose from the menu options to delete the message, hold the message while you read other messages, forward it to someone else on the network, print it, reply by attaching your own message and returning it to the sender, or save it in a folder for future reference. If the message included any *attachments* (other files sent along with the message), you also can access those attachments.

The main Mail menu also includes options for deleting messages, storing them in folders, and printing them. The Options menu enables you to configure Mail for easier use, and the Update option checks for additional incoming mail.

When you are finished using Mail, return to the main menu and press Esc. Select **Yes** to leave Mail.

Understanding Mail Command-Line Options

Although you usually can start Mail without specifying any options, several options are available to customize Mail for your system, as the following syntax shows:

> MAIL *mailboxname -lines -C -Ddrive -H -M -Nseconds -P -Sdisplay -V -Wcolor -X*

Table A.6 summarizes Mail's command-line options.

Table A.6 Mail Command-Line Options

Option	Description
-<25-50>	Specifies number of lines on-screen
-C	Specifies color monitor
-D<drive>	Specifies drive letter assigned to post office (by default Mail uses M:)
-H	Displays help
-M	Loads MICRO
-N<1-199>	Sets number of seconds before Mail checks for new messages
-P	Bypasses password prompt
-SCGA,-SEGA,-SHERC, -SVGA,-SMONO	Specifies type of monitor on your system
-V	Reduces screen snow on CGA
-X	Sets notification method to polling instead of instant
-W<1-15>	Sets border color to one of the following: 1-Blue 9-Bright blue 2-Green 10-Bright green 3-Cyan 11-Bright cyan 4-Red 12-Bright red 5-Magenta 13-Bright magenta 6-Brown 14-Yellow 7-White 15-Bright white 8-Gray

Using Micro

If Mail is running when an incoming message arrives, it notifies you that a message was received. You probably want to use your PC for other purposes than simply to receive electronic mail, though, so it's not very likely that you will want to dedicate your system to Mail. Fortunately, Workgroup Connection includes a small, memory-resident program, Micro, that notifies you when new mail messages arrive.

You must start the Workgroup Connection and set up Mail on your computer before you can use Micro.

To load the memory-resident Micro program so that you will be informed of incoming messages, use the following syntax:

MICRO mailboxname *-C -Ddrive -Fminutes -Nminutes -Ppassword -U -Xseconds*

Table A.7 summarizes the command-line parameters you use for Micro.

Table A.7 Micro Command-Line Options

Option	Description
mailboxname	Specifies your mailbox name. You must include your mailbox name.
-C	Displays the screen in color.
-Ddrive	Specifies the drive letter for your workgroup post office (by default, drive M). Use this option only if your post office uses a drive letter other than M.
-Fminutes	Specifies that when new mail arrives, a Mail notification appears on your screen. This option does not interrupt an application to check for mail. The *minutes* parameter specifies how many minutes the Mail notification remains on-screen.
-Nminutes	Displays a message on your screen when new mail has arrived, halting your current application. You must press Esc to continue using the application. The *minutes* parameter specifies how many minutes the notification message should remain on-screen before it is removed and your application can continue.
-Ppassword	Displays information about the sender and subject of new mail. Include your Mail password.

continues

Table A.7 Continued

Option	Description
-U	Removes Micro from your computer's memory.
-Xseconds	Specifies that Micro should use polling to check for new messages, instead of instant notification. The *seconds* parameter specifies how often Micro checks for new mail. The default value is 30 seconds. The maximum value is 360 seconds (one hour).

Figure A.20 shows how Micro displays a message box informing you that incoming mail has arrived. When you press Enter, the message box is cleared from the screen. You then use the MAIL command to read your mail.

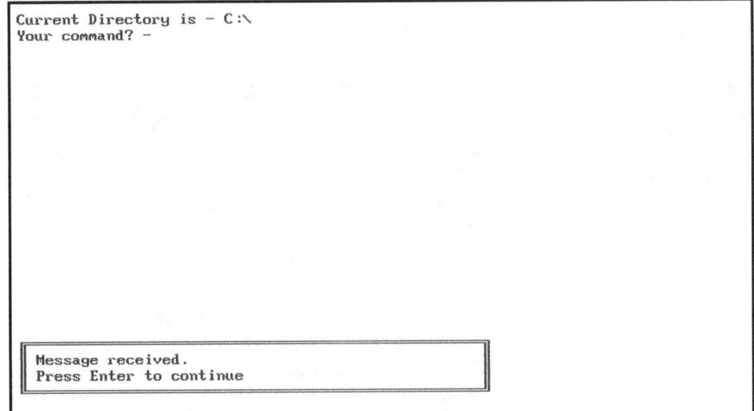
Current Directory is - C:\
Your command? -
Message received.
Press Enter to continue

Fig. A.20

Micro informing you of incoming mail.

If you have access to a compatible network, the Workgroup Connection provides many useful features—including file- and printer-sharing and electronic mail. If you do not have a network, but you do want to share files between two PCs or you use a printer attached to a different PC, refer to the description of DOS 6's Interlnk in Chapter 8.

As computers become faster and more powerful, the capability to connect PCs so that they can share data and peripherals is becoming very important. This appendix introduced you to Workgroup Connection, the powerful connectivity system and stand-alone product sold separately from DOS 6. You learned how to share files between PCs, and how to access printers connected to another PC.

You also learned how to use Microsoft Mail, the electronic mail system that is part of the Workgroup Connection. Using Mail, you easily can send and receive messages over a network.

INDEX

Symbols

A

B

C

D

E

F

G-H

I

K

L

M

N-O

P

Q-R

S

T-U

V

W

X-Z

Egghead gives you huge selection and personal attention!

The following pages are filled with Eggsclusive rebate offers on software products that work well with the new MS-DOS 6 Upgrade. Trust Egghead to bring you more selection and more value for your software-shopping dollar.

Choose the software eggsperts.
When you want a wide selection of software and computer accessories, forget those big warehouse stores. They stock a lot of copies of a few titles to give the impression that they're well equipped. We know better. We're Egghead, the Software Eggsperts.

Our selection includes over 2,000 titles.
Every one of our more than 200 stores stocks over 2,000 titles. So, when you come to us, you get a *real* selection. And, since our stores are sized for people and not airplanes, you won't need a map to find your way around. You *will* find lots of software and friendly, knowledgeable store Eggs who are ready to answer your questions and show you how a program works. That's right—we have IBM-compatible and Macintosh computers in all our stores so you can "test-drive" featured applications before you buy them.

We're your multimedia source.
Multimedia is the hottest new category in personal-computer software. You can now bring CD-quality sound and music, animation, video, and an eggstraordinary amount of text-based data to your desktop. We've got more than 100 multimedia titles for DOS or Windows, besides our eggstensive listings for the Macintosh. That includes software and hardware such as CD-ROM drives, stereo speakers, and microphones. We have a multimedia demo station in every store as well, so come see and hear for yourself what all the eggcitment is about!

multi M media

We're your multiplatform source.
Whether you work in DOS, Windows, OS/2, or Macintosh, we're the place to come for software. We make it easy. We make it fun. We make it affordable. We're the largest software reseller in North America for a reason—we do it better than anyone else.

We're your special-order source.
Even with our broad selection, there may be times when you want something that we don't carry. But we're *still* the place to come to, because we'll gladly special-order anything you need. We have access to thousands of titles in addition to those you'll find on our shelves.

So, when you want more than just a big room with some software thrown in; when you want big selection and big value *and* personal service; you can have it—at Egghead. If there's not an Egghead store in your area, call us at **1-800-EGGHEAD** for "Eggspress Ordering" and ultimate convenience!

Eggspress Ordering
1-800-EGGHEAD
Call Direct

Egghead Eggsclusive Mail-in Rebate

Buy Quicken (DOS) and get a $10 rebate!

Money management is a snap with this award-winning program! Features include a self-balancing electronic checkbook, automatic data-entry and credit-card tracking, financial-planning calculators, and more than 30 charts and graphs for quick "reads" on your budget! For **DOS** from Intuit.

Not valid with any other Intuit offer.

Egghead Eggsclusive Mail-in Rebate

Buy QuickBooks or QuickBooks & QuickPay and get a $20 rebate!

Make your small business run like clockwork! **QuickBooks** quickly organizes bills, invoices, income, accounts, assets, and cash flow. **QuickPay** easily generates payroll checks and calculates taxes and other employee deductions. For **DOS** from Intuit.

Egghead Eggstra Value Offer

Buy Alpha Four and get a FREE ZIP Code database (a $49.95 value)!

Current users of Paradox, dBASE, Professional Developer, DataEase, or other relational databases can switch to this network-compatible tool and save! Alpha Four's relational features include PowerScripts that make it easy to create professional applications—even without programming eggsperience. For **DOS** from Alpha Software.

Offer applies to Upgrade and LAN 2-Pack Editions of Alpha Four.

Egghead Rebate Offer

Quicken (DOS)

Name: ______________________________

Company name (if applicable): ______________________________

Address: ______________________________

City: ______________________________

State/Province: ______________________________

ZIP/Postal Code: ______________________________

Telephone: (   )______________________

Here's how to get your software rebate:

Proof of purchase: Mail this original certificate along with a copy of your Egghead store-identified cash-register receipt or packing slip with qualifying purchase circled.

Rebate certificate: Fill in the information requested at left. Please print clearly. Place in an envelope, along with the receipt/packing slip, and mail to Egghead Software Awards Center, Dept. #932032, Lubbock, TX 79491-1767. Rebate checks will be mailed in approximately six to eight weeks.

Important: Offer limited to one rebate per product purchased per name, family, household, or address. Egghead reserves the right to request further proof of purchase. Mail-in rebate only. Qualifying purchase must be made between March 30, 1993 and June 30, 1993. Rebate submission must be postmarked by July 10, 1993. Offer valid in U.S. and Canada; rebates will be paid in U.S. funds. Questions? Call the Egghead Software Awards Center at 1-800-825-4344.

Product: Quicken (DOS)

EGGHEAD SOFTWARE.
North America's Software Eggsperts.

Egghead Rebate Offer

QuickBooks or QuickBooks & QuickPay

Name: ______________________________

Company name (if applicable): ______________________________

Address: ______________________________

City: ______________________________

State/Province: ______________________________

ZIP/Postal Code: ______________________________

Telephone: (   )______________________

Here's how to get your software rebate:

Proof of purchase: Mail this original certificate along with a copy of your Egghead store-identified cash-register receipt or packing slip with qualifying purchase circled.

Rebate certificate: Fill in the information requested at left. Please print clearly. Place in an envelope, along with the receipt/packing slip, and mail to Egghead Software Awards Center, Dept. #932033, Lubbock, TX 79491-1767. Rebate checks will be mailed in approximately six to eight weeks.

Important: Offer limited to one rebate per product purchased per name, family, household, or address. Egghead reserves the right to request further proof of purchase. Mail-in rebate only. Qualifying purchase must be made between March 30, 1993 and June 30, 1993. Rebate submission must be postmarked by July 10, 1993. Offer valid in U.S. and Canada; rebates will be paid in U.S. funds. Questions? Call the Egghead Software Awards Center at 1-800-825-4344.

Product: QuickBooks
QuickBooks & QuickPay

EGGHEAD SOFTWARE.
North America's Software Eggsperts.

Egghead Eggstra Value

Alpha Four

Name: ______________________________

Company name (if applicable): ______________________________

Address: ______________________________

City: ______________________________

State/Province: ______________________________

ZIP/Postal Code: ______________________________

Telephone: (   )______________________

Here's how to get your FREE software:

Coupon certificate: Fill in the information requested at left. Please print clearly. Then, bring your coupon to any Egghead Software store and receive a **FREE** ZIP Code database with your purchase of Alpha Four 2.1 or Alpha Four 2.1 LAN 2-Pack.

Important: Offer limited to one coupon per product purchased per name, family, household, or address. Qualifying purchase must be made between March 30, 1993 and June 30, 1993. Coupon must be redeemed by July 10, 1993. Offer valid in U.S. and Canada. Questions? Call the Egghead Software Awards Center at 1-800-825-4344.

Product: Alpha Four

EGGHEAD SOFTWARE.
North America's Software Eggsperts.

Egghead Eggsclusive Mail-in Rebate

Buy Aldus IntelliDraw and get a $50 rebate!

Choose the smart draw program! Special tools automatically create symmetrical shapes, and objects whose sides remain attached when moved. You can also design "flip book" stacks of images. The Windows and Mac versions share files seamlessly and include built-in clip art. For **Windows** or **Mac** from Aldus.

Egghead Eggsclusive Mail-in Rebate

Buy AutoSketch and get a $30 rebate!

Create production-quality technical illustrations! AutoSketch's natural drawing interface, graphic tools, symbol library, and powerful CAD features make it easy. Save time with the pull-down menus and macros. Pan and zoom through drawings for easy editing. For **DOS** from Autodesk.

Egghead Eggsclusive Mail-in Rebate

Buy InstantArtist and get a $25 rebate!

Produce your own signs, banners, and letterheads with this eggcellent graphics tool! Choose from more than 500 professionally designed layouts, and select graphics from the library of more than 700 images. Move, scale, and rotate the graphics, and eggsperiment with special type effects. For **DOS** or **Windows** from Autodesk.

Egghead Eggsclusive Instant Rebate

Buy The Best of ClickArt and get a $20 rebate!

Start a clip-art library with Egghead's eggsclusive sampler! This collection includes 100 of ClickArt's most popular images. Choose from bitmapped, EPS, and color graphics that are sure to bring eggcitement to your signs, banners, newsletters, and other documents. For **DOS** and **Windows** from T/Maker.

Egghead Eggsclusive Mail-in Rebate

Buy Direct Access and get a $30 rebate!

Create a custom, graphical interface for launching your favorite programs! Build menu screens that give you instant access to applications, even grouping a number of programs together under a single menu entry. Password protection and a built-in screen saver are also featured. For **DOS** or **Windows** from Fifth Generation.

Egghead Eggsclusive Mail-in Rebate

Buy Close-Up and get a $40 rebate!

Enjoy remote computing between any two PCs linked by modems! Winner of PC World's "Best Buy of 1992," Close-Up supports both DOS and Windows. The program automates rapid file transfers, remote operations, and calls to information services and mainframes. For **DOS** and **Windows** from Norton Lambert.

Egghead Rebate Offer

The Best of ClickArt

Name: ______________________________

Company name (if applicable): ______________________________

Address: ______________________________

City: ______________________________

State/Province: ______________________________

ZIP/Postal Code: ______________________________

Telephone: (   )______________________________

Here's how to get your software instant rebate:

Proof of purchase: Bring this original certificate to present at time of purchase to qualify for the instant rebate.

Important: Offer limited to one rebate per product purchased per name, family, household, or address. Limited to stock on hand. Instant rebate only. Qualifying purchase must be made between March 31, 1993 and June 30, 1993. Offer valid in U.S. and Canada.

Product: The Best of ClickArt

EGGHEAD SOFTWARE.
North America's Software Eggsperts.

Egghead Rebate Offer

Direct Access

Name: ______________________________

Company name (if applicable): ______________________________

Address: ______________________________

City: ______________________________

State/Province: ______________________________

ZIP/Postal Code: ______________________________

Telephone: (   )______________________________

Here's how to get your software rebate:

Proof of purchase: Mail this original certificate along with a copy of your Egghead store-identified cash-register receipt or packing slip with qualifying purchase circled.

Rebate certificate: Fill in the information requested at left. Please print clearly. Place in an envelope, along with the receipt/packing slip, and mail to Egghead Software Awards Center, Dept. #932042, Lubbock, TX 79491-1767. Rebate checks will be mailed in approximately six to eight weeks.

Important: Offer limited to one rebate per product purchased per name, family, household, or address. Egghead reserves the right to request further proof of purchase. Mail-in rebate only. Qualifying purchase must be made between March 30, 1993 and June 30, 1993. Rebate submission must be postmarked by July 10, 1993. Offer valid in U.S. and Canada; rebates will be paid in U.S. funds. Questions? Call the Egghead Software Awards Center at 1-800-825-4344.

Product: Direct Access

EGGHEAD SOFTWARE.
North America's Software Eggsperts.

Egghead Rebate Offer

Close-Up

Name: ______________________________

Company name (if applicable): ______________________________

Address: ______________________________

City: ______________________________

State/Province: ______________________________

ZIP/Postal Code: ______________________________

Telephone: (   )______________________________

Here's how to get your software rebate:

Proof of purchase: Mail this original certificate along with a copy of your Egghead store-identified cash-register receipt or packing slip with qualifying purchase circled.

Rebate certificate: Fill in the information requested at left. Please print clearly. Place in an envelope, along with the receipt/packing slip, and mail to Egghead Software Awards Center, Dept. #932043, Lubbock, TX 79491-1767. Rebate checks will be mailed in approximately six to eight weeks.

Important: Offer limited to one rebate per product purchased per name, family, household, or address. Egghead reserves the right to request further proof of purchase. Mail-in rebate only. Qualifying purchase must be made between March 30, 1993 and June 30, 1993. Rebate submission must be postmarked by July 10, 1993. Offer valid in U.S. and Canada; rebates will be paid in U.S. funds. Questions? Call the Egghead Software Awards Center at 1-800-825-4344.

Product: Close-Up

EGGHEAD SOFTWARE.
North America's Software Eggsperts.

Egghead Eggsclusive Mail-in Rebate

Buy Micro Kitchen Companion and get a $5 rebate!

Organize your kitchen with this advanced cooking reference system! Compile your own recipe library with Micro Kitchen Companion. Plan special diets, keep track of what you served and to whom, even print shopping lists organized by store aisles! For **DOS** or **Windows** from Lifestyle Software Group.

Egghead Eggsclusive Mail-in Rebate

Buy Typing Tutor 5+ and get a $10 rebate!

Develop your typing technique! Master the keyboard in short order, using a series of lessons, tests, and arcade-style games. Split-screen views simulate real-life typing environments, while graphs track your performance. The games Letter Invaders and Mouse Invaders sharpen your skills. For **DOS** or **Windows** from Que Software.

Egghead Eggsclusive Mail-in Rebate

Buy any title from The Learning Company and get a $10 rebate!

Treat your children to software that teaches valuable skills while it entertains! The Learning Company is a leading manufacturer of educational software, specializing in programs that develop reading, math, and problem-solving skills in ways that children love. From The Learning Company.

Egghead Rebate Offer

Micro Kitchen Companion

Name: ____________________

Company name (if applicable): ____________________

Address: ____________________

City: ____________________

State/Province: ____________________

ZIP/Postal Code: ____________________

Telephone: (   ) ____________

Here's how to get your software rebate:

Proof of purchase: Mail this original certificate along with a copy of your Egghead store-identified cash-register receipt or packing slip with qualifying purchase circled.

Rebate certificate: Fill in the information requested at left. Please print clearly. Place in an envelope, along with the receipt/packing slip, and mail to Egghead Software Awards Center, Dept. #932044, Lubbock, TX 79491-1767. Rebate checks will be mailed in approximately six to eight weeks.

Important: Offer limited to one rebate per product purchased per name, family, household, or address. Egghead reserves the right to request further proof of purchase. Mail-in rebate only. Qualifying purchase must be made between March 30, 1993 and June 30, 1993. Rebate submission must be postmarked by July 10, 1993. Offer valid in U.S. and Canada; rebates will be paid in U.S. funds. Questions? Call the Egghead Software Awards Center at 1-800-825-4344.

EGGHEAD SOFTWARE.
North America's Software Eggsperts.

Product: Micro Kitchen Companion

Egghead Rebate Offer

Typing Tutor 5+

Name: ____________________

Company name (if applicable): ____________________

Address: ____________________

City: ____________________

State/Province: ____________________

ZIP/Postal Code: ____________________

Telephone: (   ) ____________

Here's how to get your software rebate:

Proof of purchase: Mail this original certificate along with a copy of your Egghead store-identified cash-register receipt or packing slip with qualifying purchase circled.

Rebate certificate: Fill in the information requested at left. Please print clearly. Place in an envelope, along with the receipt/packing slip, and mail to Egghead Software Awards Center, Dept. #932045, Lubbock, TX 79491-1767. Rebate checks will be mailed in approximately six to eight weeks.

Important: Offer limited to one rebate per product purchased per name, family, household, or address. Egghead reserves the right to request further proof of purchase. Mail-in rebate only. Qualifying purchase must be made between March 30, 1993 and June 30, 1993. Rebate submission must be postmarked by July 10, 1993. Offer valid in U.S. and Canada; rebates will be paid in U.S. funds. Questions? Call the Egghead Software Awards Center at 1-800-825-4344.

EGGHEAD SOFTWARE.
North America's Software Eggsperts.

Product: Typing Tutor 5+

Egghead Rebate Offer

Your choice of any title from The Learning Company

Name: ____________________

Company name (if applicable): ____________________

Address: ____________________

City: ____________________

State/Province: ____________________

ZIP/Postal Code: ____________________

Telephone: (   ) ____________

Here's how to get your software rebate:

Proof of purchase: Mail this original certificate along with a copy of your Egghead store-identified cash-register receipt or packing slip with qualifying purchase circled.

Rebate certificate: Fill in the information requested at left. Please print clearly. Place in an envelope, along with the receipt/packing slip, and mail to Egghead Software Awards Center, Dept. #932046, Lubbock, TX 79491-1767. Rebate checks will be mailed in approximately six to eight weeks.

Important: Offer limited to one rebate per product purchased per name, family, household, or address. Egghead reserves the right to request further proof of purchase. Mail-in rebate only. Qualifying purchase must be made between March 30, 1993 and June 30, 1993. Rebate submission must be postmarked by July 10, 1993. Offer valid in U.S. and Canada; rebates will be paid in U.S. funds. Questions? Call the Egghead Software Awards Center at 1-800-825-4344.

EGGHEAD SOFTWARE.
North America's Software Eggsperts.

Product: Any title from The Learning Company

Egghead Rebate Offer

Your choice of any title from Individual Software valued at $39.99 or more

Name: ______________________________

Company name (if applicable): ______________________________

Address: ______________________________

City: ______________________________

State/Province: ______________________________

ZIP/Postal Code: ______________________________

Telephone: (   )______________

Here's how to get your software rebate:

Proof of purchase: Mail this original certificate along with a copy of your Egghead store-identified cash-register receipt or packing slip with qualifying purchase circled.

Rebate certificate: Fill in the information requested at left. Please print clearly. Place in an envelope, along with the receipt/packing slip, and mail to Egghead Software Awards Center, Dept. #932047, Lubbock, TX 79491-1767. Rebate checks will be mailed in approximately six to eight weeks.

Important: Offer limited to one rebate per product purchased per name, family, household, or address. Egghead reserves the right to request further proof of purchase. Mail-in rebate only. Qualifying purchase must be made between March 30, 1993 and June 30, 1993. Rebate submission must be postmarked by July 10, 1993. Offer valid in U.S. and Canada; rebates will be paid in U.S. funds. Questions? Call the Egghead Software Awards Center at 1-800-825-4344.

EGGHEAD SOFTWARE.
North America's Software Eggsperts.

Product: Any title from Individual Software valued at $39.99 or more

Egghead Rebate Offer

PC Globe

Name: ______________________________

Company name (if applicable): ______________________________

Address: ______________________________

City: ______________________________

State/Province: ______________________________

ZIP/Postal Code: ______________________________

Telephone: (   )______________

Here's how to get your software rebate:

Proof of purchase: Mail this original certificate along with a copy of your Egghead store-identified cash-register receipt or packing slip with qualifying purchase circled.

Rebate certificate: Fill in the information requested at left. Please print clearly. Place in an envelope, along with the receipt/packing slip, and mail to Egghead Software Awards Center, Dept. #932048, Lubbock, TX 79491-1767. Rebate checks will be mailed in approximately six to eight weeks.

Important: Offer limited to one rebate per product purchased per name, family, household, or address. Egghead reserves the right to request further proof of purchase. Mail-in rebate only. Qualifying purchase must be made between March 30, 1993 and June 30, 1993. Rebate submission must be postmarked by July 10, 1993. Offer valid in U.S. and Canada; rebates will be paid in U.S. funds. Questions? Call the Egghead Software Awards Center at 1-800-825-4344.

EGGHEAD SOFTWARE.
North America's Software Eggsperts.

Product: PC Globe

Egghead Rebate Offer

The Norton Utilities

Name: ______________________________

Company name (if applicable): ______________________________

Address: ______________________________

City: ______________________________

State/Province: ______________________________

ZIP/Postal Code: ______________________________

Telephone: (   )______________

Here's how to get your software instant rebate:

Proof of purchase: Bring this original certificate to present at time of purchase to qualify for the instant rebate.

Important: Offer limited to one rebate per product purchased per name, family, household, or address. Limited to stock on hand. Instant rebate only. Qualifying purchase must be made between March 31, 1993 and June 30, 1993. Offer valid in U.S. and Canada.

EGGHEAD SOFTWARE.
North America's Software Eggsperts.

Product: The Norton Utilities